D1217339

The Psychology
of Social Movements

The Psychology
of Social Movements

BY

HADLEY CANTRIL

Institute for International Social Research
Princeton University

ROBERT E. KRIEGER PUBLISHING COMPANY
HUNTINGTON, NEW YORK

Original Edition 1941
Reprint 1973

Printed and Published by
ROBERT E. KRIEGER PUBLISHING CO., INC.
BOX 542, HUNTINGTON, NEW YORK, 11743

©Copyright 1941 by
Hadley Cantril

Reprinted by arrangement with
John Wiley & Sons, Inc.

Library of Congress Catalog Card Number 73-89079
ISBN 0-88275-133-6

Printed in U.S.A. by
NOBLE OFFSET PRINTERS, INC.
New York, N.Y. 10003

To

GORDON W. ALLPORT

PREFACE

Within the past twenty-five years we have seen millions of people swept into mass movements, leaving among their unhappy victims kings and emperors, religious and educational institutions, political and economic systems. Although no great wave or revolt has recently engulfed our American culture, the domestic sea has not been entirely untroubled. Social movements of various kinds have recruited many followers but have proved abortive.

Whether a person is eager for social change or whether he resists it, he can hardly be complacent at the course of events. He wonders if this country will be caught in the vortex of Fascism or Communism, if some ideology indigenous to American soil will arise to attract multitudes of his fellow citizens.

Such a person will know that social movements flourish when the times are out of joint. In an effort to understand the contemporary scene, he may turn to the historian who has carefully recorded the events and causes of past critical periods; he may follow some columnist or radio commentator whose interpretation of news makes sense to him; he may read books written by able journalists and correspondents who tell in their own way how men and movements rise to power.

But, after examining history, listening to commentators, reading eye-witness accounts of social movements in formation or in action, the person may still feel that something is lacking. He wants to know more precisely what it is that motivates men to follow an untried leader, what the social environment does to make people so suggestible, what people are thinking about, are puzzled about, and are hoping for when they lose themselves in some cause that seems strange or esoteric to the observer. If a person does ask these questions, he is likely to turn to the psychologist for the answers. And no psychologist in recent years has tried systematically to provide the answers.

The present book is an attempt to fill this need. Strictly speaking, the book belongs in the field of social psychology, although the line between social psychology and other areas of psychology is tenuous indeed.

In Part I, I have tried to give a systematic framework for the interpretation of certain social movements considered in Part II. The particular social movements selected for examination in Part II should be regarded only as prototypes. The number from which I might have drawn is almost limitless. Because of their intrinsic interest and because information was available, I have chosen for consideration certain movements from the recent past. They range from the lynching mob, specific in time and space, to the Nazi movement which aims, according to its leader, to alter the course of world history for the next one thousand years. Although the movements treated are all more or less spectacular, the reader should not carry away the false impression that *all* social movements are spectacular. Many of them are. But many others, such as reforms occurring within the democratic framework, progress with comparatively little fanfare. For my purposes, it does not matter greatly what movements are chosen for final study. My aim is not primarily to understand these *particular* movements but to have, through an understanding of them, an insight into all social movements: those of the past, those of the present, and those others yet to come. Each movement arises in a particular social context; each has its characteristic followers; each, its special appeals. My primary aim is to provide a basic conceptual framework for the explanation of any social movement, to show individuals what to look for when they themselves set out to understand whatever movement may interest or involve them. The social movements discussed in Part II cannot be properly understood unless the background of Part I has been read.

Chapter 5 of this volume appeared in substantially the same form in the *Journal of Abnormal and Social Psychology* and is reproduced here with permission. I wish to thank the Messrs. Arthur Raper, Ralph Davis, Munro Work, and Walter White for their discussions of the problem of lynching mobs. Mr. Jerome Bruner helpfully read several chapters of the manuscript. Dr. Hans Gerth criticized the chapters on the Nazi movement in great detail. He will by no means be satisfied with the present account. Earnest Jandorf excerpted from life histories and translated some of the quotations used in Chapters 8 and 9. Dr. H. S. Langfeld gave me valuable critical suggestions.

Some unpublished figures, obtained from tabulations made on data gathered by the American Institute of Public Opinion, are presented in various chapters. I am deeply indebted to Dr. George Gallup for permitting me to reproduce all the Institute's findings and to use them for purposes of social research.

The conceptual framework used throughout the book is essentially an elaboration of that originally presented by Muzafer Sherif in *The Psychology of Social Norms*. Although frequent references acknowledging Sherif's contributions are made in the volume, they still do not convey my debt to Sherif. The early systematic chapters have been formulated in discussion with Gordon Allport. He has read the entire manuscript and has given constructive criticism throughout. In addition, as the person who first interested me in the field of psychology, he must share the responsibility for this volume. Carolyn Taylor has patiently typed and retyped the manuscript.

HADLEY CANTRIL

PRINCETON, N. J.
January, 1941

INTRODUCTION

Before any social movement can be understood, it is necessary to have some appropriate conceptual tools. Just what these tools will be depends upon the investigator's own conception of the nature of explanation. Some men may regard only as rough *description* what other men hold to be *explanation*. The more "exact" the scientist, the more is he likely to frown on other scientists whose accounts of various phenomena seem global and crude by comparison. Thus, the chemist may cast a skeptical eye on the biologist, the biologist on the psychologist, and the psychologist on the sociologist and the philosopher. Within the single field of psychology there is already a variety of conceptual frameworks from which an investigator may choose his instrument of thought. Some psychologists, for example, cling to the conditioned response and all its ramifications; others prefer a modified Freudian interpretation; others put their faith in a more detailed analysis of instincts or needs. Each approach slices the mind in a different way; each may have special explanatory advantages for certain types of problems. The final justification for any accounting relationship must be the extent to which it enables us to understand the problems with which we are dealing and to predict the type of behavior with which we are concerned.

Some explanatory systems completely leave out of account the normal man in his everyday setting. They direct their attention instead to neurotic segments of personality or to the rat in the maze. Other approaches, while concerned with man and his social life, construct a fictitious, schematic man who represents abstract "human nature," endowed with a bundle of fixed needs or capacities but with none of the personal characteristics which make of man a full-bodied, distinctive individual. Still other approaches stress individuality and the variety of men's capacities and traits, but somehow neglect the relationship of men to the social context in which they live.

No ready-made conceptual scheme, to me, seems adequate to explain the problems of mass psychology. In Part I, therefore, I have attempted to extend the concepts of social psychology so that they will be adequate to account for the type of problem considered in this volume. The system of explanation outlined leaves many vexing questions unanswered, but at least it makes a start, and students of social psychology will see for themselves what problems must be faced squarely before explanation is entirely complete.

The particular "explanation" I have evolved is a purely functional one. The mechanistic, positivistic approach has been rejected in favor of a phenomenological analysis that hopes to straighten out in part the tangle of mental context and motivation found in the individual who is adjusting himself to the social world. In the present state of our psychological knowledge, a functional approach seems the most sensible. For, if functional relationships are not first clearly examined, investigators who are seeking mechanisms may get completely sidetracked or led up blind alleys because of the limited or false frame of reference within which their search occurs. This does not mean, however, that functional analysis can wander foot-loose and fancy-free without any regard for the biological organism with which the psychologist is dealing. Still, it does mean that the psychologist is not circumscribed in his understanding of psychological relationships by limitations of knowledge concerning structural relationships: he does not, for example, have to restrict his terms to those describing demonstrable structural counterparts to conditioned responses or to terms employed by sensory psychologists to explain the physiological mechanisms of isolated experiences.

The search for concepts that will account for the behavior of man in his social life and that will follow the rule of scientific parsimony is by no means an easy one. For human beings are not static, not amenable to indefinite manipulation and control. Life is constantly going on, creating as the psychologist's medium a fluid personal and social environment. Behavior at any one moment must always be regarded as a function of the environment and of the particular pattern of predispositions influencing the individual at that moment. Hence, statements about men in social life are limited by both the environmental context and the motivational factors that are operating when observations are made. The social psychologist, therefore, needs explanatory concepts which will accurately describe the individual and his relationship to society at any given point in time.

In addition to this main task of outlining an explanatory framework, I have, quite frankly, a second purpose—to influence specific value judgments concerning the merits of various social movements. The social psychologist, as well as every other social scientist, is dealing with problems firmly rooted in the social context. He cannot separate his inquiries from their human environment without distorting and obscuring the inquiries themselves. Unless the psychologist retreats into trivial and specious problems where man and the social world do not disturb him, he finds it difficult to sit by with a complacent "open-mindedness." If he claims that as a "scientist" he must insulate himself from the social context, his theories and generalizations will be meaningless when extended to the everyday world of the common man; his research will take on the pseudo-objectivity of those who are blind to scientific fashions. Hence, if the psychologist is aware of the influence of the social context or the relativity of his findings, he has forced upon himself also an awareness of the implications of his findings for the individual and the society in which he lives. The psychologist's training and knowledge will, he assumes, make him somewhat of an authority on questions that involve man's adjustment to his environment. And with such authority should also come some responsibility, a responsibility to make value judgments based on information acquired by objective methods. My own value frame has as its goal the creation of a society where maximum economic and cultural opportunity will prevail for every person, where both science and the individual will have more freedom. Such a social order might be called a real democracy.

From my point of view, then, the principles of some social movements are "wrong," those of others more nearly "right." Some are cruel illusions accepted by bewildered people who follow false prophets; others uncompromisingly base policies on assumptions which the psychologist knows are untrue; some would completely prohibit the search for an understanding of man and his social world; some unnecessarily destroy the capacity and talent of man in obtaining his objectives. Will-o'-the-wisp schemes and movements founded on the presuppositions of demagogues should, I think, be discouraged. Others that rest firmly on a knowledge of human nature and society and show a real promise of improving man's adjustments should be encouraged. Any evaluation of social movements that is not based on such knowledge must of necessity spring from ignorance, bias, and prejudice. Any such evaluation will in all likelihood overlook basic causes of discontent. Thus, if the social scientist refuses to make evaluations, who else can do so with an equal chance of predicting what movements will achieve desired goals?

H. C.

Part I

BASIC CONCEPTS

CHAPTER I

MENTAL CONTEXT

At this stage of the world's development, practically every individual is born into a highly organized society. Almost all the experiences which constitute his life are likely to be prescribed roughly for him by the particular culture within which his life happens to be lived. To be sure, the individual will develop the capacity to select alternate courses of action. He may also set about changing some characteristics of his culture which are by no means to his liking. But still this selection and this desire to alter certain practices are themselves bounded and determined by the original conditions imposed by a certain way of life.

Although we must leave to the sociologists and anthropologists the task of describing precisely what it is that constitutes a culture, even the psychological story of how the individual acquires a certain mental context inevitably begins with some account of all those things in a culture which surround the individual when he enters it: those things first quite outside him, unknown to him, which gradually become a part of him, use him as a carrier, and make of him a socialized person.

THE SOCIAL CONTEXT

A child finds himself growing up in a world composed of an enormous variety of stimuli. Nature provides him with an infinite number of sights and sounds, temperatures and smells. And to this array the creations of men are added for his perception—buildings and bridges, furniture and foods, clothes and automobiles. The child also becomes aware of certain forms and rhythms, of music and language, of numbers and pictures. Less tangible but still sooner or later just as intensely experienced are other social products called *manners* and *customs*, conventions and mores, laws and institutions. All these stimuli are an inescapable part of the culture, all

3

are part of the environment to which the growing individual must adjust and orient himself.

For the psychologist concerned with the explanation of the mental life and the daily reactions of the common man, these social stimuli, these ways of talking, figuring, building, dressing, eating, thinking, buying, selling, worshipping, working, and playing take on special significance. They furnish the social framework, the superstructure of society, which tends so greatly to canalize the way in which the single man will talk, figure, build, dress, think, work, and play. All these social products which have become standardized in a society we shall call *social norms*. Many of them may be regarded as established methods of satisfying basic needs for food, sex, and shelter.

Now all of this is obvious enough. But it needs repeating for the simple reason that it is so frequently overlooked by both laymen and psychologists when they try to figure out why men act the way they do. We are apt to forget that we are members of the twentieth century Western World and that our conceptions of religion, morality, or education are relatively localized in time and space. As Americans, we may take for granted as permanent and unchangeable our natural resources, our form of government, our freedoms. As members of the white race in a society dominated by white men, we sometimes fail to realize that many of the advantages we enjoy are not available to others because they have black skins. As members of the middle or upper economic classes, we may glibly assume that ours is the best of all possible worlds with its high standard of living, its automobiles, its colleges, its substantial homes, its abundance of food, its recreational facilities, its security. Yet if we walked across the tracks and visited the slums we would see a world of poverty, of malnutrition, of insecurity and despair which, in many important aspects, might differ from our own environment much more than if we visited the better sections of Hong Kong, Moscow, Singapore, or Ankara. For not all the norms within a Western, or even American, culture are uniform. They are patterned in many ways. There are differences in the norms in various sections of the country, in different communities, in different neighborhoods, in different economic classes, and in different generations.

Thus in explaining social movements, we must always look first at the particular pattern of norms which surround the individuals who compose that particular movement. In what sort of physical and psychological environment did these people try to satisfy their needs? What desires, worries, frustrations, and prejudices did their particular community or status foster? Why did a certain social movement at least temporarily seem to be the solution for maladjustments? These are the types of questions we must ask ourselves if we are to avoid oversimplified solutions in terms of innate racial, sex, or class differences or in terms of instincts, or uniform urges, that are supposed to drive men to certain types of social behavior.

TRANSMITTING THE SOCIAL CONTEXT

Just how the accepted standards of a culture become interiorized or introcepted, how they become a part of the individual, is still a relatively unknown process.[1] Much more research is needed before we shall know the whole story. The problem is not a simple one. The process of interiorization varies enormously within different population groups, with the different norms being acquired, and with individuals of different capacities and temperaments. It would be foolish to expect that an individual living in a backward, under-privileged, bigoted, rural community would acquire his ideas in the same manner as an individual in a progressive, middle-class, urban environment. It is unlikely in such contrasting settings that two individuals' points of view regarding religion, the Turks, the Communists, government regulation of business, or birth control would be learned in similar ways. Nor would we expect a highly intelligent, introverted boy to acquire his ideas in the same way as a stupid, extroverted boy brought up in the same environment.

It is possible and useful, however, to differentiate the processes of introception of cultural standards according to the degree to which the individual himself acts as a selective agent.[2]

[1] G. Murphy, L. B. Murphy, and T. Newcomb, *Experimental Social Psychology,* New York: Harpers, 1937; E. L. Horowitz, The development of attitudes towards the Negro, *Arch. Psychol.,* 1936, 194; Otto Klineberg, *Social Psychology,* New York: Holt, 1940.

[2] Throughout the present discussion the essential task is to describe the relationships that hold between the cultural standards and the individual standards, rather than to analyze in detail the mechanism by means of which cultural standards are learned. Accounts of learning, language, and imitation as mechanisms in civilization

Acceptance of cultural norms. The relative uniformity of a culture from one generation to another, the usual slow rate of change, is clear indication that many norms of the culture are uncritically accepted by a large majority of the people. Not only do people acquire certain of the standards the culture provides regarding such characteristics as sizes, shapes, melodies, language, and institutions, but they are likely to accept in large measure the prevailing evaluations which the culture has placed on its material products or its various ways of life. For the norms of society are by no means always merely neutral stimuli from which the individual may pick and choose as he pleases, which he may regard as good or bad, as right or wrong when the spirit moves him. Most of them have already been judged by society, by the individual's predecessors, when he first experiences them. When people learn about a specific religion they generally learn at the same time that it is the "best" or that it is the "true" religion; when they learn about races they usually gather either directly or by implication that some are "superior," some "inferior"; when they become aware of sex they learn that some actions are "right," other things are "wrong." The fact that so many norms are already evaluated by society before the developing individual is even aware of their existence is, from the point of view of the social psychologist, perhaps one of the most important characteristics of social organization.

It is indeed difficult to think of any ordinary activity, institution, or point of view that is not implicitly valued in one way or another by the culture. A person's occupation, his leisure-time activities, his dress, his political beliefs, his family life, his reading habits, his orderliness, his temperance, his sense of humor, his initiative, his earning capacity are only a few of an infinite list of beliefs or behaviors that are subject to the rather uniform approval or disapproval of others around him. Seldom during the process of growing-up does the child have pointed out to him the distinction between what the norms are and what attitude he should take towards them. Like the editor or propagandist who tells his readers what to think

---

will be found in Katz and Schanck, *Social Psychology,* New York: Wiley, 1938; G. W. Allport, *Personality: A Psychological Interpretation,* New York: Holt, 1937, ch. 5. Because of its special importance, however, the role of *suggestion* is treated separately in ch. 3 of this book.

of the news at the same time he presents the news itself, society seems to tell us what we should think of its various components at the same time that we learn what those components are. These prevailing evaluations of norms we shall call *social values*.

Often a person will suddenly acquire a current value which, if it is not later contradicted, will remain permanent. A child who knows nothing of the Turks may be told about them by his parents or in story books. He learns that they are a cruel lot who once delighted in the killing of Armenians. He may forever afterwards carry with him this evaluation of a particular nationality. Or the same child may learn from his English teacher that Hawthorne and Thackeray were the world's greatest authors, and that their works will probably never again be equalled. If, in later life, the student never takes a serious interest in literature, without further question he will probably carry this judgment with him to the grave.

Other points of view may be acquired after a longer series of specific experiences. The child brought up in the United States will probably learn from a number of remarks or implications that Negroes are, on the whole, a rather sensual, unintelligent, slow, but kindly people He will also learn, no doubt, that there are "a few exceptions." Or the child may be gradually introduced to the rituals and creeds of a particular church and remain a devout Catholic, Methodist, or Baptist the rest of his life.

Some values may crystallize and become meaningful to the individual only after he has become an adult. Take, for example, the son of a well-to-do manufacturer. The boy is protected from all problems concerning the business of making a living. He goes through college by endorsing his father's checks and half-heartedly doing his assignments. When he is graduated he enters his father's plant as an executive assistant. He mingles with other young men of his class now motivated by financial profit. After three years he becomes a dyed-in-the-wool conservative.

The values which are, in these ways, uncritically accepted are generally learned not by experience with the objects, persons, or groups to which the values are related, but by secondhand contact with the values as reflected in the ideas and behavior of other people. The point of view which an individual may hold toward the Negro, the Japanese, the Communist, the union leader, the atheist, the nudist, the music of Beethoven, or the poetry of Keats is more frequently derived from the opinions of other people than it is from any knowledge of, or experience with, Negroes, Japanese, Communists, union leaders, atheists, nudists, the works of Beethoven, or the poems of Keats.[3] And since people are more likely to remember what they hear or read than where they hear or read it, the sources of the personal values or points of view engendered are generally soon forgotten. But the point of view itself can become quite autonomous of its origin and remain firmly fixed.

There are other characteristic ways in which values become interiorized. Some values may be accepted bodily as firmly established stereotypes. The individual will acquire in this event a point of view which has no reference to facts, alleged facts, or experience. A child, for example, may live in a northern town where there are no colored people. One day when he goes to the nearby city with his mother, he sees a colored man running an elevator. He asks his mother about the man, learns that he is a "nigger," hears her apply various uncomplimentary adjectives to the race, admonishing him never to associate closely with black people because they are different, "not like us." If the child accepts this notion he will grow up with a prejudice only meagerly supported with reasons.

Other values that are acquired may have some basis of information or rationalization. Whether the information is correct or not, whether the rationalization is valid or not, may be, for the individual who accepts them, unknown and irrelevant considerations. The "facts" may be entirely gossip or hearsay. A child may be raised in the South, have a colored servant in the home, and accept the servant's little boy as his closest childhood friend. When he goes to school, however, he finds that there are no colored children and soon his parents begin to tell him that he mustn't play any more with little Charlie, the colored boy. He learns that he must address his parents' white friends as "Mr." or "Mrs.," but that he should call all colored people by their first names. He learns that he can sleep under the same roof with colored people only if they are definitely regarded as servants, that he cannot ride in the same automobile with them unless a colored man drives and wears a chauffeur's cap.

[3] Muzafer Sherif, An experimental study of stereotypes, *Abn. & Soc. Psychol.*, 1935, **29**, 371-375.

He is told over and over again that Negroes must be "kept in their place." He is taught that, with few exceptions, colored people are not as smart as the whites, that they are apt to be unreliable, that the book of Genesis says they were meant to be slaves, and that they must never be allowed to get too "uppity." This child would find it relatively easy to give what, to him, would seem sound and sensible reasons for his feelings toward the Negroes.

Some values, furthermore, may be acquired as part and parcel of more inclusive values. Parents or teachers may consciously or unconsciously demonstrate to a child the patterning of what otherwise may be accepted as several isolated, specific points of view. They may show how several attitudes are all related to certain basic assumptions that are "right." For example, another child living in a large city may acquire his point of view toward the Negroes when he is told that as a native white American he has something especially to be proud of, that he is "better" than the "foreigners" and "niggers" who live in certain parts of town. For him, the Negroes become simply one variety of a whole group of people whom he regards as inferior.

Now all three children, the one who got his prejudice directly from his mother, the one who had some experience with Negroes, and the one who learned that he was superior, have accepted the values of the culture surrounding them. All three have obtained their attitudes from other people, not because of their own experience with Negroes or because of any known and reliable facts about the race. None of the children has any knowledge of the basic reasons why Negroes have the status they do or why the white people have the ideas they do about the colored race. All three will probably grow up as adults whose points of views and behavior toward the Negro will be roughly similar. But the reasons for the ideas they have, the bases upon which they are founded differ significantly. Also, there is a difference in the relationship between the opinions about Negroes and the self-interest of the individual, a relationship which may affect the stability of the opinion in later life. Sometimes opinions derived from different sources will conflict. For example, a white man was riding as the only passenger in an elevator in the South. The elevator stopped to pick up a colored woman. The man took off his hat. Then the elevator stopped to pick up a white man and the first man put his hat on again.

The uncritical acceptance of cultural standards is bound to vary with the equilibrium of the culture or the uniformity of the values of the culture. If the interests, purposes, and assumptions of people were common, then no conflicting points of view would arise to make the individual question the values he has been gradually absorbing. So happy a state of affairs, however, never exists. The times are always more or less out of joint. Confusion, divergency of opinion, disagreement on standards is the general rule. A person born into a culture where intense conflict reigns may find comparatively few clear-cut values to accept or any basic standards with which he can relate the variety of specific opinions he hears expressed around him.

Our own culture has been in a state of unusual confusion at least since the first World War, and more especially since the beginning of the depression in 1929. To be sure, standards such as those affecting language, dress, or monogamous marriage have not been seriously affected. But in many other areas of life, doubts have arisen concerning the goodness or practicability of certain norms. Older social values regarding religion, economic practices, parental authority, birth control, and a host of other issues are being reexamined. Possible ways of instrumenting new values, such as those regarding old-age security, job opportunity, government regulation of industry, are being widely discussed. The institution of the family is being modified by preschools, clubs, organized play, and the like. The school and other community, state, or federal institutions are extending their influences into more and more areas of life. The net result is that a uniformity of standards in regard to many questions concerning political, social, or economic life is, in our culture at the present time, the exception rather than the rule. The recent emergence of, and interest in, public-opinion polls is clear evidence of this fact. The polls could not possibly survive in a country where people, by and large, agreed with each other. There would be no issue to poll, everyone would know the answers beforehand.

This variation between standards in our day is undoubtedly encouraged by the mass means of communication. The newspaper, the radio, and the moving picture make it possible for larger proportions of the population to learn diverging opinions. The radio, especially, has aroused people in the lower income and educational groups to learn certain different points of view since comparatively fewer people in these groups read newspapers.[4] The result is that people in all walks of life are less sure of many of their older norms than their fathers were. Even when such people have specific attitudes regarding this question or that, it may be difficult for them to find any common rationale behind their attitudes. Hence, inconsistencies of opinion and attitudes contradictory to self-interest may be prevalent.

The individual as a selective agent. Our everyday experience with people, as well as attitude tests and public-opinion polls, reveal that by no means all persons in the same economic class, the same section of the country, or the same rural environment think alike on all subjects. To be sure, such sociological determinants as these do have an enormous effect on attitudes. People in the upper income class are usually more conservative than their poorer countrymen; people in the South do have greater Negro prejudice; farmers do differ from urbanites on many tariff questions; skilled workers do differ from unskilled workers in their attitudes toward the unions.[5] But not all rich people are conservative, and not all conservatives are conservative in the same way. A few scattered southerners are not prejudiced against the Negroes, and some southerners draw the color line much more rigidly than others. In brief, by no means do all people accept uncritically the norms and values surrounding them in their usual cultural group. In the process of interiorization the norms become modified for reasons which people may often be quite unaware of themselves. Hence any ideology which stresses the single determinant of economic class or of sectional influence tends to obscure, by oversimplification, important psychological consequences of other determinants.

There are many possible determinants operating to force this modification or alteration of an individual's opinion. One of the

[4] P. F. Lazarsfeld, *Radio and the Printed Page,* New York: Duell, Sloan & Pearce, 1940. More extensive educational opportunities are showing their slow but sure effects in the greater encouragement to independent thinking.

[5] A. W. Kornhauser, Analysis of "class" structure of contemporary American society, in *Industrial Conflict* (edited by G. W. Hartmann and T. Newcomb), New York: Dryden, 1939, ch. II.

most important, and one of the most difficult to isolate in its influence, is the personality of the individual himself. His temperamental traits, his characteristic ways of expressing himself, his intellectual capacities may all play a role in leading him to accept some norms and to reject or alter others. A sensitive, tender-minded, physically weak, mentally alert youth brought up in the home of an unskilled worker may, because of his personality alone, more readily question the conditions that keep him and his family economically insecure than will his carefree, toughminded, strong, dull brother who finds adjustment easier, who broods less, and is a more popular member of the community.

The amount of education that a person has the opportunity and capacity to absorb will also somewhat determine the degree to which he accepts uncritically the standards around him. Education will, in general, stimulate a greater readiness to question interpretations and will provide an individual with certain information that he may find contradictory to some of the ideas he meets outside the classroom. There is already some evidence that education and reading, especially in the social sciences, makes people more liberal in their views.[6] In the early days of the second World War, when most Americans felt sure that the Allies would win, an analysis of the attitudes of a sample population, regarding the type of peace treaty that should follow the war, showed that educated people were much less vindictive in their feelings and did not want Germany to suffer as badly as she had after the first World War.[7]

Individual modifications of norms may also arise because of a person's experiences. Occasionally, a single, intense experience will arouse a desire to alter some way of life or some idea that one has always had. A person may see policemen club strikers or vigilantes intimidate migratory workers and emerge with new standards of social justice. A nine-year-old girl, for example, one Christmas received from her favorite uncle a number of children's books which he had selected from a bookstore. Among other titles, he had chosen *The Jungle* by Upton Sinclair. The girl read this avidly along with

[6] G. Murphy, L. B. Murphy, and T. Newcomb, *op. cit.;* G. Murphy and R. Likert, *Public Opinion and the Individual,* New York: Harpers, 1938.

[7] Hadley Cantril and Donald Rugg, Looking forward to peace, *Publ. Opin. Quart.,* March, 1940, 119, 121.

all the other stories. From that time on she became interested in the fate of the underprivileged and is now devoting much of her time to progressive causes. More generally, however, the effect of experience is a gradual process where contradictions between things as they are and things as they are supposed to be, or as the individual would like them to be for his own interests, becomes more and more apparent.

Certain events in which the individual himself is not a direct participant may also leave their impressions. The public-opinion polls clearly show, for example, that the opinion of Americans toward the Nazis was very greatly changed when Hitler marched his army into Czechoslovakia and when his men conducted their particularly intensive persecution of the Jews on November 10, 1938. The effect of outside events is perhaps even more important than is commonly recognized or than measuring devices are able to show. For a single event may not change a person's attitude noticeably but may be the opening wedge in his questioning of that attitude, so that the attitude itself will show a discernible change months or even years later when the significance of the provocative event has long since been forgotten.[8]

If an individual's temperament, education, expression, or cognizance of certain events does affect his acceptance of current norms it is likely to be in a relatively mild rather than in a drastic way. The individual does not usually want to overthrow most of the culture. He wants rather to modify it, to amplify the meanings of some old concepts, to adjust a few traditional standards to modern conditions. There was, for example, a panel discussion in which certain religious and educational leaders participated. During the question period following the formal discussion, a gentleman in the audience asked one of the speakers if he didn't think all the problems of the world would be settled if everyone were a Christian. "That all depends on what you mean by Christianity and how far you are willing to go with it," said the speaker. "My grandfather would have readily answered 'Yes, certainly' to your question. My grandfather was a slaveholder in the South." The grandson, then, did not

---

[8] Philip Jacobs, Influences of world events on the United States "neutrality" opinion, *Publ. Opin. Quart.*, March 1940.

want to do away with Christianity, but he did want to enlarge its scope.

Not only does this selection by the individual generally suggest to him a moderate rather than a radical change of norms, but it also generally concerns specific norms rather than more basic or general ones. Thus certain people will be eager to stop war, or to improve the lot of the sharecropper, or to take politics out of their city government, or to help the aged, or to provide for unemployed youths. Yet their voting habits indicate that comparatively few of them realize that all these evils which they refuse to accept placidly are intrinsically related to a whole system of ownership and distribution which they strongly defend. Likewise, although over 95 per cent of the American people say that they believe in freedom of speech, about two-thirds of them do not think Communists or Fascists should be allowed to hold public meetings.[9]

Occasionally some individuals will refuse to accept whole patterns of norms that are highly valued by the majority. If such men can gain audiences or put their thoughts into ringing words, they are known as revolutionary thinkers. We remember Rousseau, Marx, or Lincoln as men who questioned commonly accepted, basic values. Almost every area of interest produces such people from time to time. Art has had its Leonardo da Vincis, music its Wagners, religion its Mohammeds, science its Listers. There are, no doubt, many more people of this "radical" type who remain unsung and unknown. Not only do they lack the ability or opportunity to translate their thoughts into effective action, but they are also often disposed of at early ages by guillotines or jails. Others will tend to keep their thoughts to themselves to avoid personal disaster, ostracism, or intimidation.

THE STRUCTURE OF MENTAL CONTEXT

We have roughly classified the objective standards of culture as norms and values, leaving finer distinctions to the sociologist whose problems call for them. We have reviewed the way in which these norms and values are transmitted by representatives of a culture to those who are to carry on that culture. Now our task as psychologists is to understand what the precise relationships are between the indi-

[9] American Institute of Public Opinion, June 9, 1938.

vidual and his society, what subjective standards the individual himself acquires, and how the mental context of the single man can be most accurately characterized.

All the norms and values of a culture or a group have their subjective counterparts in some or all the individuals who compose that culture or group. The social scientist whose main interest is in the description of cultural and institutional behavior, will dismiss such a statement as commonplace and tautological. He will point out that cultures or groups without individuals are unthinkable. And he is quite right. But for the social scientist whose business it is to investigate the reasons for social change or social stability, the statement poses many problems. He must constantly ask himself how certain cultural standards actually become introcepted by the individual and why others are not introcepted at all; what correspondence and uniformity there is between the subjective standards of the individual and the objective standards of the culture; what modifications individual temperaments, capacities, and experiences make on older patterns of thought.

The history of man's development clearly shows that there is not a point-to-point correlation between the laws, customs, mores, and values of a culture, as they might be described by a visiting anthropologist, and the characteristic behavior and thought of all the members of the culture, as they might be discerned by the psychologist. To be sure, the psychological worlds of almost all persons show some order and stability. Part of this stability is due to habits of behavior, society's "most precious conservative agent," as James long ago pointed out. A person gets up, goes to bed, eats his meals, listens to his radio, goes to church, and does a thousand and one other things in a more or less routine fashion month after month. Part of the stability is due to stereotyped ideas. In our own culture almost all of us reckon time with the Gregorian calendar, believe in monogamous marriage, care for sick relatives or friends, defend the right of every man to trial by jury.

In our investigation of the psychology of social movements, it is these beliefs and opinions of men, more than their routine habits of behavior, which must primarily concern us. For when these components of an individual's psychological world are violently jarred by worries, fear, anxieties, and frustrations, when he begins to question the norms and values which have become a part of him, when the customary social framework can apparently no longer satisfy his needs, then a serious discrepancy emerges between the standards of society and the personal standards of the individual. Then the individual is susceptible to new leadership, to conversion, to revolution.

Suppose a boy, named David Green, is born into a middle-class family in a small midwestern town. David's father is a general physician, a sympathetic, kind-hearted man whose duties thoroughly acquaint him with the lives of rich and poor, young and old. David's mother is a woman with a strong Christian background, preoccupied entirely with her home, family, and church work. Neither of David's parents is particularly interested in politics or in anything that is happening outside the local community. But they are both devoted to their children and anxious that their children become respectable citizens and, as they say, leave the world a better place than they found it.

David's parents are what their neighbors call "practicing Christians." Both by example and by teaching they try to give their boy a profound respect for the rights of every individual. From them he learns that there are enormous differences in the opportunities people have in life. Some people, say his parents, are born into poor homes, have to begin work when they are young, and just never seem to get any breaks in life. Others are born with silver spoons in their mouths. Some are looked down upon because they are members of a minority race or religious group, others because they are only day laborers or housemaids. All this, say the Greens, is unjust. In their own small way they try to help the underprivileged of the community. What the state or government might do to help larger numbers of such people never enters their heads. They are just too busy with other things to be concerned with complex national or international problems. They are, however, well aware that they are living in a democracy, and they teach David that democracy is a form of government where all people are able to exercise certain political rights and to enjoy certain freedoms.

David leaves the small home town to go to college. There he learns about other forms of government, about the history of our own country, about political corruption, about tariffs and the interdependency of modern nations, about monopolies, strikes, crime, and the distribution of the national income. His world becomes greatly extended and he begins to appreciate the intricacies of social organization which his parents had never known. When he leaves college, he gets a job in a large city as a construction engineer. He marries and settles down.

When young Mr. Green talks with his friends, they find him enthusiastic about a proposal for a new public school to be erected in a poor section of the city. He is in favor of more government regulation of wages and hours, wants higher income taxes to finance public works programs, more liberal admission of colored students to the state university, and public ownership of utilities. Although some of his acquaintances call him a Red, people who know him realize that he thoroughly opposes Communism as he sees it practiced in Russia, but that he hates Fascism and all it stands for even more. They call him a *progressive*. He believes in democracy. But he believes that there is much yet to be done in this country if real democracy is to be achieved.

Now suppose another boy, named Philip Jenkins, is born into an upper-class home in a suburban district in the East. Philip's father is a corporation lawyer who commutes to his office five days a week. Mrs. Jenkins is fond of her family but leaves most of the care of the children to the maid while she plays her role in the community social life. When Philip is six years old he is sent to the local private school for boys. His mother wants him to grow up with children of the right sort. She does not like to think of his sitting in the same school room with colored children or the boys and girls of ordinary workers. He is not allowed to play with the cook's little boy. Mrs. Jenkins feels quite keenly, and indirectly impresses on Philip, that he is better than most boys, deserves what she thinks is a better education, and should not have to bother with chores around the house.

As Philip grows up he hears his father talk about the restrictions the government is putting on men who have brains enough to amass large amounts of money. His father says that poor people are being spoiled, that they are happy the way they are, don't know any better, and only waste any extra money they have. It's no use to give them decent houses, the elder Jenkins contends, for they are ignorant, dirty, lazy, and won't bother to keep things in order. All they want is something for nothing. They don't seem to realize that a man who has spent four years in college and three more in law school has worked hard for his advantages. Democracy, Philip learns, is the best system of government, because it leaves people alone. The trouble now is, his father says, that the politicians in Washington won't let business men run things as they should be run.

Philip also goes to college. There he studies many of the things that David did. But somehow the problems of housing, crime, unemployment, and the utilization of natural resources seem quite foreign to him. He is concerned with these subjects as things to be passed, not as vital questions involving human welfare. Philip gets most out of the courses that teach him about the stock market and investment. Moreover, he keeps his eye open for friends whose fathers may help him get a good job when he graduates. Because he is an able and likable boy, he does land a promising job in the business offices of a large industry. He, too, marries and settles down.

When Philip Jenkins gets together with his business friends, he tries to figure out how he can help the company make more money, how he can speed up production, how he can cut overhead and labor costs. He considers labor unions only as necessary nuisances, opposes government taxes on excess profits, wants to cut out of the public school system a number of courses that are of no practical value, and thinks that white people should be given preference to colored people when they apply for jobs in the factory. Some who know Jenkins call him a *reactionary* young business man, but he considers himself a liberal. He favors a certain amount of social security and thinks the CCC camps are splendid. He says he favors many objectives of the New Deal but does not like its methods. He is an ardent believer in the democratic form of government. He would hate to have to live in a fascist state, but still he thinks that would be a lesser evil than Communism if a choice were forced upon him.

Here is a glimpse of the mental contexts of two not unusual men whom one might meet in modern American society. How can we best describe the content of their minds? It is not enough merely to say that Green and Jenkins have developed different attitudes. They have different attitudes to be sure, but some of their attitudes are toward specific and temporary affairs, such as the erection of a new public school; whereas other attitudes, such as that toward

Communism, seem broad by comparison. We suspect, too, that some of their attitudes are rather deep-seated, would be held through thick and thin, while others might be readily relinquished. Jenkins, for example, might change his attitude toward social security more readily than his attitude toward labor unions.

Attitudes, then, have various dimensions. Furthermore, the uncritical use of the term attitude obscures the relationships between essentially qualitatively different characteristics of mental life. Isn't there some important distinction as well as important connection, for example, between Green's childhood impression that some people get an unfortunate start in life because their parents are very poor and his favorable adult disposition toward wages and hours legislation? We need to describe the content of mental life in terms that will somehow throw light on cause-and-effect relationships.[10]

An examination of the cases of David Green and Philip Jenkins, observation of everyday social life, and what knowledge we have of the psychological structure of mind all help suggest that we must distinguish between three characteristics of mental context.

Standards of judgment. There were certain social norms and values in the environments of Green and Jenkins which were transmitted to these men by their parents. We recall that Green was taught that all people deserved an equal opportunity in life, but that by no means all people these days were actually provided equal opportunity. He learned that wealth was not a sign of any inherent superiority, that because a person was a Negro, a Jew, or a Catholic was no reason to lessen one's respect for him. Jenkins, on the other hand, was made to feel at a tender age that he was above others, that people in the lower classes tend to be ignorant, stupid, carefree, dirty, and callous to their physical environment.

[10] The omnibus use of the term attitude in much recent social psychology has been examined in Gordon Allport, Attitudes, in *Handbook of Social Psychology* (edited by C. Murchison), Worcester: Clark Univ. Press, 1935, ch. 17. Some of the dimensions of attitudes have been noted and examined experimentally in Hadley Cantril, General and specific attitudes, *Psychol. Monog.,* 1932, 192; W. S. Watson, and G. W. Hartmann, The rigidity of a basic attitudinal frame, *J. Abn. & Soc. Psychol.,* 1939, 34, 314-335; J. G. Darley, Changes in measured attitudes and adjustments, *J. Soc. Psychol.,* 1938, 9, 189-199; S. E. Asch, H. Block, and M. Hertzman, Studies in the principles of judgments and attitudes, *J. Psychol.,* 1938, 5, 219-251; Allen L. Edwards, Four dimensions in political stereotypes, *J. Abn. & Soc. Psychol.,* 1940, 35, 566-572.

Now all these notions of what is good and bad, right and wrong, superior and inferior are simply taken for granted by these two men. These notions are assumptions, presuppositions, unquestioned evaluations. They serve as definite points of anchorage, as standards of judgment which provide the psychological basis for interpretation. As we shall see later, they may be completely forgotten by the individual as he matures. But they leave their mark on the whole structure of his mental organization.

Frames of reference. If someone who knew both Green and Jenkins were asked what sort of men they were, he would probably answer, among other things, that Green was quite a liberal, progressive, democratic fellow and that Jenkins was conservative, almost reactionary, and tended to be snobbish about his position in life. Such characterizations as these, so frequently employed in everyday conversation, are possible only because Green and Jenkins have acquired general and consistent points of view. These points of view in turn are founded upon the whole pattern of assumptions, the standards of judgment, the two men acquired. They are as broad and general as the pattern of standards upon which they are based. They are the organized framework, the structure which directs interpretations. These generalized points of view we shall call *frames of reference.*

Attitudes. In addition to standards of judgment and frames of reference, the mental context of Green and Jenkins contains another important feature. When these men are asked their opinions regarding certain issues, when they must decide what they think about a certain labor union, a certain community housing project, a certain legislative proposal to raise more taxes, they have relatively little difficulty in making up their minds. Green would probably approve of the CIO while Jenkins would disapprove of it; Green would like to see an extension of the federal housing project, Jenkins would think it was interfering with private business; Green would contend that wealthy people should pay higher income taxes, Jenkins would argue that a sales taxes on everyone would be fairer. These are interpretations of definite situations, evaluations which these men place on certain objects or proposals. These are their attitudes. They are derived from a general frame of reference. Unlike the frame of reference, the attitude may be general or specific depending upon the stimulus which evokes it. When Jenkins refuses the application for a job of a specific man because that man happens to be a Negro, he is exhibiting a specific attitude; when he says that Negroes should not be encouraged to enter institutions of higher learning, he is showing a somewhat more general attitude; when he says that he opposes Fascism he reveals a still more general attitude. A frame of reference may be regarded as an attitude only when the stimulus itself is sufficiently general to evoke the whole frame.

The distinction between the three concepts—standard of judgment, frame of reference, and attitude—may be summed up with the example of David Green. He learns certain values and assumptions in early life: these become for him *standards of judgment*. On the basis of these he constructs or has constructed for him a pro-democratic point of view: this is a *frame of reference*. When specific situations or proposals are seen by him to have some relationship to democracy and are evaluated accordingly, he has definite opinions: these are *attitudes*.

VARIATIONS OF MENTAL CONTEXT

We have so far shown that a frame of reference is based on certain standards of judgment, and that an attitude emerges when a given situation is appraised by means of a frame of reference. But this relationship is in many instances an oversimplification or falsification of what may actually hold true for certain people at certain times. In the actual course of everyday life, the untangling of relationships is not always easy; and when the relationships are untangled, we may find certain variations in the elementary process so far described. At least four complications may enter into the illustrations we have used: complications due to overlapping, short-circuiting, varying degrees of integration, or the personal involvement entailed in standards, frames, or attitudes.

Overlapping. The first problem arises because there is by no means always complete independence between one standard of judgment and others, one frame of reference and others, one attitude and others. A certain standard of judgment may have in it some common relationships between the individual and his environment that other assumptions have. A person may believe in freedom to worship, freedom to speak, freedom to travel. All these values are somewhat similar and yet distinct. All might be subsumed under a single more general value of freedom to do as one pleases—if the individual believed that. But he probably doesn't, for he realizes that certain personal restrictions are necessary in organized social life. One frame of reference may be derived from standards of judgment that overlap to some extent with the standards of judgment which furnish the basis for another frame of reference. Thus the Fascists and Communists, if certain common values can be better achieved, may temporarily join hands. One attitude may at one time be the result of one frame of reference and at another time be the result of another frame of reference operative in the same individual. Thus a person may, at one time, approve of a political candidate because he is the member of a certain party and at another time approve of him because he discovers the candidate is, like himself, a good Catholic.

The variety of standards that may give rise to the same frames of reference and the variety of frames of reference that may produce the same attitudes must never be lost sight of if the mental contexts of different individuals or groups of individuals are to be understood properly. All too frequently the assumption is made that the same points of view held by different poeple are due to the same causes. While David Green may have disapproved of President Franklin D. Roosevelt because Green was too liberal, Philip Jenkins may have disapproved of him because Jenkins was too conservative.

Often the results of attitude tests or public-opinion polls may be misleading if one does not know the underlying frames of reference upon which the attitudes are based. Thus, in one study of the popularity of Associate Justice Black, it was found that 35 per cent of the population approved of his nomination shortly after it was made, and that the nomination was approved by approximately the same percentage a few weeks later after he had been accused of affiliation with the Ku Klux Klan. On the surface it appeared, then, that public opinion had not changed, but analysis showed that different people were approving him at different times and, probably, for very different reasons. At first, opposition to his appointment came chiefly from republican, upper-class voters; later the opposition was concentrated in Catholic, democratic, lower-class voters.[11]

Short-circuiting. A second complication arises because of the short-

[11] Paul Lazarsfeld, *J. Appl. Psychol.,* 1939, **23,** 131-144.

circuiting of the relationship we have described between standards of judgment, frames of reference, and attitudes. It has already been pointed out that an individual may acquire a frame of reference without having any knowledge of the values upon which it is based or other possible values that might be considered before a final point of view is accepted. Although standards of judgment are always implicit in the acceptance of a frame of reference, they may never be considered by the individual. Many people, for example, will accept Christianity as the only true religion. In days gone by, many people had defended this point of view with their lives. Probably then, as now, no greater proportion of them had ever really examined the assumptions upon which the religion was based and compared these assumptions to those in the teachings of Mohammed, Buddha, or Confucius. Therefore just as such frames of reference may be accepted without foundations, so isolated attitudes, completely unrelated to any frame of reference, may be acquired. People may react negatively to symbols, such as "Reds" or "Wops," or they may accept certain attitudes toward the season's fashions, toward fat men, or blonde women—attitudes that have no discernible relationship to any underlying frame of reference. Such attitudes are essentially conditioned responses. Other persons may have more idiosyncratic, disconnected attitudes. A man may, for example, disapprove of drinking alcoholic beverages although consciously his attitude is not related to any religious, moral, or scientific frame of reference. Or he may like all animals except horses, which he loathes. Psychoanalytic probing may uncover the relationship of some of these tangential attitudes to more basic systems of mental life, or such analysis may show that the attitudes have been created as the result of unique, traumatic experiences and that they never were related to the main current of belief.

This short-circuiting of the relationship tends to the familiar process of rationalization. If a person has a frame of reference without being aware of the standards from which it is derived, then he will, when questioned, attempt to defend his point of view by thinking up good reasons for it. Or if he has attitudes toward people, issues, or objects which are not derived from any frame of reference he may at times find it necessary to concoct some rationale for his

opinions—a rationale that will lead him either to the temporary
acceptance of definite values or to a larger consistent framework
which will give his attitudes some "reasonable" basis.

The usual steps in the process of attitude formation, furthermore,
may be radically shortened in situations where a stimulus will evoke
a response which is based directly on a standard of judgment. Such
situations arise when the stimulus is so unique, so specific, or so
sudden that no frame of reference is applicable.[12]

In a study of a nation-wide Hallowe'en broadcast that frightened
at least 1,000,000 Americans in 1938, it was found, for example, that
two-thirds of the people who tuned in after the announcement indi-
cating that the broadcast was a play believed they were listening to a
news broadcast. And 70 per cent of these people were frightened or
disturbed by subsequent reports of monsters from Mars who were
destroying life and property in wholesale fashion all along the north-
eastern coast. Here was a situation never before encountered by these
people. Those who were upset had no general frame of reference or
no specific standards of judgment with which they could properly
orient themselves. Uncritically they accepted a standard of judgment

[12] The literature of experimental psychology is filled with research which demon-
strates conclusively that a frame of reference is an inevitable accompaniment of any
series of judgments a person may be asked to make; and that when the situation is
unique and specific, as it is frequently deliberately designed to be in the laboratory,
the frame of reference is a function of the relationships discerned between the
series of stimuli. No matter how hard the experimentalist, especially the psycho-
physicist, may try to work on the peripheral level of judgments and side-step
central issues, he finds it almost impossible to avoid in the laboratory the phenomenon we are describing that occurs so constantly in judgments of everyday life.
Cf. M. Sherif *Psychology of Social Norms*, New York: Harper, 1936, ch. 3; W. A.
Hunt and J. Volkmann, The anchoring of an affective scale, *Amer. J. Psychol.*,
1937, **49**, 88-92.

Perhaps the most significant difference between the perceptual frame of reference
in experimental psychology and the social frame of reference considered here is
that the latter is almost always ego involving, the former seldom ego involving.
The various concepts, *Einstellung* and *Stellungnahme,* which were proposed by
the Würzbürgers and were employed in the experimental psychology of thought,
judgment, or affectivity, would, in our terminology, be essentially highly circumscribed frames of reference based on one or a few specific standards of judgment
derived either from the experimental instructions or the stimuli experienced during
the experiment as the case might be. The *Verankerungspunkte,* demonstrated by
Wertheimer and other Gestalt psychologists, would be essentially standards of judgment upon which perceptual frames are based.

which proved to be false and which resulted in some extremely narrowing experiences.[13]

Such an interpretation, based as it is directly on a standard of judgment, must not be confused with a conditioned response. A person may hurry to the telephone when he hears a bell ring in the house. Here a specific reaction to a specific stimulus has been learned. If such a conditioned response is regarded as a standard of judgment, it must be remembered that it is only one limited type of standard of judgment and in no way a substitute for the concept as we have used it. Analysis of the backgrounds of the people who became panicky listening to the Hallowe'en broadcast clearly shows that in no way had they been specifically conditioned against Martian invaders' mowing down people on this planet. Nor should we confuse the term standard of judgment with a motor habit, such as, for example the veteran automobile driver who has learned not to slam on his brakes when his car suddenly starts to skid on an icy road. Here again there is a reaction without relationship to a frame of reference. But here there is little if any connection between such a response and the type of mental organization that concerns us in the present volume.

Differential organization. A third complication arises from the fact that the components of various individuals' mental contexts are organized into systems that vary in their completeness of integration. Furthermore, the organization of the mental context within a single individual may change radically with his experience and education. Some people have comparatively few standards of judgment which furnish the basis for a limited number of generalized frames of reference. But these few frames of reference, in turn, can lead to a host of highly consistent attitudes. Sometimes this *Zusammenhang* in mental life may be due simply to the fact that an individual has to an extraordinary degree accepted a few primary values from his culture. Other persons may attain such integration as the result of wide experience, years of study or reflection. Both an ignorant peasant and a great scientist may have a simple, consistent organization of mental context. But while the peasant has accepted bodily the few beliefs of his ancestors without any question, the scientist

[13] Hadley Cantril, *The Invasion from Mars,* Princeton: Princeton University Press, 1940.

may have sought some factual basis for certain standards and arrived at others after a serious comparison of the values of many cultures. In certain rare cases, integration apparently may approach completeness, a single value may seem to determine an individual's frame of reference and all his attitudes. Tolstoy's principle of the simplification of life, Lenin's concern with social revolution, Hitler's dream of Pan-Germanism, and the single-mindedness of great religious leaders are examples.

Other people may have a larger number of different standards of judgment, some of which may even be contradictory. Hence, their frames of reference are apt to be more circumscribed, their attitudes less consistent. Still other people are found with comparatively few socially important values, a situation which may be due either to inherent instability of personality or, what is more common, to the failure of the culture to provide them directly or through education with any clear-cut standards that they can uncompromisingly accept as anchoring points for interpretations.

Just how well-integrated the mental context of any person is cannot easily be determined.[14] Introspectively we are aware of the different components of our mental contexts in varying degrees. For most people, the ordinary current of mental life flows on the attitudinal level. And while we are more or less aware of our attitudes, we may quickly forget their sources, if indeed they were ever known. People tend to feel satisfied if they can evaluate this situation or that event. The business of making ends meet, of adjusting to an ever-changing environment pushes them on to more and more evaluations of concrete situations. They have comparatively little time and interest to discern why they have the attitudes they do or why they have any attitudes at all. Even in such moments of reflection it is not easy to reconstruct and to conceptualize one's frame of reference. Such a process involves more insight than most men possess.

It is even more difficult introspectively and requires even more perspicacity to detect the values and assumptions which one has taken for granted. They are even further hidden from consciousness. The net result is that people lose perspective not only concerning

[14] Experimental attempts to differentiate between the strength and pervasiveness of standards are found in Darley, *op. cit.*; Watson and Hartmann, *op. cit.*; Asch, Block, and Hertzman, *op. cit.*

themselves and others like them, but also concerning people whose ways of life are very different from their own. They become encapsulated in psychological worlds which are held together by their own presuppositions. They can be thoroughly understood and can understand themselves only when the boundaries which form their worlds are discovered. The perspective which an individual has on himself, on other people, or on other cultures is directly proportional to his awareness of his own standards of judgment.[15]

Ego involvement. A fourth complication in unraveling the nature of mental context develops because certain standards of judgment, with the resultant interpretations they provide, are felt by the individual to involve him personally. Subjectively, he, his ego, is more concerned about some things than others. Some of his standards have a strong, felt significance for him; others he accepts in a matter-of-fact way without any strong feeling. Thus in our own culture a person will be more disturbed if his right to live in peace with his family is threatened than if his right to travel to Canada or Mexico is taken away; he will sacrifice more to maintain his economic values than he will to preserve his aesthetic values.[16]

[15] Scores of examples of lack of perspective might be cited. The literature of anthropology is rife with descriptions of different cultural standards. Within our own culture, sociologists are accumulating accounts of discrepancies between the things different people take for granted. For example, *These Are Our Lives* (Federal Writers' Project, Chapel Hill: University of North Carolina Press, 1939) reports many instances such as the following:

The narrator is a young man in charge of a WPA supply room.

Folks that ain't never been poor just don't know nothin' a-tall about doin' on nothin'. I get so all-fired full of laugh when some o' these women from the higher ups comes down to the welfare department. Nice ladies, but it ain't a salt spoon of sense about poor folks in their heads. Pretty little thing come last week to tell the women come here about cookin'. Before she started spielin', she seen them cans of salmon I took from the big case and put on that shelf back there. That gave her a start. She aimed to tell 'em how to make up a pot dish from salmon. We ain't really got no salmon here. Just a cheap grade of canned mackerel. She sailed in. 'Brush the baking dish with melted butter,' says she. If she hadn't been so pretty and young, I'd like to asked right off, where they going to get the butter? Ain't two in the rooms got butter for their bread. You'll have to shift to a skillet for the cookin'. That's about the best they got for greasin' up. Of course I didn't say so such to her. She was just plumb wore out time she got dat salmon out of her head and into the cook stove.

[16] Some standards of judgment and the frames of reference derived from them have little or nothing to do with the ego. One's frame of reference concerning speed, light, the shape of buildings, or the western musical scale seldom acquires any personal significance. These are essentially specific perceptual frames, based on

The amount of ego involvement any standard of judgment entails is best discovered perhaps by means of the disturbance felt if an accepted value is destroyed or by means of the sacrifice an individual will make to preserve a value. The religious martyr, the political revolutionary, and the patriotic citizen are willing to sacrifice life itself rather than relinquish certain of their cherished ideals.

The extent to which a person feels that either his standards of judgment or his frames of reference involve what he regards as "himself" provides the intensity with which he holds these standards and frames.

This dimension of intensity is to be distinguished clearly from the dimension of direction. The difference between these dimensions may be seen most clearly in relation to attitudes. The *direction* of an attitude is the extent to which it indicates approval or disapproval of the object, person, or issue to which it is related; the *intensity* of an attitude is the personal significance and importance which the individual who holds the attitudes assigns to it. Thus two people may be equally opposed to child labor according to an attitude scale. But whereas one person merely may vote against child labor or express his opinion whenever he is asked, another person may devote much of his time, energy, and income furthering legislation to prevent child labor. In America the widespread fear of Communism undoubtedly is due in part to popular knowledge of the intensity with which Communists hold their beliefs, as well as to exaggerated ideas of the Communists' numerical strength.[17]

This dimension of intensity is another reason for the variation in the stability of a frame of reference or an attitude. The more a frame involves the ego, the more permanent and inflexible will it be. Because this is true, people with essentially the same amount of education or intelligence will often cling tenaciously to diverging frames of reference. It is a well-known fact, if a discouraging one, that the way a person votes is determined much more by his self-

---

single standards of judgment and evoked almost entirely by some external stimulus. They generally give rise to judgments, not to attitudes. Such non-ego frames of reference, important as they are in the psychology of perception and learning, are, for our present understanding of mental context, of much less consequence than ego frames.

[17] D. McGregor, *J. Abn. & Soc. Psychol.,* **34,** 1939, 179-199.

interest or his unquestioned frames of reference than by his knowledge of social problems or his intellectual ability to appraise issues.[18] Other frames of reference, such as those concerning religion, the family, or the nation, are also likely to become thoroughly ingrained. They, too, will probably be little influenced by education or by new experiences that might, on the other hand, radically alter points of view about which the individual does not feel so strongly. It is for this reason that propaganda is not uniformly the all-powerful weapon that some people assume. Propaganda, like other methods of influencing opinion, is limited by the nature of the personal context which it arouses or of the social context within which it must operate. The essential difference between a highly intelligent, well-educated, widely experienced man who has a certain frame of reference and a dull, uneducated, inexperienced man with the same frame of reference is that the former is able to rationalize his point of view more lucidly and persuasively than the latter.[19]

The distinction between standards of judgment, frames of reference, and attitude, the relationships between them, the complications that arise in tracing their interdependence will clarify some of the problems we shall confront in our later analyses of social phenomena. They will help us understand why people become members of mobs, why they are taken in by utopian schemes, why they follow a self-appointed messiah, why they join a revolutionary political movement. Unlike the older, static, elementaristic context theory of meaning, which existed *in vacuo*, the theory we have outlined here has imbedded meaning and interpretation into both a social and a personal context. Moreover, as we shall see in the next chapter, this context becomes a very necessary and integral part of the psychology of motivation.

[18] John Dewey, *The Public and Its Problems*, New York: Holt, 1927.
[19] K. Diven, Aesthetic appreciation test, in H. A. Murray *et al.*, *Explorations in Personality*, New York: Oxford University Press, 1938, 447-453.

Chapter 2

MOTIVATION IN SOCIAL LIFE

In everyday life people feel themselves pushed or pulled by some goal, some drive, some ambition, some devotion, some frustration or need. When they are asked the reasons for their activities, people say they are hungry and want food, tired and want rest, mad and want to fight, interested in a particular kind of work or play, anxious to solve a scientific or commercial problem. The motives of men are almost as numerous as men themselves, ranging from the comparatively simple desire for shelter or a mate to the search for an all-embracing metaphysics or for the South Pole. No matter how inaccurate an account a person may give of his motivation, he feels that his behavior is somehow purposive, that his behavior is somehow directed toward a goal.

Of all the problems facing psychologists, that of motivation most defies simplification. Some psychologists reject the concept of motivation as too teleological for science. It is, they say, too subjective to be susceptible of study and they talk, instead, of incentives, of instigations, of means-end relationships. Mechanists, although implicitly recognizing purposive behavior as obvious and important, hold that to speak of purposes and motives is too easy a way out of the dilemma, and they attempt to explain away purpose. Their only self-defense is to deny that motivation exists. As Whitehead observes, "Many a scientist has patiently designed experiments for the *purpose* of substantiating his belief that animal operations are motivated by no purposes."[1] The problem of motivation cannot be easily side-stepped if we are to extend our interest from the rat in the maze to the man in the street.

The particular way the psychologist attacks the problem will depend upon his own purposes and his own interests. If he is a physiologist, he will regard his task as essentially that of discovering

[1] A. N. Whitehead, *The Function of Reason,* Princeton: Princeton University Press, 1929, 12.

the physiological processes related to behavior and described in terms of rewards or punishments; if he is a clinician, he will search for the causes of the anxieties or perversions which keep his patient from feeling or acting like a "normal" person; if he is a laboratory experimentalist, he may be chiefly concerned with the role of incentives in learning or perception. The concept of motivation is thus attacked from many different angles.

And it is well that this is the case. Some investigators will insist on what they call *scientific validity*. They will demand experimental proof for any hypothesis and condemn as poetry or philosophy any account of goal-seeking activity that cannot be neatly demonstrated under controlled conditions. Other investigators will insist above all else on psychological adequacy. They will refuse to admit that the complexity of man's purposive striving can be reduced altogether to an explanation whose validity they believe is restricted to a particular organism in a particular situation.[2]

The emphasis in this volume is frankly on adequacy, for we are primarily concerned with analyses of certain social phenomena as they occur in everyday social life. We want to discover what it is that drives men to become members of crowds, mobs, political movements, or revolutions. If we restricted our accounts of motivation to theories that claim rigid scientific "proof," we would distort or obscure our problems, fitting problems to a limited conceptual scheme rather than formulating a conceptual scheme to account for the problems. We would also fail to discover strictly psychological relationships which may later on in some modified form be problems for the laboratory psychologist to test or for the physiological psychologist to underpin with a mechanism. In brief, our justification for our emphasis on adequacy is merely our interest.

APPROACHES TO THE PROBLEM

Certain major conceptualizations have arisen in social psychology to account for the purposes of men. Following Gordon W. Allport,

[2] In the recent history of social psychology, the contrast between these two approaches is exemplified by E. B. Holt and the early text of F. H. Allport, on the one hand, and the writing of William McDougall or E. A. Ross, on the other hand. The arguments between such men are due not so much to disputes about facts as to divergent points of view concerning the relative emphasis to be placed on scientific parsimony and on adequacy in the psychological explanation of motivation.

we may divide these approaches into two groups: those that seek original, basic energies common to all men and those that emphasize the variety and individuality of personal motives.[3] A brief review of the implications of these approaches will show why neither of them is as yet sufficiently adequate to explain social movements.

Search for original energies. A number of attempts have been made to describe the innate endowments which furnish for all human beings a basis for their motivational life. Behaviorists have looked for universal prepotent reflexes;[4] others have posited lists of instincts or propensities which unfold and push men on;[5] Freud gave man an *Id,* or storehouse of instinctual energy;[6] some psychologists assign to all people certain uniform wishes or needs. Although each classification of innate drives may satisfy the purposes of its author, no two classifications are sufficiently overlapping to be called alike, and the accumulation of psychological data seems to bring us no nearer to agreement on any one classification. Even if the whole search for any such dichotomizing is a scientific will-o-the-wisp,[7] we cannot deny that there are certain basic, biological needs, such as those for food, shelter, and sexual gratification, more or less common to all men. They become so conditioned or regulated by cultural influences that later on they may be scarcely recognizable. And while we must reject as inadequate for our purposes any theory of motivation based entirely in terms of such basic needs or their modifications, we must at the same time not overlook the possibility that tensions created by needs so fundamental may be, at times, important parts of the story of some social movements.

The reason why such accounts of motivation are inadequate is that they fail to give satisfactory reasons for the enormous flexibility and variety of motives found in modern everyday life—they fail to show why socialized men, often only indirectly motivated by any

[3] G. W. Allport, *Personality: A Psychological Interpretation,* New York: Holt, 1937, ch. 7.

[4] F. H. Allport, *Social Psychology,* Boston: Houghton Mifflin, 1924; E. B. Holt, *Animal Drive and the Learning Process,* New York: Holt, 1931.

[5] William McDougall, *An Introduction to Social Psychology,* Boston: Luce, 14th ed., 1921.

[6] Sigmund Freud, *The Ego and the Id,* London: Hogarth, 1927.

[7] G. W. Allport, Motivation in personality: Reply to Mr. Bertocci, *Psychol. Rev.,* 1940, **47**, 533-554.

search for food, sex, or shelter, display the directed behavior they do. As Allport says, "Not four wishes nor eighteen propensities, nor any and all combination of these, even with their extensions and variations, seem adequate to account for the endless variety of goals sought by an endless variety of mortals." It is essential, then, to find some way to account for this variety of motives without positing a total host of instincts or needs or without trying to classify all specific motives as some permutation of one of a more restricted number of basic drives.

Functional autonomy. This inadequacy of theories which seeks uniform dimensions of mind in general has been met by the theory of functional autonomy elaborated most systematically by G. W. Allport.[8] According to this theory, the variety of adult motives can be accounted for by the fact that learned behavior which originally stems from innate needs may become functionally independent of its origins and itself possess a dynamic quality. "Just as a child gradually repudiates his dependence on his parents, develops a will of his own, becomes self-active and self-determining, and outlives his parents, so it is with motives. Each motive has a definite point of origin which may lie in the hypothetical instincts, or, more likely in organic tensions and diffuse irritability . . . Theoretically all adult purposes can be traced back to these seed-forms in infancy. But as the individual matures the bond is broken. The tie is historical, not functional . . . The life of a tree is continuous with that of its seed, but the seed no longer sustains and nourishes the full grown tree. Earlier purposes lead into later purposes, but are abandoned in their favor."[9]

Presumably, if one could obtain a complete case history of an individual, one could uncover the sources of his present motives. But whether or not the real origins of derived drives are ever discovered, there would seem to be overwhelming evidence from personal experience and observation that men's interests, when once formed, are by no means necessarily sustained by some original urge. It becomes more possible, then, to understand why men may become absorbed by such a variety of activities. The wheat farmer, the architect, the carpenter, the concert pianist, the life-insurance salesman, the fisherman, the sea captain, the cook, the devoted mother

[8] Allport, *Personality, op. cit.,* ch. 7.
[9] *Ibid.,* 194.

are all motivated by derived drives. A search for some earlier, more primitive need as the source for the contemporary energy of these drives forces one to indulge in highly imaginative speculation.

The theory of functional autonomy may be regarded, then, as much more satisfactory for our purposes than theories which seek basic, innate drives common to all men. But even this theory is not wholly suitable. For it fails to place the individual and his motives sufficiently in their social context. It obscures the significance of any motive to the whole life of the individual and thereby neglects the intimate relationship between the person, the *me*, the self, and its cultural surroundings.

For illustrative purposes, let us consider two typical cases. Suppose, for example, that a Mr. Lewis has a derived drive to earn as much money as he can. Originally Mr. Lewis needed money to eat, to provide his personal needs and later those of his family. His industry, his luck, and his business acumen make him a millionaire by the time he is 45 years old. He has plenty of money to supply all the needs of himself and his family. But he goes on earning more and more money and the more he earns the more he returns in taxes. Does Mr. Lewis merely have a derived drive to earn money? Or is the process of earning money somehow a means to some other personal end, some other value which he has incorporated as part of himself? Suppose Mr. Lewis is offered the presidency of a great university, the city-managership of a large metropolis, or the post of United States ambassador to some European capital. The chances are that he would accept these new positions which, in themselves, would decrease his net income. Or, to take another example, suppose a Miss Beech graduates with honors in English from her college, does postgraduate work, and becomes a brilliant and absorbed scholar of Elizabethan literature. Her chief interest in life seems to be to understand a certain literary period and to uncover and publish new bits of information concerning it. But suddenly a man appears in her life. She falls in love with him, has a family, and only occasionally and in a comparatively non-professional way returns to her former literary pursuits.

These are not far-fetched illustrations. Functionally autonomous motives in mature adults frequently seem to change overnight. Yet they change only when the individual involved can increase his own self-respect or improve his status. *Derived drives are autonomous of their origins but not autonomous of the ego* or of the values in the culture which the individual has somehow interiorized as part of *him*.[10] Before we can outline a theory of motivation satisfactory for our purposes we must, then, see what this ego is and just how it is rooted in and affected by the social context.

THE EGO

Development of the ego.[11] In the last chapter we pointed out how the individual acquired certain standards of judgment, frames of reference, and attitudes. We showed how these different characteristics of mental life determined an individual's reactions and gave consistency and congruence to his thought and behavior. Although this is half the story of motivation in social life, it is not the whole story. For throughout the chapter there was an important implication: we assumed, without elaborating the point, that most of these standards, frames and attitudes were somehow an integral part of the individual self. When a person's national flag is torn down, *he* is insulted; when disparaging remarks are made of his parents, *he* is involved; when his football team or political party loses a contest, *he* has been defeated. Certain standards, frames and attitudes the individual feels are a part of him. How does this come about?

All evidence would indicate that the child at birth has no notion that he is a separate individual. His world, as James pointed out, is a "buzzing confusion." He experiences undifferentiated forms, tastes, sounds, and temperatures. All are vague and inseparable and he does not know that these experiences are happening to *him*. He does not differentiate between himself and the objects around him, between the person of his mother, for example, and the warmth and satisfaction she provides. But gradually, as he matures, he learns that *he* is something separate and distinct.

A number of influences which help the infant and the growing child to distinguish what is himself from what are other things in

---

[10] G. W. Allport, Motivation in personality: Reply to Mr. Bertocci, *op. cit.*

[11] The concept of the ego as developed here was stated by M. Sherif in his *Psychology of Social Norms*. The discussion in this chapter and the final theory adopted is essentially an elaboration and extension of the points outlined by Sherif. The ego as conceived here includes the super-ego of the psychoanalysts.

the world have been suggested by various psychologists.[12] By manipulating various parts of his body and other objects around him, relating visual to kinaesthetic cues the child learns what is the physical *me* as contrasted to the physical *not me*. Later he finds that *he* can be a cause of events or action; with a howl he can make his mother run to comfort him, with a slight push he can knock over a tower of blocks. He finds that he is always referred to by a certain sound, "Johnny." *He* has a name. He sees that *his* physical self is separated from the outside environment by clothes. His developing memory enables him to recall that certain experiences are familiar to *him*.

Soon the ego or me becomes extended far beyond the simple confines of the physical self. The child is told that certain objects or that a certain room belongs to *him*. As he adjusts himself to his expanding world, he is constantly instructed that some things are good or right to do, to say, or to believe, while other things are bad and wrong. He learns that he is an American, a white man, a Methodist, a Democrat, a midwesterner. And consciously or unconsciously he learns that these affiliations are "good." For the norms of the culture surrounding the individual are, as we have seen, generally evaluated already by those who compose that culture. In the process of learning these values, the individual acquires them as part of himself. His ego, therefore, becomes enormously extended. It transcends time and space. The individual who may believe both in democracy and in the beauty of Byzantine art will himself feel upset if anti-democratic forces win a victory in a distant battle field or if someone makes a derogatory comment about the ancient art he loves.

Variations in egos. The relativity and complexity of individual egos are bound to be enormous and to defy any simple typologies such as

[12] See William James, *Principles of Psychology,* New York: Holt, 1890, ch. 10; William Stern, *Psychology of Early Childhood,* New York: Holt, 1930, 2nd ed., chs. 30-34; S. Freud, *op. cit.;* K. Lewin, *Dynamic Theory of Personality,* New York & London: McGraw-Hill, 1935; K. Koffka, *Principles of Gestalt Psychology,* New York: Harcourt, Brace, 1935; William McDougall, *Energies of Men,* New York: Scribner's, 1933; W. Preyer, *Mental Development in the Child,* New York: Appleton-Century, 1896; J. Piaget, *The Child's Conception of the World,* New York: Harcourt, Brace, 1929. The contributions of each of these and other writers and their disagreements are not analyzed in detail here since our main concern is with the result, the phenomenon of self-consciousness, rather than with the genesis. Sherif, *op. cit.,* ch. 9, and Allport, *op. cit.,* ch. 6, review briefly some of the major contributions.

the four *selves* of James or the six *types* of Spranger.[13] Differences in cultural influences, differences in training, differences in temperament and intellectual capacity will all play their role in shaping the ego of every individual. The child's conception of what is himself will differ from the adult's; the primitive man's conception will differ from that of his civilized contemporary; the ignorant, apathetic man's conception from that of an educated, alert individual. We can list at least four conditions that contribute to the variety we observe in the egos of different individuals.[14]

1. There is variability in the patterns of social values which so largely compose the ego. As was pointed out in the last chapter, different cultural patterns contain different established ways of satisfying needs which the individual must uphold if he is to become an acceptable member of the culture. What one culture regards as "moral" another culture will regard as "immoral"; what one culture calls "honesty" another may call "dishonesty"; what one culture calls "success," another may call "failure." Furthermore, as we have already seen, by no means all persons in the same limited culture will accept to the same extent the characteristic values of the culture. The experience and education of one person will develop in him a critical ability and perhaps lead him to incorporate as his standards of judgment, not certain commonly accepted social values, but values shared by only a few individuals who cherish them as ideals. Such people may become reformers, evangelists, or radicals. Other individuals become dissatisfied with certain values surrounding them but cannot find any consistent, ideal standards with which they may identify themselves. They turn out to be malcontents or dilettantes.

Some people will regard certain objects with so great a value and will identify themselves so completely with these objects that it may be difficult for them to orient themselves in what might seem to the outside observer as the most intelligent or appropriate way. Just as the child may regard a toy or a particular corner of the room as part of him, just as some primitives regard their excrement or some pos-

---

[13] W. James, *op. cit.*, ch. 10; E. Spranger, *Lebensformen*, Halle: Niemeyer, 1927, Pt. 2.

[14] Some of the points in this discussion have been suggested by H. Werner in his *Comparative Psychology of Mental Development*, New York: Harper, 1940 Werner discusses these conditions in relation to the syncretic nature of primitive thought, imagery, and action.

session as part of themselves, so do some men in our own society identify themselves completely with their houses, their land, or their fortunes. It therefore becomes impossible for such people to consider their own actions without thinking at the same time of the fate of the things that are also bound to them. Adjustment becomes less flexible, choices are more circumscribed. Thus, some penniless families living on marginal land which they call theirs, will not willingly move to richer soil provided them by the Resettlement Administration; some wealthy people may prefer to face the risk of revolution or dictatorship in which all their money would be confiscated rather than pay larger taxes to ease the lot of disgruntled workers.

Other people will make comparatively little distinction between their own goals and the goals of their community, between their own frames of reference and the norms of their society. The child may find it difficult to distinguish himself as a separate member of his family; the Australian primitive holds that his brothers have all the rights he has, even over his children and his wife; some people in our own culture will become so engrossed in the affairs of a local club, fraternity, or movement that "it becomes their whole life" and may, depending on its purposes, give them an air of self-importance and self-righteousness. One psychological consequence of this identification of the self with the social world is that a person depends upon external social circumstances for his personal stability. If the social context with which he identifies himself is altered, then a violent disturbance of the ego occurs. If the lodge goes bankrupt or if he has to move into another community, he is thoroughly lost until he can find some new identification. And since his ego is so dependent on some part of his social environment, his ego drives may change their direction with any change of policy in the lodge, with any new project started in the community. His ego is labile and flexible, and has little independence from the social situation. The more mature person is self-contained, his motivation is more consistent, his personal integrity is not blown thither and yon by the winds of social change.

2. The differences between the values people incorporate into their egos and the relative differentiation they make between their egos and external objects or social environments will create for indi-

viduals differences in their psychological worlds, in the inclusiveness of their life space. The world of the child is especially likely to be circumscribed in both time and space. His world is his room, his home, his yard, or his neighborhood. His life is running its course in a temporal space that consciously has little past and little future. There is a nearness of everything. The dimensions in the psychological worlds of modern adults vary so enormously that it is difficult for any single individual to imagine what the world must be like for many of the contemporaries even in his own society. Think of the differences between the worlds of a wheat farmer and a plumber, a nurse and a Maine fisherman, a sailor and a coal miner, a college professor and an air-mail pilot. How, for example, during the summer of 1939, could a complacent, uneducated, politically disinterested, small-town grandmother possibly project herself into the world of a secretary of state who was busy night and day telephoning distant ambassadors and reading cables from European capitals? For one, Europe and war would seem as distant as the moon; for the other, they would seem as close as the next-door neighbor.

3. There is variability between individuals in the understanding of causality. It is a familiar fact that children in a certain stage of development and many primitives possess what modern, sophisticated adults regard as naive ideas of causal relationship. Animistic and egocentric thinking are often the rule for them. The child turns a stick of wood into an airplane; the primitive attributes life to the sun. The child believes in Santa Claus; the primitive thinks he is sick because his enemy is casting a spell over him. Neither has the training nor the experience necessary to understand contemporary, mature notions of causality. So it is often with men in modern society.

The difficulties people encounter in their search for explanation will be treated in detail in the next chapter. It should be pointed out here, however, that the nature of the ego is affected by differences in the validity of explanations, the reliability of standards of judgment. For some people will so identify themselves with a certain interpretation of events that they are deeply hurt when that interpretation is questioned. For example, the person who firmly believes in a single dynamic force, such as God, economic determinism, or Aryan superiority, will be more intolerant, more rigid in his adjustments, more fanatical in his devotion than an agnostic, than someone who accepts an idea of multiple causation, or than someone who believes no final explanation for a given problem is yet possible because information is insufficient.

4. There is variability in the degree to which different values are regarded as personally significant by different individuals. Two individuals in the same culture may be exposed to the same values. Each may make the same values a part of himself. But the core of one person's ego may be composed of certain values which are to another person of relatively little importance. Thus one mother may sacrifice for her children her health, her leisure, potential luxuries, the love of her husband, or the approval of former friends. Another mother may also love her children but not give up her comforts, her social life, or the companionship of her husband for what might be regarded as the children's benefit. Two skilled workers may both accept the principle of collective bargaining. But whereas one of them may be willing to undergo all the deprivations necessary to win a prolonged strike and strengthen the union, another may soon decide that the union is not worth the hardships which its support at times involves. Two business men may both accept the golden rule as a standard of behavior. But one may be willing to take exception to it occasionally if profits can be increased, whereas the other does not believe more profits are worth compromise with allegiance to his standard.

The number of variations and permutations of egos is probably almost as large as the number of people who inhabit the earth. What any one person regards as *himself* will in all probability not be identical in its nature to what another person regards as *himself*. The egos of some people will closely fit the values of the immediate environment, others will range far and wide in both time and space; some will include many objects of the external world, others will be completely independent of material things; some will be tied to creeds and symbols, others will be indifferent to any ideology; some will cause sacrifice and suffering for objectives that others would lightly dismiss. When we use the term *ego*, therefore, it must be understood that we are not referring to some mystic, universal characteristic which has the same complexion in all individuals. The ego is only a concept to describe what each person subjectively regards as *me*. When the concept is used it must be remembered that the ego is in large measure composed of the acquired values with which the individual identifies himself and that to understand the ego of any single individual requires knowledge of his whole background and personality.

SELF-REGARD

For the individual, a subjective counterpart of what the psychologist describes as the ego is the feeling of self-respect. A person "takes a look at himself," "is proud of himself," "ashamed of himself," "has a guilty conscience." People are continually evaluating their behavior, their social affiliations, their goals, and their ideals with respect to the significance certain behavior, social affiliations, goals, and the like have for *themselves*. "It's rotten of me not to have written poor old Aunt Nell," says the busy nephew. "I deserve a raise in pay," says the worker. "It would be better for me to die on a battlefield than to live under foreign domination," says the patriotic citizen. "If I were willing to give up my ideas of what is right, I could sell out and make some money," says the honest labor leader. A person evaluates the felt significance of any action or any standard of judgment by referring it to his own feeling of self-regard.

The analysis of self-respect and self-regard is still, as McDougall pointed out, very much in the "backwaters of psychology." For McDougall the "sentiment of self-regard" was the cornerstone of a systematic psychology. This sentiment he believed had "as its most essential constituents, the propensities of self-assertion and submission."[15] These instinctive tendencies were the prime movers, the forces behind the sentiment. From our point of view, such a foundation for the feeling of self-regard is untenable and unnecessary for, as we have already pointed out, the psychology of motivation does not seem to be forwarded by assuming the existence of a fixed number of instincts common to all men. The feeling of self-regard, like the ego, is composed of the values and standards of judgment

---

[15] W. McDougall, *Energies of Men,* New York: Scribner's, 1933, 234. McDougall is mentioned here especially since his treatment of the sentiment of self regard has been so widely discussed in social psychology. Other psychologists, notably James, Freud, and Koffka, have stressed the desire for self-esteem.

an individual interiorizes as part of himself. The difference between the feeling of self-regard and the ego is simply that the feeling of self-regard is experienced when an individual (the knower) introspects on his ego (the content, what there is to be known).

By tying the feeling of self-regard to the ego and by showing how the ego develops in the social context, we are better able to understand why the "sentiment of self-regard," as McDougall pointed out, has the peculiar characteristic of extending "itself to whatever objects express one's personality, or can in any way be regarded as parts of one's larger self" or why "the self-sentiment is also commonly extended in some degree to other groups than a man's own family."[16] From our point of view, this extension of the feeling of self-regard is not a "peculiarity" of the sentiment; it is not some inherent quality of a particular personal endowment. It is, on the other hand, an inevitable, logical development. The feeling of self-regard does not "extend" itself to objects or groups, it simply includes certain objects or groups because these have become interiorized as part of the ego. In short, while we must thank McDougall for pointing out "the immense importance of self-respect," we cannot agree with him that it is founded on hypothetical propensities which extend themselves during the course of life. It is founded, rather, on known or ascertainable values with which the individual identifies himself.

Status. Since the ego is for most individuals so largely composed of common social values, almost every person to some extent evaluates himself in terms of the norms of his particular society. This relationship between a person's interiorized values and the norms of his society we shall call *status.* A person "places himself" in some definite relationship to his social world. In one public-opinion poll, for example, 88 per cent of the American population was found to identify itself with the *middle* social class, 6 per cent with the *lower* class, and 6 per cent with the *upper.*[17] Within any such broad grouping, most individuals would place themselves in definite hierarchies in relation to other members of their immediate community. Thus, a white man in a white man's world believes he is superior to other racial groups; a rich man in a world where wealth is highly valued, believes he is somehow above the poor man; a professional man in a

[16] *Ibid.,* 235 f.
[17] American Institute of Public Opinion, release of Apr. 2, 1939.

world where professional men are rated "higher" than unskilled workers believes he is "better" than they are. From the point of view of both the individual and the outside observer, status is synonymous with social recognition.

This social recognition is relative to the particular norms found in a culture at any given time. When the norms are stable and unquestioned a person can more securely "place" himself in society. If this cultural stability lasts for many years and if the individual does not move up or down the social ladder, he begins to take his status for granted; it becomes unconscious. The person is unlikely to be very aware of his status unless he comes in contact with groups of people or environments where his own values and his own way of life are brought into sharp relief. Thus a wealthy matron who spends 98 per cent of her life with the families of other wealthy matrons may become relatively oblivious to the superior position she enjoys. However, when she drives with her chauffeur to take an occasional basket of food to poor people in the slums, she becomes more fully aware of the role she is playing. The discrepancy between her own position and that of other people is brought into her consciousness. This conflict between statuses obviously holds for individuals who have joined together in groups, parties, or movements, as well as for single individuals. People in the upper income brackets are more aware of their position when they find that position threatened by legislation or revolution; people in the lower income brackets realize their plight more fully when they become more aware of how others live or how they themselves might live if things were different.

To an outside observer there may be an enormous discrepancy between the status an individual assigns himself and the objective criteria a person exhibits to qualify in that status. Thus, in selecting respondents in the proper proportion according to their economic status, experts who poll public opinion realize that an aristocratic old man who carries a cane, who once possessed a fortune but now is poverty-stricken and lives in a garret, will still identify himself with the upper class and have all the opinions characteristically held by the wealthy.[18] Some people who call themselves Negroes have no negroid complexion or features whatever and are treated by whites

[18] Elmo Roper, Classifying respondents by economic status, *Publ. Opin. Quart.*, 1940, 4, 270-272.

as Negroes only when they care to reveal what they regard as their true identification.[19]

Frequently the status in which an individual regards himself is apparently determined merely by familiarity. There seems to be a tendency for people to hold as "good" or "right" those objects, ideas, or ways of life with which they are familiar. By no means does familiarity always breed contempt. It often breeds complacency and satisfaction. An American Babbitt traveling in Europe will compare unfavorably the food he eats, the plumbing he encounters, the trains he rides on with those back in the good old U.S.A.; the housewife will listen impatiently while her neighbor Mrs. Jones tells how she makes a chocolate cake and then eagerly relates how *she* does it; the husband may dote on an old moth-eaten sweater which he could well afford to replace but which he regards as a good and faithful friend; one man will listen to another tell why he is voting for the Democrats and then, completely neglecting the other man's arguments or assumptions, tell why *he* is voting for the Republicans. Each of these individuals likes what he is familiar with. Even people who have lived in slums and have eaten cheap food are often discontented for some time when their standards of living are improved by federal aid. It takes a while to adjust even to better things.

Self-integrity. However, a person's ego and, consequently, the way in which he regards himself are by no means always *entirely* bound by the surrounding culture. We saw in the last chapter that many people, by nature, by training, or by a combination of both, refuse to accept bodily and in uncompromising fashion the norms of society. Some people are progressive in politics, liberal in their religious views, dissatisfied with certain features of their community or national life. For such persons, a feeling of self-regard is not completely derived from the accepted standards of the majority. For them, social recognition and social status are not synonymous with self-regard. They identify themselves with goals not yet achieved, with ways of life not yet approved by the majority. Their self-regard is determined by standards derived from a small minority

---

[19] For a fascinating autobiography of a "white" Negro and the role of social status, as dependent in our culture partially on skin color, see J. W. Johnson, *An Autobiography of an Ex-colored Man,* published anonymously, 1912.

group, from reading, from discussion, or from their own creative intellectual activity.

Other people may be rebels against the culture which surrounds them and, consequently, frown on or laugh at the common criteria of status. The Bohemian, the nudist, the reformer, and the revolutionary are examples.

Still other people may be quite indifferent to the norms of a culture or to the standards of the majority. They may conform to a certain mode of thought or behavior but in no way identify themselves with such ways of thinking or acting, harboring their own ideas about how people should act but taking no interest in what others think of them or in propagandizing for their own way of life. Individuals who isolate themselves on remote hilltops, vagabonds who choose to wander and make a living doing odd jobs, recluses who hide in one-man offices and somehow seem to disappear from society when the day's work is done are examples of people indifferent to ordinary standards.

Every man's life, his *inner self*, is more or less of a secret to other people. Most of us probably do certain things clandestinely just to maintain our own self-respect. Although we do conform in large measure to the common values of society and do desire a certain amount of social recognition, in addition to this—and often much more important in terms of felt significance—we cherish certain values which may be shared by our family circle, a few professional colleagues, a local community group, or a political party. And sometimes we cherish, as most important of all, those values which we have worked out for ourselves and think of as our own. Conformance to these more personal standards maintains our feeling of self-regard through self-integrity. In such instances, we care about recognition only from a very few people, or the status we may want is status only in our own eyes.

Ego Drive

We may now return to our original problem of motivation. The ego becomes an integral part of the story. For only by understanding the development of the ego can motivation be put into its proper *social* context, and only by understanding the relation of needs, derived drives, frames of reference, and attitudes to the ego can motivation be placed in its proper *personal* context. If we leave the ego out of account, our picture is inadequate and we deal only with some abstract or incomplete man.

Maintaining self-regard. Our own introspection and our observation of the behavior of other people indicate that *an individual is constantly trying to maintain or enhance his own feeling of self-regard.* This "force propelling the Ego upward," as Koffka describes it,[20] must be considered as a basic principle in the psychology of motivation. For, the individual whose ego is composed so largely of interiorized values must maintain respect for these values if he is to remain himself or if he is not to become a disintegrated, abnormal personality. If the values are not maintained, the individual has neither respect for himself nor the respect of others. Some broken spirits of this sort may be found among the ne'er-do-wells, the members of chain gangs, the inmates of county poor farms or mental hospitals. The normal man, the one in the vast majority, is one whose feeling of self-regard is intact.

People strive for this self-regard in an infinite number of ways.[21] The particular behavioral pattern adopted by any individual depends, of course, upon his temperament and capacities, his training and education, and the physical and social environments in which he lives. Since self-regard, for most people, is so often achieved through social recognition, through status, a good deal of behavior is motivated by the attempt to preserve or to enhance status so that it will be recognized objectively for what it is felt to be or desired to be subjectively. In our own type of culture, where class and caste lines

[20] K. Koffka, *Principles of Gestalt Psychology,* New York: Harcourt, Brace, 1935, 670-673.

[21] An interesting experimental demonstration of this desire for self-esteem has been made by C. W. Huntley, Judgments of self based upon records of expressive behavior, *J. Abn. & Soc. Psychol.,* 1940, **35,** 428-448. Without the knowledge of his subjects, he got various recordings of their expressive movements—photographs of their hands in different positions, copies of their handwriting, silhouettes, records of their voices, etc. They were asked to give their reactions to these recordings of their own expressive movements when these were mixed with similar recordings of the behavior of other people. Huntley found, confirming an earlier experiment of Wolff, that people rated their own expressions more favorably than the expressions of other people even though they failed in general to recognize which expressions actually were their own. There was, then, an unconscious recognition of self-characteristics, and the consequent ego involvement produced the more flattering judgments.

re not irrevocably drawn and forcefully perpetuated, where some ways of life, some achievements, some statuses are more highly valued than others, and where "ambition," "getting-ahead," "progress," and the like are praiseworthy personal characteristics, the individual is probably more conscious of and more motivated by the drive for social recognition than he would be in a less flexible, less democratic society. Status cannot be maintained without some effort. It cannot be enhanced without some recognized signs of accomplishment, possession, personal capacity, or way of life, all of which symbolize to others in a recognized way the subjective status of the individual. Even a king occasionally must take the trouble to put on his medals or his crown and be drawn by gold-bedecked steeds through the lines of his admiring subjects; even the modern dictator, no matter how plain his dress or absolute his power, occasionally must show himself on a balcony to receive the salutes of the masses.

However, since social recognition for most people is by no means the only way in which their self-regard may be maintained and since for some people the desire for status plays a comparatively small role in their lives, self-regard for them must be achieved in other ways. For some persons like progressives, reformers, or revolutionaries who do not identify themselves completely with current social values, there is a desire to change the criteria of status, to have society recognize as "good," "right," or "desirable" the values which the individual holds and which he himself believes are good, right, or desirable. Such persons maintain their self-regard by maintaining their self-integrity, and their self-integrity motivates them to judge both their own behavior and that of others in terms of the values which are a part of them but which are not shared by the majority. Their motivation may lead them to social ostracism and disgrace, to the status of the prison inmate—but they still have their self-respect.

Other people, as we have seen, may also be malcontents but have no desire to disturb the accepted cultural hierarchy of values. Unlike the progressive or the reformer, their values and their life spaces do not include the welfare of other people. Hence they can maintain self-integrity by conforming obediently to the minimum number of social norms, by detaching their own values from any social context, and by behaving and believing as their values dictate. Even for the conformist who yearns for social recognition and even for the discontented man who would like to change the world, much behavior is motivated by the desire to do certain things toward which society may be relatively indifferent but which the individual personally values. One man may feel that he loses his own self-respect if weeds grow in his garden; another, if he does not keep up his stamp collection; another, if he cannot solve a crossword puzzle; another, if he cannot play the piano as well as he would like to; another if his muscles get flabby.

A backlog for almost every person's feeling of self-regard is found in the familiar process of rationalization. Rationalization may be used to increase one's status, as is true of the janitor who was asked his occupation by a public-opinion-poll interviewer, and who answered "stationary engineer." Whether one is a janitor, a factory worker, a lawyer, a doctor, or a professor, the chances are that one often tends to rationalize one's position as more "important" than it is actually. Rationalization also comes to the rescue of self-integrity by relieving pangs of conscience created by temporary lapses from social or personal standards. A boy may take the last piece of cake from the pantry and, when reprimanded by his mother, say that he did it to keep his little brother from getting sick if he should spy it; or, the war lord will assure citizens in a besieged town that he hates to have them suffer and die but that the whole trouble lies with their own leaders.

Sources of discontent. Under the pressure of the environment, then, a person is continually motivated to some activity if he is to be satisfied with himself. At least four characteristic relationships between the individual and his social world contribute to dissatisfaction. In the first place, the values with which a person has identified himself may not be those which his behavior actually reflects. A discrepancy arises between his ego level and his achievement level, between his aspirations and his performances.[22] Sometimes the discrepancy may be temporary and of comparatively little consequence, as with the

[22] This concept of ego level has been developed by Kurt Lewin and his co-workers. See F. Hoppe, Erfolg and Misserfolg, *Psychol. Forsch.*, 1930, 14, 1-62; J. D. Frank, The influence of the level of performance in one task on the level of aspiration in another, *J. Exp. Psychol.*, 1935, 18, 159-171. Earlier work has been critically analyzed by R. Gould, An experimental analysis of "level of aspiration," *Genet. Psychol. Monog.*, 1939, 21, 1-116.

ootball player who misses his tackle, the salesman who turns in a
oor monthly report. At other times, and more important for us,
here are the enduring discrepancies between what a person is or does
nd what he believes he is or should be doing. An intelligent, honest,
ardworking laborer may feel that he deserves more recognition and
ecurity than he has; a Negro will resent the limited occupational
pportunities offered him. An inferiority feeling may result and the
ndividual may try to restore equilibrium by various forms of direct
ction, disguise, or compensation.[23] Or else, ego frustration may re-
ult in various forms of aggression.[24]

Another source of irritation to a person's ego is caused when his
tatus, his values, are not properly recognized by other people.[25] The
3oston Brahmin may be treated as an ordinary mortal by the west-
rner; the prestige of a business executive may vanish when he
eaves his office; the professional pride of a college professor may be
urt when he is asked to join a labor union; the cultured Jew may
e disrespectfully treated by members of a Gentile community. In a
housand and one different ways the ego is violated, and in a thousand
nd one different ways people try to insure recognition and to mini-
nize violation. Most societies have established mores whose essential
unction is to enable individuals to display their status. Joining clubs,
lriving high-priced automobiles, wearing fashionable clothes, "being
een" at exclusive places, having one's name in the news, wearing
igh-heeled shoes or having long fingernails, indulging in mutual
lattery, counting some prominent person as a friend, and attending

[23] Cf. A. Adler, A study of organ inferiority and its psychical compensation, *Nerv.
Mental Disease Monog.*, 1917, 24; R. Dodge and E. Kahn, *The Craving for Superi-
ity*, New Haven: Yale University Press, 1931; G. W. Allport, *op. cit.*, 173-181.

[24] J. Dollard L. Doob, *et al., Frustration and Aggression*, New Haven: Yale Uni-
ersity Press, 1939.

[25] Allport, *Personality, op. cit.*, 164, says, "self-consciousness in its popular sense of
mbarrassment is a hypertrophy of the natural awareness of self, intensified by frequent failure and consequent experiences of shame." In our terms, self-conscious-
ess of this type would be most likely to result when there was a recognized wide
liscrepancy between the values reflected by others in the immediate environment
nd the lack of conformity to these values exhibited by some action of the indi-
idual. The opposite extreme of "losing oneself" in a situation is attained when
ne's own values temporarily coincide entirely with those of the immediate social
nvironment as they do, for example, in certain crowd or mob behavior. See chs.
and 7 of this book.

expensive schools are only a few random illustrations of such ac
cepted behavior in our own culture.[26]

A third cause of dissatisfaction to the ego results from the fac
that a person can by no means always satisfy his innate or acquired
needs and at the same time identify himself with the values he
believes are his.[27] Sexual cravings must be suppressed, sublimated
redirected; emotions of anger or fear must be curbed; curiosities mus
be inhibited; desire for scores of material satisfactions or for educa
tion must be thwarted. The unconscious provides some indirec
outlets for these repressions in the form of dreams, phantasies, slip
of the tongue, and other more personal forms of behavior related by
psychoanalysts. And again society has partially come to the rescue by
establishing approved ways by which these needs may be vicariousl
satisfied. The movies, the pulp magazines, novels, dances, crowds
ball games, and scores of other social media and mechanisms thrive
partially at least because they indirectly accommodate needs or suffi
ciently reduce the tension created by the needs in order to keep the
discrepancy between them and the accepted values from becoming
too patent.

A fourth source of discontent is the failure of society to provide
any recognition for certain values that individuals may cherish. Many
people are upset because others in their society do not appreciate wha
they regard as their own talents or valuable creations. A man may be
an accomplished zither player, have his heart set on perfection with
the instrument, but find few people willing to pay enough to hea
him perform so that he can keep body and soul together. Literature i
rife with stories of artists, inventors, and intellectuals whom the
world shunned in their own day but whose contributions later were
called valuable. More important for our own story are the cases o
reformers, idealists, and revolutionaries who have no way to share
their own conception of status, their own ego values, until they have
acquired a cohort and mass following.

Use and misuse of the ego concept. For various reasons, then, and

[26] For an account of the devices used by a particular group in a particular cultur
to display their status, see T. Veblen, *Theory of the Leisure Class*, New York: Mac
millan, 1899.

[27] This important emphasis of Freudian psychology is popularly treated by Freud
in *The Psychopathology of Everyday Life*, London: Benn, 1914; also in Karen
Horney, *The Neurotic Personality of Our Time*, New York: Norton, 1934.

n various ways individuals seek to preserve or to enhance their egos. But to claim that the explanation of motivation in social life is *merely* hat people strive to preserve or to enhance their egos is to leave xplanation on so abstract a plane that generalization can never be ufficiently particularized to give any understanding of a concrete erson or a concrete social phenomenon. For, in a sense, all behavior s motivated directly or indirectly by some ego drive. And the concepts of *ego* and *ego drive*, if carelessly employed, are all too likely o become redundancies.

Furthermore, we must not confuse ego drive with what we commonly know as *egotism*. Egotistical behavior, as the term is used, is behavior obviously carried out to satisfy some relatively unsocialized lesire, to achieve some goal clearly related by the observer to some ersonal ambition or to the individual's self-esteem. Altruism and umility, on the other hand, are generally regarded as signs of a nature, highly socialized individual whose personal interests are less rudely identified with his own personal advantage.[28] To be sure, the *gotist* who proudly boasts of the wealth he has accumulated and the *ltruist* who secretly distributes his wealth to help deserving people re both motivated by ego drives. Each gets satisfaction out of his articular activity; each is maintaining self-respect in his own personal way. But the type of ego enhancement involved in these two nstances varies enormously. One is crude, direct, socially disapproved; the other more subtle, highly derived, admired.

The justification for the use of the concept ego drive is simply that *without knowledge of the way in which values of society may become a part of an individual's mental context, without the realization that an individual is seeking in some way to maintain or to enhance his own self-regard, any more specific account of motivation ails to relate the dynamic aspects of behavior to the context of the otal personality as it develops in the social world.* Quasi needs, unonscious desires, or functionally autonomous motives run the risk f existing in a relatively personal and social vacuum unless their elationship to and dependence on ego-involving values are recognized.[29]

Let us return for a moment to our example of Mr. Lewis, the man

[28] Cf. Allport, *Personality, op. cit.,* ch. 8, for a discussion of the mature personality.
[29] Allport, Reply to Mr. Bertocci, *op. cit.,* 533-554.

who acquired a derived drive to earn money and then accepted a position as a university president at a financial sacrifice. Unless we understand something of Mr. Lewis' ego values, this behavior is baffling. But the probable explanation is that he, like most persons in his culture, learned to accept wealth and education, business executive and university presidents as good things. As we saw, by his industry luck, and business acumen he acquired wealth and the social prestige and the status it provided. Yet once he became wealthy, his status, though higher than that of 99 per cent of his countrymen was not clearly above that of the other wealthy people with whom he associated. He already knew and was continually reminded of the fact that men who devoted their lives unselfishly to some prominent public service acquired great prestige. Both in his social world and in his own estimation, they were more highly regarded than millionaires who did nothing but increase their fortunes. Consequently when an opportunity was presented to him to identify himself with so highly valued a public service and to increase his own feeling of self-regard, the transformation of his apparent motives was accomplished without any disturbance whatsoever to his ego. The apparent motivation of the man was changed to the observer, but not to the man himself or to those who knew him well.[30]

[30] One may, to be sure, speak of satisfying a basic need such as that for food, sex or shelter. But needs, too, become in most people so modified that the more primitive urge cannot be satisfied without some concession to cultural or personal tastes Civilized explorers have been reported to have starved to death rather than eat the food of cannibals. In less extreme cases, hungry Occidentals may prefer their hunger to pickled mice or snakes and beetles, that may be offered them by Oriental hosts

CHAPTER 3

THE INDIVIDUAL'S PURSUIT OF MEANING

So far we have seen that an individual acquires standards of judgment, frames of reference, and attitudes through which he interprets much of his environment. We have also seen that the social values accepted are subjectively an integral part of a person's ego, becoming dynamic forces within the person. By a combination of innate capacities, environmental opportunities, and chance, a person also acquires certain habits and derived drives which function essentially as instrumentations for these ego motives. We have also pointed out the enormous complexity and variability in both the mental contexts and the egos of different people. Now, both the variability in mental contexts and the variability in the make-up of egos converge on a final major problem which must be analyzed. That problem is to discover how and why different people accept or construct the variety of interpretations we observe in social life. Why are some people interested in certain interpretations while others are not? Why are some people unwilling to subscribe to certain points of view even if they are interested?

The environment of any individual is to a greater or lesser extent meaningful to him. Different cultures ascribe different meanings to similar events, depending upon custom and the particular state of "development" that culture has reached. People in a primitive culture who suffer from a long drought may agree that it is provoked by an angry sun god who must be propitiated by the sacrifice of a lovely maiden or of a fatted calf; people in another drought-suffering area may set aside a day of prayer to a somewhat less personal god; whereas people in a third culture may authorize the government to build dams and reservoirs as an insurance against such crises, the direct cause of which they believe they know. In one culture, if a prominent and beloved member dies, a medicine man may assign the death to a magic spell cast by neighboring enemies; in another culture, such a death may be ascribed to the will of God; in a third culture, to an illness known as pneumonia, whose symptoms and causes may be explained in great detail. The literature of cultural anthropology is replete with descriptions of the interpretations which various peoples have placed on natural, social and personal occurrences. And within any one culture, different people obviously find meaningful and understandable to them certain phenomena that baffle their contemporaries. The veteran politician will know how nominating conventions finally choose a candidate whom the bewildered citizen must later decide upon; the garage mechanic readily understands what is wrong with the car of a politician who may be helplessly stranded on the road; the physician can prescribe for both politician and mechanic when they are ill and wondering what they can do to recover.

Something that makes sense to one man may be regarded by another man as nonsense or superstition; and the concern of one person to figure out how presidential candidates are nominated, how automobiles run, or how the human body functions may be of no interest whatever to another person. Some people will feel strongly that the interpretation of what to them are important social problems is best furnished by the Ku Klux Klan, the Communist Party, the Catholic Church, the Townsend Plan, or Fascism. Other people will be relatively indifferent to almost any social or political philosophy or movement, care little about it until, perhaps, some circumstance affects their own needs or status. Why different interpretations arise at all, why they elicit the approval, allegiance, or disdain of certain people, why some persist and others quickly fade are problems which we must examine somewhat more precisely before we have a conceptual framework adequate to understand specific social phenomena.

THE ORGANIZATION OF EXPERIENCE

One of the chief characteristics of experience is that it generally seems organized, meaningful, somehow structured. In everyday life we perceive forms, rhythms, colors, speeds, and sounds to which we can usually attach some significance: we go about our daily tasks, see other people following expected routines, observe seasonal changes, social developments, distant wars. Usually we either take these experiences for granted or in some fashion manage to assign an interretation which places them in our mental contexts. To be sure, the order and significance of experience are relative and sometimes completely lacking—conditions of great importance to us as we shall soon see. But in our desire to explain the unusual, we must not overlook the usual. By and large, experience is constituted preponderantly of meaning rather than of chaos. Why is this so?

Conditioning. The common and obvious answer is that individuals learn the responses they should make to sounds, objects, people, and other stimuli in the long process of adjusting to a particular physical and social environment. Just how this learning occurs and just what is learned are now, and probably will long remain, subjects for psychological debate and research. Behaviorists, dissatisfied with the mentalism of the theory of the association of ideas, have proposed conditioning as the objective, scientific way to account for learning. People become conditioned to keep their hands from flames, to respond appropriately to the word "fire," and to use fire in specific ways to warm their bodies, cook their food, and heat their blast furnaces. All learning, for the behaviorists, is the result of elaborate conditioning and cross-conditioning of specific stimuli and responses. All meaning is reduced, therefore, to a readiness to respond, an implicit response, a tonic reaction, a sustained reflex, or some behavioral counterpart of what we have called *meaning* (and what most people subjectively experience as meaning), a concept which behaviorists eschew as meaningless in itself.[1] Frequently the concept of conditioning is so loosely employed that it explains nothing at all. More systematic proponents of the theory use it more cautiously, and therefore more appropriately, in accounting for the ever-increasing range of man's adaptive responses.[2]

The behaviorist's characteristic lack of concern for what appears to be creativity, the purposive planning, and the feeling of human beings, seems to confirm the statement that "the main evidence a methodology is worn out comes when progress within it no longer deals with main issues."[3] Problems seem to be falsified or obscured

[1] For a critical discussion of the behavioristic theory of meaning, see W. Köhler, *Gestalt Psychology,* New York: Liveright, 1929, ch. 1.

[2] Cf. E. R. Hilgard and D. G. Marquis, *Conditioning and Learning,* New York: Appleton-Century, 1940.

[3] A. N. Whitehead, *The Function of Reason,* Princeton: Princeton University Press, 1929, 13.

by a limited conceptual framework. And, despite the fact that theories of conditioning have enormously contributed to our understanding of much of the behavior of animals and of some of man's more elemental and specific responses to verbal and non-verbal stimuli, these theories are by no means adequate to explain the apparent meaningfulness of man's experiences. Behaviorists have no use for certain concepts simply because their theories automatically exclude them. Also, if main issues for the social psychologist are to be accounted for, the conditioned response must be supplemented with other explanations.[4]

Internal structuration. The whole description of mental context developed in Chapter 1 suggests some of the major reasons why experience seems organized. There we found that acquired standards of judgment and the derivative frames of reference based on them enable men to "place," to interpret a variety of stimuli which they are able to relate to those frames. Newspaper headlines, reporting that a thief has been put in jail, that a strike has been called in a certain plant, that airplanes have dropped bombs on a certain foreign city, are all significant only because they can be related by the reader to a certain mental context. When a person holds some frame of reference that is especially rich with experience and information, he may detect great significance in an occurrence which, to less sophisticated observers, is regarded as of little consequence. Thus, while the ordinary layman may remain unperturbed when he reads of the resignation of a certain minister from the cabinet of a foreign government, a seasoned diplomat or a veteran correspondent may foresee in the resignation the overthrow of a whole government with drastic consequences for his own nation; the military expert may find a whole new type of military strategy foreshadowed by a single enemy manoeuvre; the physicist may construct a new theory on the basis of certain facts which may be of only passing interest to the average citizen. Such an increase in the range of experience and in the factual knowledge underlying a frame of reference makes

---

[4] For a vigorous discussion of this point, see G. W. Allport, The psychologist's frame of reference, *Psychol. Bull.*, 1940, **37**, 14 f. Some limitations of conditioning for the psychologist interested in personality and human beings are pointed out by Allport in *Personality, op. cit.*, 151-158.

possible more specific interpretation, greater objective verification, and more precise prediction.

On the other hand, as we have already pointed out, frames of reference may be broad and inclusive even though the assumptions upon which they are based have little factual data to support them. Nevertheless, to the individual, they may be just as adequate or just as helpful in interpreting his environment as the more verifiable frames of the sophisticate. If a person firmly believes that God directs all the activities of nature and of man, there will be few things to puzzle him; if he believes in the superiority of the white race, many of the questions that baffle the social scientist will for him be easily answered. No matter what the source or validity of a person's standards of judgment or of his frames of reference may be, experience will be meaningful to him so long as he can relate it appropriately to his particular mental context. Hence, experience aroused by specific stimuli appears to an individual to be so well organized simply because the mental context, upon which it impinges before a response is made, is itself structured.

What about creative experience? Why do we generally find so meaningful and orderly conscious experience that results without any apparently adequate, external stimulus or learned responses—men's plans, daydreams, inventive schemes, visions of skyscrapers, symphonies, poems, airplanes, and the like? At least part of the answer is, we have already seen, that standards and frames are seldom autonomous of the ego, that the individual sets for himself a certain ego level and strives through some derived drive, some talent, some knowledge, or capacity to satisfy the values that have become a part of himself.

External structuration. In addition to the specific learning of responses and the structuration of mental context, two other processes contribute to the organization of experience. One of these is what we may call *external structuration: the organization that appears in the stimulus itself and that is perceived directly by the individual as organization or as meaning.* This patterning of stimuli has long been discussed in the psychology of perception by Gestalt psychologists. Certain figures, sounds, melodies, movements, and other stimuli can be demonstrated to have an inherent organization which is perceived as such, irrespective of past learning or association.[5] The concept has been extended into experimental social psychology by the studies of Lewin and his pupils on "social atmosphere" where they have shown, for example, the effects on the individual of membership in democratic or autocratic "group atmospheres."[6]

The meaning experienced because of the patterning of a social-stimulus situation may, to be sure, be difficult for an individual to verbalize, and its full significance may by no means be clear. It may, nevertheless, be sufficient to enable the person to characterize it vaguely and to differentiate the effects it has produced on him from the effects produced on him by another social situation. The traditional man from Mars, for instance, who knew nothing of social life on this earth, who was ignorant of our language, our symbolic gestures, and the like, would probably experience a different reaction at a funeral from that at a dance, in a church from that at a vaudeville, in a lecture room from that at a football rally.

There is nothing mystical about this process. Nor is there any denial of the contention that might be made that, if this patterning of the social stimulus is to be thoroughly understood, it must be broken down and its characteristics analyzed as Lewin and others have done. When we say that the social pattern, the "atmosphere" of a funeral, a dance, a vaudeville, and a football rally may be experienced as such, we are simply recognizing the fact that the complexity of sights, sounds, and other specific stimuli that constitute such situations is often experienced directly as a pattern and that the various stimuli composing that pattern are discerned only when the participating individual assumes an analytic set. An ardent

[5] See W. Köhler, *Gestalt Psychology, op. cit.*, chs. 5 and 6; K. Koffka, *Principles of Gestalt Psychology*, New York: Harcourt, Brace, 1935. Behaviorists and specifists deny that such organization is a "given" and believe it is due to conditioning; older introspectionists accounted for such "givens" on the basis of association. Gestalt psychologists have often been accused of overstatement, and the "movement" has attracted those who have used Gestalt concepts loosely. We are not contending here that *all* sensations are organized, but we do agree that *some* stimuli are so structured. The criterion for such organization must be the individual's own introspection.

[6] K. Lewin, R. Lippitt, and R. K. White, Patterns of aggressive behavior in experimentally created "social climates," *J. Soc. Psychol.*, 1939, **10**, 271-299; R. Lippitt, An experimental study of the effect of democratic and authoritarian group atmospheres, *University of Iowa Studies*, 1940, **16**, No. 3, 45-198.

football fan, for example, may become greatly excited during a game. He may also be a psychologist and, during the excitement, deliberately begin to introspect on the various causes of his emotion and the components of the whole stimulus situation to which he is reacting. As we shall see later, the elaborate stage setting of the crowd leader, the Quiet Time of the Oxford Grouper, and the fanfare of the dictators are all studied, social situations whose characteristics are designed to create a particular mood. Although social situations which have a configuration of their own may be relatively uncommon in normal social life, and although their effect can be determined only by a study of the individual case, still this "external structuration" that exists independently of learning or mental context should be added to our reasons why experience is organized.

The desire for meaning. In many everyday-life situations a person finds himself faced with no clear interpretation of a stimulus or problem because there is no meaningful patterning to the stimulus itself or because his own standards of judgment and frames of reference do not provide immediate understanding. Yet for one of several possible reasons, the individual is dissatisfied, annoyed, bothered, and tense until his understanding is more complete, until he can make sense out of the problem, until his tension is somehow resolved. A desire for meaning is aroused. Although the postulation of a highly derived, intellectualistic desire for meaning may seem to go against the rules of scientific parsimony, and although its physiological bases may be completely unknown, still few people can deny that subjectively it is a desire that occasionally *is* most poignantly felt.

Under what psychological circumstances does such a desire arise? There are several relationships between the individual and his environment that seem to create it. For one thing, some fundamental, biological need, such as that for food, may arouse in the individual a desire to make some adequate response to satisfy that need. An unemployed man may get enough from relief or from a few odd jobs to buy just enough food to keep body and soul together. But he and other members of his family know that such products as milk, meat, coffee, oranges, and the like exist in relative abundance for those who can afford them. The man tries ceaselessly to get work. Law and custom forbid him to take the food he wants from the store or to cultivate a garden on the estate of a wealthy townsman. The man begins to wonder what it's all about, why he and many others are in this condition although the majority of people are not. He wants to understand the situation so that he can do something to remedy it. He seeks an interpretation, a meaningful solution to his problem.

The desire for meaning may also emerge if some derived drive is not satisfied. Defeated candidates, whether they were nominees for president of the senior class in high school or for state senator, must frequently ask themselves why they lost, as they first survey the returns; the advancement, promotion, and success of some persons must genuinely puzzle disappointed colleagues or workers who may not understand their own limitations or the inside machinations and wirepullings which leave them behind. Frequently, too, a person will have a desire to interpret a particular situation because his own status is involved and may be threatened if he cannot provide that meaning. Thus a person who regards himself as an "expert" will be challenged to understand the newest developments in his field so that he will not be caught offguard. Or he may pretend to have such knowledge, "explaining" a problem to less sophisticated persons even though he may realize that his scientific colleagues would laugh at his accounts. Furthermore, as we have seen, an individual may have a derived drive which serves as a particular mechanism to enhance his status, to give him more prestige and authority and more respect from those whose values he himself respects. In this case, the person will often deliberately look for problems to which he may attempt to give meaning, whether the problems are in the field of business, politics, psychology, geographic exploration, architecture, or in any other area of activity with which he has identified himself.

The desire for meaning may also result when some event is not understood but, because of its potential personal significance, motivates the individual to seek an understanding. The strange noises one hears downstairs in the dark of night when one has awakened from a sound sleep often keep one awake until they have been figured out; the nomination of a dark-horse candidate will cause the serious citizen to look up his record and qualifications so that he may place him in a scheme of values; the invasion of a small neutral nation by a distant foreign power will cause the international banker, the advocate of democracy, the isolationist, and others to look for the significance of the event in terms of personal values. Shortly after the German conquest of France in the summer of 1940, a correspondent in describing the "extremely complex situation" that had emerged reported that the gravest problem facing the new government was to tell people what it was all about. "Public opinion yearns for guidance; certainly also that guidance must not be long deferred."[7]

Meaning may also be sought because one has accepted some temporary task, has become momentarily involved and identified with the achievement of a particular goal.. If a person is a crossword-puzzle fan and finds himself unable to work out the puzzle presented in today's newspaper, he eagerly awaits the solution in tomorrow's edition; if a person becomes impatient and anxious about the outcome of a story, he may turn to the last chapter before he reads the middle of the book. If the individual cannot achieve his goal directly he may seek some substitute solution to the problem or else continue the search for a solution in his phantasies.[8] Thus an individual who fails miserably in pitching horseshoes may stand, when the game is ended, right over the peg and make the desired ringers, whereas the jilted lover in his daydreams will achieve his conquest by hook or by crook.

These are some of the psychological conditions creating the desire to give meaning to a particular problem that presents itself. In all these situations there is a need for closure, a tension that demands resolution.[9] This concept is another indispensable tool in our psychological kit if we are adequately to account for social phenomena. For the desire to obtain meaning, related as it generally is to the ego, motivates the individual to seek a solution, causes him to be dis-

[7] *New York Times*, July 6, 1940. The same eagerness to have a perplexing situation rationalized is shown in an advertisement for a book, published in 1940, which aims to tell people how to argue for democracy. Many persons merely may be conditioned to the word democracy and consequently have an insufficient mental context to give the concept meaning. It is no wonder such people buy a book which claims to give pat answers to skeptics who might argue that "democracy's processes are too slow, too inefficient" or that "most people are too ignorant to vote."

[8] T. Dembo, Der Aerger als dynamisches Problem, *Psychol. Forsch.*, 1931, **15**, 1-144; B. Zeigarnk, Über das Behalten von erledigten und unerledigten Handlungen, *Psychol. Forsch.*, 1927, **9**, 1-85. See also H. A. Murray, *Exploration in Personality*, New York: Oxford University Press, 1938.

[9] The possible physical counterparts of these subjective tensions are discussed by Köhler in his *Die Physischen Gestalten*, 1920.

satisfied, anxious, and bewildered until meaning is obtained. It thus accelerates the organization of experience observed by the psychologist. It helps us to understand why it is that we ourselves cannot forever remain in a state of indecision. It helps us to see why a war of nerves—a deliberately created, widespread, and prolonged state of indecision and tension—is a serious war that must inevitably lead to some action.[10]

CRITICAL SITUATIONS

The usual organization of experience which we have described must in no way blind us to the fact that such organization is always relative, that it is by no means uniformly satisfying, that it is occasionally entirely absent. Although an automobile driver usually is able to proceed smoothly enough because of his knowledge of traffic regulations, his conditioning to symbols, or his ability to figure out how to get to his destination, he does sometimes run into fearful traffic jams or flood or hurricane areas where apparent chaos reigns and where he is baffled as to what he should do. A naive observer will pronounce surrealist art or some modern music completely senseless; a devoted mother, listening to her mechanically minded son explain the operation of the family radio receiver, will admiringly

[10] Foreign dispatches published during the first six or seven months of the second World War frequently described the unrest and the strain created by the inactivity of the major warring powers. For example, a Paris correspondent wrote, "Irritation and resentment were noticeable today both in the Senate and in the Chamber of Deputies. The placidity of the past few months has been shaken, and the usual French procedure of looking for someone on whom to put the blame has begun . . . There is some confusion as to whether Germany or Russia is the enemy, but there seems to be a realization that more must be done, if the war is to be won, than merely sit it out behind the Maginot Line at a cost of a billion francs a day." *New York Times,* Mar. 15, 1940. When major hostilities began in the North Sea and in Norway, reports from both England and France said that people had "regained their cheerfulness and enthusiasm," that they were glad "it had finally started." Relief from indecision, even though the relief means intensive warfare, is preferable to a tenuous peace.

This point was also illustrated in the case of a woman who grew very nervous listening to the international news on the radio prior to the declaration of war Sept. 3, 1939. Her husband, a physician, forbade her to listen to the radio because he knew her heart was ailing and that she should try to keep calm. One afternoon in October, he came home unexpectedly and found her listening to radio news. When he reprimanded her she answered, "But I don't get excited now that the war has begun."

and honestly say that "it's all over my head"; a worried father, listening to news regarding the second World War brought to him by the mysterious radio, may say that he can't understand clearly what it's all about; a small business man, farmer, or middle-class housewife may wonder why capital and labor don't get together and settle their differences without having all these silly strikes.

As we have already implied, this lack of organization and meaning in experience will vary with the interests and needs of the individual. A romantic young girl, driving with a beau who is trying to get out of a traffic jam, may never even notice the traffic; a person who cares nothing for art or music will find surrealist art or modern music not much different from other art; a woman without an inquisitive son may never even give a thought to the radio mechanism; a father whose whole life revolves about his family or his work may not care what is happening in Europe; whereas a society matron may be no more concerned about strikes and their causes than she is about a minor eruption of Mount Etna. The same objective conditions that disturb and bewilder some people may have no influence whatsoever on the mental equilibrium of others. The botanist, the plumber, the reliefer, the banker, the lawyer, all obviously become disturbed by different things because their psychological worlds are composed of so different values and motives.

A critical situation may be said to arise when an individual is confronted by a chaotic external environment which he cannot interpret and which he wants to interpret. The more directly an individual's ego is involved, the more critical is the situation. If the person is trying merely to decide what to do for an evening's entertainment, he may achieve the desired resolution by flipping a coin to choose between possible alternatives; if a person is invited for the first time to a church wedding, he may consult Emily Post to resolve his habiliment perplexities. However, when a young man is trying to decide on his career, a young woman on a husband, a reliefer on a course of action, an unemployed man on a better economic order, or a citizen of a small neutral nation on the possible effectiveness of resistance against a major power, then coins, Emily Post, and perhaps friends, newspapers, books, and even experts may fail to provide satisfactory answers to problems of enormous personal consequence. Events move so swiftly these days that few people can fully comprehend even a small part of them.

When critical situations like these exist among large numbers of a cultural group, the culture itself may be said to be in a critical condition. The whole social environment, current affairs, and attempted solutions of difficulties may be relatively meaningless and directionless to the masses. The impression was left with one observer in our own culture after his travels in the United States: " 'If I could believe. I want belief.' It is a cry going up out of the American people. I think it is about the absolute net of what I have been able to find out about Americans in these last few years of traveling about, in all of this looking at people and talking to them. 'I want belief, some ground to stand on. I do not want government to go on being a meaningless thing.' "[11] It is during such periods that people accustomed to the established order of things become frightened, that old values are apt to be overthrown, that new standards may arise.

SUGGESTION

Critical situations, such as those we have just described, furnish one of the two major psychological conditions that make individuals suggestible. A person is susceptible to suggestion when (1) he has no adequate mental context for the interpretation of a given stimulus or event or (2) when his mental context is so rigidly fixed that a stimulus is automatically judged by means of this context and without any examination of the stimulus itself. The first condition results from bewilderment; the second from the "will to believe."

In general, the psychology of suggestion has been traditionally explained almost entirely in terms of the latter condition, the stereotyped nature of certain values and opinions. The former condition, however, is perhaps even more important for our understanding of social movements and must be analyzed in some detail.

Although the essential characteristic of this first condition is the lack of an appropriate standard or frame for interpretation, such a variety of states of mind may accompany this characteristic that it is useful to distinguish among at least three different ways in which people may be suggestible because they are puzzled. (a) They may

[11] Sherwood Anderson, *Puzzled America*, New York: Scribner's, 1935.

be bewildered and consciously desire some standard or frame; (*b*) they may be bewildered but may not consciously realize that they are seeking some solution to their predicament; or (*c*) they may realize their condition, try to make some examination of the interpretations offered them, but have no adequate way to determine whether or not these interpretations are reliable. The discussion of suggestion examines these conditions in more detail.

CONDITIONS OF SUGGESTIBILITY

1. Lack of adequate mental context:
    a. With a desire to find out appropriate interpretation.
    b. With no realization that an interpretation is being sought.
    c. With a desire to check interpretations but an inability to do so.
2. Fixed mental context.

(1*a*) *An individual has no standard of judgment or frame of reference adequate to interpret a given situation and wants some standard or frame of reference.* A person simply is puzzled, knows that he is puzzled, and would like to get things straightened out in his own mind. People in such a condition have no reliable signposts in their mental contexts by means of which they can test an explanation given them. And because they are eager to free themselves from a state of indecision and bewilderment, they are unusually likely to accept whatever interpretation is offered as long as it seems plausible, that is, as long as it does not conflict with any standard they feel they can rely on. Thus the curious child who asks, "What causes the wind?" may believe whatever his parents tell him; the ignorant, perplexed and anxious citizen may accept uncritically the oversimplified schemes of a crackpot utopian.

There are two important variables to this particular psychological condition of suggestibility. One is the extent to which a mental context is lacking that would provide any sort of anchorage for interpretation; the other is the intensity of the desire for interpretation. Both of them are prerequisites: a person must both lack an adequate mental context and possess a certain desire for interpretation. Yet the degree to which an individual is suggestible may vary according to either variable alone. For example, if two people have an equal desire to increase the national wealth of this country, the person with even a rudimentary knowledge of economics will be less likely to believe in the efficacy of simple inflationary schemes than the person who thinks valuable money can be turned out indefinitely by the printing press. On the other hand, if two people have equally inadequate mental contexts, the individual who is extremely anxious to know how to orient himself in a given situation that may have important consequences for him will be more likely to accept a hearsay rumor than the individual who is not so personally involved. Thus the Germans, in their march through the Low Countries and northern France in the summer of 1940, had their agents in distant towns spread the news that nearby villages had just fallen into German hands. The people in the towns, anxious to know the course of a war which might at any moment threaten their lives, readily believed the false news, became panicky, and started their trek west, thus congesting the roads used by advancing Allied troops the way the Germans wanted them to. Obviously, people in towns much farther removed from the scene of hostilities who knew just as much or just as little as the unfortunate Dutch, Belgians, or French would not have been so suggestible.

As we shall see later in our discussions of various social movements, it is these critical situations that furnish fertile soil for the emergence of the mob leader, the potential dictator, the revolutionary or religious prophet, or others with new and untried formulae. Such leaders arise because they provide people with an interpretation that brings order into their confused psychological worlds. The clever leader will sense the causes of dissatisfaction, will realize which old loyalties remain unshaken and which are being seriously challenged. He will spread among the confused and eager souls a rationalization that, from their points of view, combines the best of the old and the best of the new—the new usually being some concrete proposal, some apparent way out of what had been a dilemma, some statement or program which seems to crystallize for the followers their own disorganized, contradictory worries and aspirations.[12] Frequently the solutions offered are highly

---

[12] Leaders in the scientific, literary, or art world often arise under the same circumstances. Kenneth Burke contends, for example: "Psychoanalysis effects its cures by providing a new perspective that dissolves the system of pieties lying at

oversimplified and the leader himself may suspect that they are unworkable. But he also knows that, without such simplification, his proposals will be incomprehensible, will only prolong confusion.

Among the tools of the leader during any critical situation when people are highly suggestible are slogans and symbols. These are short-cut rationalizations which fire the imagination and spread because they somehow express the dissatisfactions from which people have been suffering and at the same time imply a new direction and purpose. The chances are "that the more correctly and the more objectively a set of slogans expresses the underlying forces in a critical situation, the more vital and lasting they will prove to be."[13] Such slogans as the "No Taxation without Representation" of the American Revolution, the "Liberty, Equality, and Fraternity" of the French Revolution, the "Peace, Bread, and Land" of the Russian Revolution all helped to give meaning to bewildered people. During the early days of the second World War when the Germans were apparently still wondering what the war was for, a correspondent reported that Hitler had conferred with party chiefs to find some way of "translating Germany's war aims into concrete, effective slogans with meaning for the German people."[14]

Symbols, such as flags, insignia, or caricatures of the enemy, are further short cuts crowded with meaning. People seem to get worked up into a higher emotional pitch when they are reacting to symbols than to general programs or ideologies. The anti-New Dealer will probably hate some specific person who symbolizes the New Deal more than he will hate the whole complex of legislation which composes the New Deal; the Communist will probably despise the capitalist more than capitalism; the anti-Semite will probably get more angry when he talks about "the Jew" or a specific Jew

---

the roots of the patient's sorrow or bewilderments. It is an *impious* rationalization, offering a fresh terminology of motives to replace the patient's painful terminology of motives. Its scientific terms are wholly incongruous with the unscientific nature of the distress. By approaching the altar of the patient's unhappiness with deliberate irreverence, by selecting a vocabulary which specifically violates the dictates of style and taboo, it changes the entire nature of his problems, rephrasing it in a form for which there is a solution." *Permanence and Change,* New York: New Republic, 1935, 164 f.

[13] M. Sherif, The psychology of slogans, *J. Abn. & Soc. Psychol.,* 1937, **32,** 461.

[14] Joseph Barnes, *New York Herald Tribune,* Oct. 23, 1939.

.than when he talks about "Jews"; the believer in democracy will no doubt dislike Hitler more than National Socialism. The probable explanation for this rather common behavior of normal individuals is that specific objects or persons are much easier to conceptualize, to focus attention on, than are more general and complex causes of dissatisfaction. Such symbols furnish a definite objective toward which action, if only verbal, can be directed. If an enemy cannot be concretized, then the emotion aroused by thoughts of the enemy will probably be a vague anxiety or fear rather than a specific anger or hatred. And since anger and hatred, rather than anxiety and fear, are more likely to lead to positive, purposive action, the leader will make every attempt to personalize the system, the nation, the evil against which he is rebelling. Christianity had its "devil"; England its "Hun" and "Jerry"; Nazi Germany its "plutocrat."

It would be quite false to assume that slogans and symbols of all kinds are entirely the work of clever propagandists, scheming warmongers, politicians, or idealistic leaders. Popular slogans and symbols are frequently created by the people themselves. They spread not so much because of any organized effort of a given group but because they provide a very definite psychological function. No amount of advertising or publicity can sell a slogan or a symbol if it does not fit the social context.

It is during these critical situations, too, that "escapist" solutions of one brand or another are likely to arise. Some people may regress to a rationalization which once brought them satisfaction, but which they had discarded or outgrown because it did not seem to square with the conditions or forces of the modern world. In times of social tension, for example, it is not difficult to understand the huge popular sale of certain books that advocate a return to religion or to the good old days.[15] Other people may accept some streamlined model of escape that simply avoids central social problems, such as moral rearmament, Christian Science, or mental telepathy.

It is not surprising at critical times to find that individual differences, in the usual sense of the term, are comparatively unimportant

[15] A public opinion survey reported by the Psychological Corporation on the question "Do you think religion is losing or gaining influence in the United States?" shows an increase of 23% from 1940 to 1942 in the number of people who say religious influence is growing.

in determining whether or not a given person will be suggestible to a new rationalization. Innate capacities, expressive traits, or temperamental characteristics play a minor role when an individual is caught in a critical situation where a reordering of values is in the air.[16] To be sure, these individual differences will determine whether or not the person will be a clever or stupid, neat or slovenly, cheerful or grouchy member of what may be a new social movement that has arisen at a critical time. Almost any large political, religious, or social movement probably contains about the same number of extroverts, submissive souls, borderline morons, or neurotics as these characteristics would be measured by current tests. Republicans and Democrats, Fascists and Communists, Catholics and Protestants, prohibitionists and non-prohibitionists, nudists and decency leaguers—all would undoubtedly be found to have their rough, statistical share of personality traits and capacities, no matter how vehemently they might deny that their group's membership contained any people with traits that society values as less desirable. Whatever differences might eventually be discovered would almost certainly be insufficient to ascribe as the main reason for the affiliation of the members. Whether or not a person becomes a member of a particular organization or movement will be determined essentially by his personal values as these are acquired from experience and knowledge and by his derivative ego drives and frames of reference.[17]

(1b) *An individual not only lacks an adequate frame of reference or standard of judgment by means of which he may orient himself but he also lacks even the awareness that he needs and is seeking a new frame of reference.* In such instances it never occurs to the individual to evaluate the alternative solutions offered, to question

[16] For some experimental evidence on this point, see M. Sherif, A study of some factors in perception, *Arch. Psychol.,* 1935, 187; S. E. Asch, H. Block, M. Hertzman. Studies in the principles of judgments and attitudes. *J. Psychol.,* 1938, **5,** 219-251.

[17] We are not implying here that temperamental traits and intellectual capacities are *never* important in their determination of allegiance to old or to new standards. Occasionally, as with an extremely submissive, introverted, timid person who eschews any cause advocating violence, personality traits may directly affect participation in a certain movement and directly affect the selection of values which become part of the ego. But, as was pointed out in chs. 1 and 2, the more usual condition would seem to be that these capacities and temperamental traits are exhibited *within* a mental context and motivational system.

the notion that a proposed explanation or a course of action might not be the only one possible. Whatever solution is proposed, whatever interpretation first "occurs" to the individual, will be unhesitatingly accepted and acted upon. In this extreme condition, created by the lack of any internal structuration, the law of primacy may be considered operative: the interpretation accepted is the interpretation the individual is first aware of. The interpretation may not be held for any great length of time but it at least furnishes a temporary orientation.

There are various reasons why an individual may react in this irrational fashion. All may be illustrated from evidence obtained in the study of a Hallowe'en broadcast, purporting to describe an invasion from Mars, which frightened so many people in this country in 1938.[18] For some persons, the situation portrayed by the radio drama appeared so immediate and so urgent that their first thought was to escape or to prepare to deal with the monsters. "We'd better do something instead of just listen," said one woman. So she started to pack. Another woman reported, "I wasn't frightened until they said the gas was within a few miles of us." Other people immediately resigned themselves to the situation so that any attempt to check the program, like any other possible course of action, seemed pointless. "What difference does it make?" reflected a high-school girl. Others were so overwhelmed by environmental pressures that they lapsed from their normal skepticism. Frightened relatives or friends telephoned or rushed into the homes of uninformed persons who promptly turned on their radios only to have the harrowing reports confirmed. Still others were extremely susceptible because of a pattern of personality characteristics. People who felt insecure, who constantly worried, who lacked self-confidence, who were fatalistic were more readily frightened than others.

(1c) *An individual's mental context fails to provide him with a needed interpretation or with any reliable standards by means of which he can make a desired check on alternative interpretations offered.* This condition differs markedly from the one just mentioned. For in this instance the individual is not only aware that he is trying to select a new interpretation but also he further realizes that, because none of his present frames or standards are completely

[18] Hadley Cantril, *The Invasion from Mars, op. cit.*

relevant, he should try to validate new interpretations before accepting them as the basis for orientation. But for any one of several reasons, he fails to make a thorough check and finally he accepts the general frame of reference or specific standard of judgment offered.

These reasons may also be illustrated from the panic resulting from the supposed Martian invasion. Some people attempted to check their own interpretation against data which were themselves already influenced by the interpretation they were trying to check. Thus certain people who were moderately disturbed by the news telephoned friends, who were also disturbed, to ask them what they thought. Other people tried to verify their interpretation by making certain observations which they then proceeded, however, to rationalize as consistent with the interpretation they thought they were checking. Thus, while one person would look out the window, see no cars on the street, and conclude that they had all been destroyed, a second person would look out the window, see the street full of cars and conclude that everyone was driving to safety. Still other people very genuinely sought to validate the interpretation presented but simply did not have sufficiently rich and well-grounded standards of judgment to know whether or not the evidence they uncovered was reliable. When they turned their dials to other stations they thought the other stations might not yet know about the disaster; when they saw the program listed as a drama in the newspaper, they thought it was not the same program. How, for example, can the average citizen, no matter how sincere his motives, conclusively prove one way or the other who sunk the *Athenia* or which belligerent power first violated Norwegian territorial neutrality in the second World War?

(2) A more familiar condition of suggestibility arises *when an individual's mental context is so patterned that a stimulus or interpretation presented is thoroughly consistent with the frames of reference and standards of judgment that constitute the mental context.* In this instance, the stimulus is experienced by the individual as thoroughly consistent with what he already thinks or "knows." It is therefore accepted. Frequently this type of suggestibility is reduced to the simplicity of a conditioned response. An individual

may react to the word "Fascist" or "Red" without the slightest knowledge of what these symbols stand for, without being able to relate them to anything in his mental or behavioral repertoire except the responses he has already learned. But by no means is all such suggestion explicable on the theory that specific responses to specific stimuli have been learned. Men show an ability to generalize on the basis of accepted frames of reference, to interpret entirely new stimuli and situations by means of their existing standards, to take the initiative in imitating the behavior of others when that behavior is useful in preserving or enhancing their status. The Lynds report, for example, that "Middletown's working class appears today to be less sure of many of the old values than is the business class; but in Middletown they have developed no ideology of their own, and they lack security on any basis of their own, such as labor organization. Hence, doubtful and uncertain, they tend to straggle after the wealthier, pace-setting fellow citizens in their affirmations of established values in the midst of confusion."[19]

The operation of this type of suggestibility is apparent to everyone. The ardent New Dealer enthusiastically approves each new foreign and domestic policy of President Roosevelt; the Communist accepts, without qualification, proposals which have the stamp of party leaders; the conservative gleefully welcomes, and repeats as his own, specific rationalizations of his general frame of reference provided him by paid columnists;[20] the Bible-beating fundamentalist cheers the pronouncements of any scientist who states that the world was made and is controlled by God; the American Legionnaire routinely condemns anyone who deviates from that brand of Americanism which insures his own place in the world.

The extent to which individuals are suggestible under this condition will depend, for one thing, upon the breadth of their frames of reference, the inclusiveness of the assumptions on which the frames are based. Thus a person who has acquired a thoroughly liberal point of view will reflect his liberalism in accepting the suggestions that new political parties, new moral codes, new fashions, and new

---

[19] Robert S. Lynd and Helen Lynd, *Middletown in Transition,* New York: Harcourt, Brace, 1937, 493.

[20] Hadley Cantril, The role of the radio commentator, *Publ. Opin. Quart.,* 1939, 3, 654-663.

religions be tolerated.[21] Whether the point of view is based on knowledge and experience or whether it has merely been accepted uncritically from the culture is irrelevant *if* it adequately provides the desired meaning to the individual. The Jesuit and the un-schooled, backwoods Baptist preacher are both likely to accept some fresh evidence of God's omnipotence; the learned economist of the laissez-faire school and the propertied corner grocer are both likely to disapprove proposals for cooperative stores; the naive aviation enthusiast and the skillful airplane designer are both likely to believe in the possibility of stratosphere planes; the erudite musicologist and the untutored radio listener are both likely to accept Beethoven's music as good. As we shall see directly, this by no means implies that the knowledge or factual basis, upon which frames of reference are based, is never conducive to a higher threshold of suggestibility. But it does imply that when a frame of reference is tenaciously held, knowledge and facts serve chiefly as stepping stones for more elaborate rationalizations.[22]

Another determinant of the extent to which this condition of suggestibility will hold in any given instance is, as we have stated before, the personal significance of the frames of reference, the degree to which the values from which they are derived involve the ego. The more the self, the me, is sustained or enhanced by a suggestion, the greater the likelihood that it will be accepted. Thus the Jesuit, the learned economist, the airplane designer, and the musicologist just mentioned all have personal, vested interests in the points of view they defend. When a person has no such vested interests, or when he feels completely secure, then he can afford to be tolerant and more openminded. We find, for example, that college students who are the children of middle-class parents are more intolerant than college students whose parents are wealthy;[23] that first- or second-generation immigrants are often most insistent on the passage of teachers' oath bills or other legislation designed to promote "Americanism." Both the student with a middle-class background and the naturalized citizen are hanging more tenuously

[21] G. B. Vetter, The measurement of social and political attitudes and the related personality factors, *J. Abn. & Soc. Psychol.*, 1930, 25, 149-189.

[22] See K. Diven, Aesthetic appreciation test, in H. A. Murray, *op. cit.*, 447-453.

[23] S. P. Rosenthal, Change of socio-economic attitudes under radical motion picture propaganda, *Arch. Psychol.*, 1934, No. 166.

to a status they cherish: the middle-class student who has hopefully identified himself with the values of the upper class does not want his aspirations questioned; the immigrant has to make up in fervor what he lacks in background.

Conditions of suggestibility. Discussions of the psychology of suggestion all too frequently define suggestion in some terms such as "the acceptance of a proposition for belief or action in the absence of critical thought processes." Such definitions, with phrases like "the absence of critical thought" or the "lack of active intelligence," completely beg the question and leave the crux of the problem very much up in the air. We have tried here to show more precisely what is meant by these terms and what psychological relationships between the individual and his environment account for this "absence of critical thought." Another danger in many of the "explanations" of suggestion is that their proponents entirely neglect the psychological problems merely by stating that people are susceptible to "prestige suggestion" or to "majority opinion."

Take, for example, the question of suggestibility to majority opinion. This has often been demonstrated in experiments,[24] and is often exhibited in everyday life. But this suggestibility to majority opinion is always highly relative, dependent upon the particular circumstances of the situation, cut across by numerous other influences that may be operative at the moment, and circumscribed by what the individual regards as the majority in *his* world. If people are suggestible to majority opinion, why, for example, did they not vote for Landon in 1936, when the widely publicized Literary Digest poll showed Landon the choice of the majority? Why do we still have two major political parties in the United States? Why do members of minority groups continue fervently to preach their causes when they know public opinion is ranged against them? Why do new values ever arise at all? Majority opinion is probably effective as a suggestion only when an individual has no clearly structured mental context adequate to interpret a situation and when the majority opinion does not conflict with other frames of reference or

---

[24] C. H. Marple, The comparative suggestibility of three age levels to suggestion of groups vs. expert opinion, *J. Soc. Psychol.,* 1933, 4, 176-186; C. E. Smith, A study of the autonomic excitation resulting from the interaction of individual opinion and group opinion, *J. Abn. & Soc. Psychol.,* 1936, 31, 138-164.

ego values. Neither the opinionated, financially insecure conservative nor the more tolerant, wealthy utility executive is likely to accept the suggestion of government ownership and operation of electric power even if the great majority of people should want it. The effectiveness and limitations of suggestibility to majority opinion can only be understood if one has some knowledge of the mental contexts, the needs, the aspirations, and the social setting within which majority opinion penetrates. The same considerations hold for "prestige suggestion." The term explains nothing unless we know the reasons for the prestige.[25]

The psychology of suggestion is sometimes further obscured by loose generalizations to the effect that children, women, primitive peoples, fatigued or excited persons are more suggestible than others. Although all these statements may be true, they are true only within a certain context, and our psychological understanding is not enlarged by mere statements that age, sex, or certain physiological conditions affect suggestibility. These are only substitute indices with psychological counterparts that remain to be discovered. If, under certain circumstances, children and women are found to be more suggestible, further psychological probing would probably reveal that they had fewer pertinent standards of judgment and frames of reference to use in the particular interpretations presented to them. If fatigued or excited individuals are found to be more suggestible, then the problem remains to determine how these conditions affect mental context and motivation. All too frequently psychologists, particularly those interested in measuring and testing rather than in understanding, are willing to accept as "explanation" a correlation between observable behavior and some sociological or physiological index. Such findings are of immense value but they are only propaedeutic to psychological explanation.

Critical ability. The reverse side of the psychology of suggestion is the psychology of critical ability. Critical ability may be defined as the *capacity to evaluate a stimulus in such a way that a person is able to understand its inherent characteristics and to judge and act appropriately.* To say that a person is highly suggestible is to say that he lacks critical ability. But to say that a person is highly suggestible *because* he lacks critical ability and to say nothing more is

[25] M. Sherif, A study of some factors in perception, *op. cit.,* 47-52.

to indulge in the tautology we have just condemned. Under what conditions does an individual possess critical ability?

If it is, as we have said, the opposite of suggestibility, it should therefore emerge when the individual's mental context and motivation contrast to the conditions we have described as underlying suggestibility: (1a) If all other things are equal, people who have standards of judgment or frames of reference, which they feel can be relied upon to interpret a given stimulus or event, are likely to display critical ability to some extent. The greater the relevant knowledge or experience upon which standards are based, the greater will be the individual's critical ability. The modern physician is more likely to give his patient appropriate remedies than is the medicine man of a primitive tribe.

(1b) People who have no standards of judgment or frames of reference appropriate to interpret a given stimulus, people who desire some interpretation, but who have developed a *readiness to question* the interpretations offered them, show critical ability. In such instances, critical ability will be proportional to skepticism. In the Martian broadcast, for example, it was found that educated people who had learned not to take everything at its face value were least disturbed by the fanciful news.[26]

(1c) People who are not able to interpret a given event directly by means of existing standards or frames may, nevertheless, have other tangential standards or frames which they can rely on and which they can use as trustworthy pegs to test evidence which they gather. Thus the majority of people who tuned in late to the Martian broadcast, who at first did not know what to make of it, but who checked by referring to the newspaper or by turning to other stations, accepted as reliable standards of judgments the newspaper's listing of a drama, "War of the Worlds" or the news-gathering efficiency of other stations which would also surely report such a major catastrophe. (2) When people have a mental context so patterned that a stimulus or interpretation seems thoroughly consistent with it but also have sufficient insight to know their own biases and prejudices, to check the interpretation and if necessary to enlarge or alter their mental contexts, then they may be said to have critical ability. This critical ability due to "self-objectification"

[26] Hadley Cantril, *Invasion from Mars, op. cit.,* ch. 5.

is probably the rarest form of all.[27] For more than any other condition that might give rise to critical ability, this one is bound up with ego drives, the desire for status and self-regard which we have already shown act as blinders for the ordinary mortal who so often is unaware of the things he takes for granted.[28]

[27] Allport, *Personality, op. cit.,* 220-225.

[28] This does not mean that a person who is completely devoid of any personal point of view, completely "objective" in the popular sense, has the greatest critical ability. As James pointed out, "If you want an absolute duffer in an investigation, you must, after all, take the man who has no interest whatever in its results: he is the warranted incapable, the positive fool. The most useful investigator, because the most sensitive observer, is always he whose eager interest in one side of the question is balanced by an equally keen nervousness lest he become deceived." *The will to believe and other essays in popular philosophy.* New York: Longmans, Green, 1896, 21. For a discussion of objectivity in social psychology, see Hadley Cantril and Daniel Katz, The problem of objectivity in the social sciences, *The Psychology of Industrial Conflict* (edited by George Hartmann and T. Newcomb), New York: Dryden, 1939, 9-19.

CHAPTER 4

THE LYNCHING MOB

Mid-morning of September 10, 1930, "Pig" Lockett and Holly White, Negroes, were taken from two Kemper County deputies and lynched. The masked mob came upon the officers while they were taking the Negroes, accused of robbery, from the jail at DeKalb to Scooba for preliminary trial. Later in the afternoon one of the mob leaders bought coffins so the lynched pair could have "decent burial."

On the last day of January, 1930, in a rural community southeast of Ocilla, Irwin County, Georgia, the dead body of a sixteen-year-old local white girl was found in a puddle of water by the side of the road. Circumstantial evidence and suspicion pointed to James Irwin, a Negro of a nearby community. He was captured next morning and taken to the place of his alleged crime. There he was tortured and mutilated and then burned. Great crowds rode out to see the body during the day.

Shortly after nine o'clock on a Monday in September, 1930, George Grant, Negro, alleged slayer of the Brunswick Chief of Police, was shot to death in a second floor cell of the McIntosh County jail at Darien, Georgia. He had been placed there only a few minutes before by the National Guardsmen and the county sheriff. A member of the Guard was in the jailhouse yard and the commanding officer of the Guard was within hearing distance of the fatal shots; the county sheriff was in a downstairs room of his house which opens upon the narrow corridor leading to the second floor cells.

Shortly after midnight on October 1, 1930, an organized group of men—an "orderly" mob—went to the Bartow County jail, and without opposition from officers, took from his cell Willie Clark, Negro, and carried him to the fair grounds on the eastern edge of town where they swung him up by the neck. According to an elderly resident of Cartersville, who claimed to have seen many Negroes dispatched by mobs, it was the "nicest lynching" he had ever seen.

About midnight of April 23-24, 1930, Allen Green, fifty-two-year-old Walhalla Negro, was taken from the Oconee County jail at Walhalla by a mob of a hundred or more, carried two miles into the country, tied to a tree, and shot to death. Accused of having criminally assaulted a young white woman, Green had been arrested and bound over to court at a preliminary hearing. The mob assembled and organized in the adjacent cotton mill village, attacked the jail, clubbed the sheriff into helplessness and secured the keys from his wife.

These are reports selected at random from an account of the twenty-one lynchings that occurred in the United States in 1930.[1] In the past decade under private and public auspices, a wealth of material has been accumulated describing lynchings and conditions under which they have occurred.[2] Probably no more adequate records exist concerning the causes and actions of any mobs than the data now gathered in this country on the lynching mob. Although this type may differ from other varieties of mob in the objective circumstances which create it, still the underlying psychological reasons for lynching mobs are sufficiently basic to mob behavior in general to give us an insight into an important phenomenon of social life. Our task here, then, is to translate the objective descriptions of lynching mobs into their probable subjective psychological counterparts. Why, from the point of view of the individual involved, does he participate in or condone a lynching? Why do people indulge in lynchings at certain times? Why are people in one area more prone to lynchings than people in other areas?

A lynching has been defined as the *"killing or aggravated injury of a human being by the act or procurement of a mob."*[3] A mob may be defined as a *congregate group of individuals who feel strongly that certain of their values are threatened and whose attitudes direct*

---

[1] Arthur Raper, *The Tragedy of Lynching,* Chapel Hill: University of North Carolina Press, 1933.

[2] Cf. Raper, *ibid.;* Walter White, *Rope and Faggot,* New York: Knopf, 1929; Frank Shay, *Judge Lynch—His First 100 Years,* New York: Washburn, 1938; Hearings of the Senate Judiciary Committee on the Anti-lynching Bill, Feb. 6-7, 1940; Commission on Interracial Cooperation, *The Mob Still Rides,* 710 Standard Building, Atlanta; Southern Commission on the Study of Lynching, *Lynchings and What They Mean,* Atlanta, 1931. Also cf. Erskine Caldwell, *Trouble in July,* New York: Duell, 1940, for a vivid story of a lynching and the circumstances which led up to it.

[3] J. H. Chadbourn, *Lynching and the Law,* Chapel Hill: University of North Carolina Press, 1933, 47.

their overt behavior toward a common goal.[4] A *lynching mob,* therefore, is a *congregate group of individuals who feel strongly that certain of their values are threatened and whose attitudes direct them to kill or injure a human being.* The method by which the killing or injury is accomplished is irrelevant: the victim may be burned, shot, hanged, beaten or may receive any combination or all of these and other punishments.

SOCIAL SETTING

The lynching mob gives us an unusual opportunity to place a specific type of social movement in a broad cultural context. For lynchings, especially during the last few decades, have been localized in a roughly bounded geographical area which has had its own rather novel history and has suffered from events and conditions somewhat peculiar to itself.

Statistical trends. The beginning of lynch law is attributed to Charles Lynch, born in what is now Lynchburg, Virginia, in 1736.[5] The original purpose of lynchings was to enforce law in local communities where courts of law were inaccessible. The Vigilantes, so characteristic of an accompaniment of western expansion, had a similar origin.[6] With the growth of abolitionist sentiments in the 1830's, lynching rapidly spread into the southern states. During the Reconstruction Period, after the Civil War, the lynching of freed slaves was conducted with new vigor. Wholesale "nigger hunts" were organized and scores of Negroes were rounded up and killed in bunches. As late as the decade between 1889 and 1899, there were 1,875 lynchings reported.

Since that time there has been a gradual decrease in lynchings, owing to public opinion and more efficient law enforcement. The

---

[4] The essential difference between *crowds* and *mobs* is that the members of a crowd do not undertake any common, directed, overt action and that the common emotions they experience are generally felt less intensely. A *crowd* may be defined as a *congregate group of individuals who have temporarily identified themselves with common values and who are experiencing similar emotions.* Crowds frequently and relatively easily turn into mobs; mobs are more difficult to turn into crowds.

[5] Cf. White, *op. cit.,* ch. 5, and Shay, chs. 1-3, for a more complete history of lynching.

[6] Cf. H. H. Bancroft, *History of the Pacific States,* New York: Bancroft.

average number of persons lynched per year in recent decades is as follows:[7]

From 1889	through	1899		187.5
"	1900	"	1909	92.5
"	1910	"	1919	61.9
"	1920	"	1924	42.6
"	1925	"	1929	16.8
"	1930	"	1938	12.7

Within these over-all figures there are certain trends. The proportion of white people lynched is steadily diminishing. In the decade between 1889 and 1899, 32 per cent of all persons lynched were white, a figure which would be even lower if the Mexicans, lynched in such states as Texas and Arkansas, were omitted from the total. The odds now stand about 40 to 1 that the lynching victim will be a Negro.[8] As these figures imply, lynching, furthermore, is becoming more and more of a phenomenon characteristic of the South. Whereas in the decade between 1889 and 1899, 18 per cent of all lynchings occurred outside the 14 southern states, from 1935 through 1929, less than 3 per cent were outside these states.[9]

The crimes or alleged crimes of the persons lynched show a variety of causes for mob action. The classification of the 4,686 lynchings recorded by the Department of Records and Research of Tuskegee Institute, from the years 1882 through 1938,[10] is as follows:

For homicide	1928
" rape	910
" attempted rape	282
" robbery and theft	228
" felonious assault	200
" insult to white person	82
" other causes	1056

The popular stereotype that lynchings are almost always for rape

[7] Raper, *op. cit.,* 25; Munro Work, *Negro Year Book,* 1939, 156 ff. Since these figures are used on "reported" lynchings, they represent the very minimum. A senate committee to examine lynchings found that "reports of investigators show that successful efforts are being made to keep lynching news away from channels of publicity in the localities where the crime occurs. The new technique seems increasingly to be to have lynching carried out by small groups and in secluded places." Senate Report, 76th Congress, 1940, No. 1380.

[8] Raper, *op. cit.,* 43.

[9] *Ibid.,* 27.

[10] Work, *op. cit.*

is quite unfounded. Rape or attempted rape accounts for only a quarter of the accusations. Among the "other" causes of lynching reported are: "being a witness," "improper conduct," "insisting on eating in a restaurant," "trying to act like a white man," "being a strike breaker," "discussing a lynching," "making boastful remarks," "slapping a boy," "insisting on voting," "throwing stones," "being a member of Labor's Non-partisan League," "alleged disrespectful utterance against President Wilson," "giving poor entertainment," "riding in a train with white passengers," "being too prosperous," "not turning out of the road for automobile driven by white person."[11] An examination of specific cases gives incontrovertible evidence that a large proportion of the accusations are unsubstantiated, and many of the homicides reported appear legally justifiable. The nature and authenticity of a crime are, however, unimportant considerations for potential mob members.

Here is an illustration of the attitude:

"Who was the white man who was killed—whose killing caused the lynchings?" I asked.

"Oh, he was a hard one, all right. Never paid his debts to white men or niggers and wasn't liked much around here. He was a mean 'un, all right, all right."

"Why, then, did you lynch the niggers for killing such a man?"

"It's a matter of safety—we gotta show niggers that they mustn't touch a white man, no matter how low-down and ornery he is."[12]

Only in rare instances are mob members arrested and punished. In the five years, from 1931 through 1935, for example, lynchers were punished for only 3 of the 84 lynchings that occurred.[13] Sometimes law-enforcement officers are part of the mob. In one lynching studied, for example, "Evidence in affidavit form indicated rather clearly that various law-enforcement officials, including the sheriff, his deputies, various jailers and policemen, three relatives of the then governor of the state, a member of the state legislature, and sundry individuals prominent in the business, political, and social life of the vicinity, were members of the mob."[14] Even when they are not

[11] Raper, *op. cit.,* 36 f.; Work, *op. cit.*; Shay, *op. cit.*

[12] Walter White, I investigate lynchings, *Anthology of American Negro Literature* (edited by Calverton), New York: Modern Library.

[13] Commission on Interracial Cooperation, *op. cit.,* 11.

[14] White, *op. cit.*

lirectly involved, they remember that they are, after all, elected by local public opinion and it is usually political suicide for them to go against the wishes of the mob, even if they want to. Individual protests of whites or Negroes, or even of local, organized minority opposition to the mob, are apt to bring further disorder in the form of incendiarism, boycott, intimidation of workers, or personal violence.[15] One mob participant in answer to a query concerning the role of law-enforcement officers replied:

> We elected them to office, didn't we? And the niggers, we've got them disfranchised, ain't we? Sheriffs and police and governors and prosecuting attorneys have got too much sense to mix in lynching bees. If they do they know they might as well give up all idea of running for office any more—if something worse don't happen to them . . .[16]

The statistically average lynching, then, is one that occurs in the South, has a Negro for a victim, native whites as mob members, none of whom is arrested or punished for his actions.

Economic foundations. It is by now firmly established that the roots of mob actions that lead to lynchings lie deep in the economic context of the culture. Although the economic basis of some lynchings may be dubious and in others tenuous and indirect, it cannot be doubted that, by and large, lynchings as we know them in this country are inextricably interwoven with economic conditions.[17] Although the reason for the economic duress may vary, some economic determinant is almost inevitably found somewhere in the story of the lynching mob of any period. Thus Walter White[18] points out that the lynchings between 1830 and the Civil War were due, in large measure, to the increased necessity of slavery in the South when the invention of the spinning frame, the fly shuttle, and the like had skyrocketed the demand for cotton; after the Civil War and during the days of reconstruction, when Negroes no longer had a market value, the Ku Klux Klan and less organized groups took upon themselves the job of reenslaving the Negro and making him

[15] *Ibid.*, 11 f.; Chadbourn, *op. cit.*
[16] White, *op. cit.*
[17] Cf. Frank Tannenbaum, *Darker Phases of the South*, New York and London: Putnam's, 1924, and H. W. Odum, *Southern Regions of the United States*, Chapel Hill: University of North Carolina Press, 1936, for a picture of southern economy.
[18] White, *Rope and Faggot, op. cit.*, ch. 5.

impotent; in the latter part of the nineteenth century and up to the
World War, the Negro was beginning to make himself felt both
politically and economically, while the whites were losing their
economic advantage and drifting more and more into the propertyless, economically insecure tenant-farmer class; during the World
War, began the great migrations of Negroes to the North with the
consequent determination of southern landowners to persuade their
workers by mob terrorism to stay at home; while, immediately after
the war, returning Negro soldiers were shown that mere service in
the nation's armed forces was no reason for them to assume that
their status had changed. At times the Negroes have threatened the
economic power of controlling interests by their organization and
initiative; at times when labor is needed they are kept in sub-
servience; at times when jobs are scarce, they are regarded as unnecessary competitors.

Analysis of the lynchings occurring during any given period
clearly reveals the economic dislocations of the communities where
the lynchings took place. When the counties in which the 21 lynchings of 1930 are compared, for example, to other counties in the same
states, they are found to be far below the average. "In approximately
nine-tenths of these counties the per capita tax valuation was below
the general state average; in almost nineteen-twentieths the bank
deposits per capita were less than the state average; in three-fourths
the per capita income from farm and factory was below the state
average, in many cases less than one-half; in nine-tenths fewer and
smaller income tax returns were made per thousand population than
throughout the state; in over two-thirds, the proportion of farms
operated by tenants was in excess of the state rate; and in nearly
three-fourths of the counties, automobiles were less common than in
the state."[19]

The close relationship between lynchings and dollars and cents is
further shown by the correlation obtained when the number of
lynchings is compared to the price of cotton—the higher the price
of cotton, the fewer the lynchings.[20] The fact that more lynchings

[19] Southern Commission on the Study of Lynching, op. cit., 31.

[20] Raper reports an analysis made by T. J. Woofter, Jr., for the years 1900 through
1930. Cf. Raper, op. cit., 30 f. Woofter's correlation between the price of cotton and
the number of lynchings for those years is —.53. A later study of Hovland and
Sears shows a correlation of —.67 for the years 1882 to 1930 (reported in Dollard,
Doob, et al., Frustration and Aggression, Yale University Press: 1939, 31).

occur in the summer months with the high point in July is added evidence that economic strife is an important part of the lynching background.[21] For at that time, in addition to any effects owing to the weather, there is the most tense relationship between tenant and landlord. The tenant has been paid off, finding himself with practically nothing after the landlord has discounted his debts to the company store, while the landlord becomes dictatorial with his bewildered and irritated tenants. However, it is not the landlord who is lynched.

The role of economic competition is also indirectly seen in the fact that lynchings are most frequent in areas that have been relatively recently settled, where rivalry for jobs and opportunities is keen and where long-established mores have not so clearly defined the expected status of racial groups.[22] Likewise the number of lynchings varies indirectly to the proportion of the colored population within a given area.[23] In the Black Belt counties of Mississippi (those with a population over 50 per cent Negroes), between the years 1900 and 1930, there were, for example, 2.1 lynchings per 10,000 Negro population; in counties where Negroes represented one-fourth to one-half the population the rate was 2.9, while in counties having less than one-fourth Negro population the rate rose to 3.9. Part of this is obviously because in areas with dense Negro populations there is less chance for contact between the races. But in addition to this, these counties have more rigidly defined racial boundaries and distinctions, and custom dictates what the colored man can and cannot expect.

Cultural level. The South has long been the nation's problem child number one. Its economic difficulties and its history have produced a retarded cultural development. Southern states on the whole spend less per child for education than other states—the literacy rate even of native whites in the South is lower than for other parts of the country. And the South is traditionally known as the backbone of fundamentalist, anti-scientific, primitive religion. There is, for example, a high relationship between the percentage of illiteracy and the number of Baptists in a state.[24] Also, when the relationship between

[21] R. Steelman, The study of mob action in the South, a Ph.D. dissertation, University of North Carolina, 1929 reported in Lynchings and what they mean, 10 f.

[22] Southern Commission on the Study of Lynchings, *op. cit.,* 13.

[23] *Ibid.,* 12 f., 74.

[24] White, *op. cit.,* 59.

religious affiliation and income of people in the southern states alone is compared, we find a definite tendency for members of what in this area are the more narrow, Bible-beating organizations to be found also in the lower income groups. Hence, it is not surprising

Table I

RELATIONSHIPS BETWEEN CHURCH AFFILIATION AND
ECONOMIC STATUS IN SOUTHERN STATES[25]
(FIGURES INDICATE PER CENT)

	Economic Status		
	Above Average	Average	Below Average
Baptists	4	48	48
Methodists	8	47	45
All other Protestants	11	55	34

to discover that a high relationship is found between the proportion of Methodists and Baptists in a southern state and the number of lynchings in that state,[26] or that the ministers of the small Methodist and Baptist churches in the South sympathize by and large with the members of their flock when they indulge in a lynching.[27]

PSYCHOLOGICAL SETTING

Although statistical and economic orientations are necessary backgrounds before we can understand the cultural context within which mobs arise, they are in themselves by no means enough for our purposes. The relationships between the objective conditions of the culture and its norms and values must be sought before we are ready to give any final account of the reasons why any given individual within that culture participates in mob behavior. In this particular case, we must examine briefly some of the standards peculiar to the South which produce mob phenomena that are also now almost exclusively confined within its borders.

In the South, two distinct races have had to live side by side for more than three centuries. And since the Negro did not migrate to

[25] Analyzed from data obtained by the American Institute of Public Opinion.
[26] Raper, *op. cit.,* 248 f.
[27] Southern Commission on the Study of Lynching, *op. cit.,* 58.

North America of his own accord but came under bondage, it was inevitable that a whole complex of cultural standards should be erected by the whites to see that such bondage was sustained. The history of the Negro and his relationships with the whites in this country reflects throughout a systematic perpetuation of rigidly established norms which would insure the white man of the Negroes' economic, political, and cultural servitude.[28] No one can set foot below the Mason-Dixon line without observing the operation of the established pattern which is, of course, only an extension and elaboration of the pattern found in the North. In every phase of life, the Negro is provided less freedom and fewer opportunities than the white. His houses, his jobs, his recreations, his medical care, and his schools all reflect his subservient position.

Psychologically, these cultural norms are reflected in the standards of judgment, the frames of reference, and the attitudes of the people themselves. The common phrase is that "the Negro must keep his place." This means to the white person essentially that "the white man must keep *his* place." A few reports of scattered interviews made with southern whites who were asked what they thought of Negroes will show how these cultural standards are reflected in individual mental contexts.[29]

Leslie Needham is fifty years old and lives in Atlanta. He was a brakeman but is now a watchman on WPA. He was graduated from high school and spent about a year in a business college.

> They are all right if you keep them in their place. But they must be kept in their place. I don't approve of associating with them myself.

[28] Racial antagonisms seem inevitably to grow where there is economic discontent. Frequently such antagonisms are encouraged by interested parties to prevent the organization of racial groups along other lines inimical to such interests. The modern variation of this strategy is to place distinctly separate national groups near each other in factories so that their internal quarrels will keep them from joining into a self-conscious working class. It is also perhaps not without interest that the Allied armies in the Near East during the second World War were composed almost entirely of native troops or foreign legions rather than of regular French or British soldiers who might as a group be more susceptible to Soviet propaganda in the event of close contact.

[29] These excerpts are taken from material especially gathered for the writer. The names and identifying characteristics of the respondents are fictitious, but the true flavor of the interview is preserved. For other accounts, see Allison Davis and John Dollard, *Children of Bondage,* Washington: American Council on Education, 1940, ch. 10.

These WPA jobs are full of Negroes. If everybody was the way I am
with them, it would be all right; for example, some men will drink
out of the same cup after a Negro—but I'd never do that. Give 'em a
separate bucket and cup. *I am not prejudiced against them.* We have
plenty of 'em in Atlanta—when you go downtown to a market on
Saturday night they are everywhere. I don't believe in stepping aside
for a Negro, I just shove 'em out of the way . . . They are treated
too well. They get too much pay for what they do . . . I used to be an
agent (selling) and traveled quite a bit. Most maids and butlers and
help in the home was colored. They work cheaper and will do things
that a white person wouldn't . . . If I had my way they'd be put in a
section by themselves and keep them there. They shouldn't be allowed
to move into white neighborhoods. There are lots of houses they are
now tearing down that are good enough for Negroes . . . Oh yes,
they are gettin' an education. They'll keep on improving, sure. But
they won't improve so much that we can respect 'em. Some people will
respect 'em. But I don't care who they are or how much education
they have, I wouldn't. They are black to me. I am afraid that the
white people are not going to take this serious enough in time. They
shouldn't have let the Negroes get as far as they have.

Ella Ferguson is a house servant in Alabama. She is in her early
thirties, was raised on a farm, and had a high-school education.

I think their mentality is low, I do . . . Niggers oughta have their
own social life like the whites—among themselves, but they oughta
stay with their kind. They are beings like us but their skin is a different color and they oughta stay to themselves. I don't think much
about it myself. They oughta have their own schools and churches, yes
sir, their own churches and schools. They can do the same work as the
whites—laboring work—if they provide their own labor. The better
jobs 'tho should be kept for the whites. I want a better job myself
and maybe that's why I say that. I don't know. Some folks would say
that I'm doing nigger work myself, but that ain't so. I think that the
good jobs oughta be for the whites. If they can't have busses and
street cars for the niggers and one for the whites, they oughta have a
place in 'em for the niggers. But they oughta have busses and cars
for both. I was on a bus one time that had niggers on it and we put
'em in the back. I don't know how they do in the North or other
places, but that's the way it oughta be.

Sarah Lee is a middle-aged housewife living in a small town in

Arkansas. Her husband is unemployed. She is slouchy and un-educated.

I was about thirteen when we come to Arkansas. That was the first time I'd ever lived 'mongst niggers and had any dealins' with 'em. Oh my goodness! I 'jest couldn't 'git used to 'em. They've got a funny turn and funny ways. A lotta niggers down here don't stay in a nigger's place. One of the agents at the depot and his wife used to "mister" the niggers. They'd call us by our first names and call the niggers Mr. and Mrs. We thought that was awful. Mrs. Goodman ask my daughter to help her teach a nigger Sunday school class. It 'jest *killed* Marie. She never *did* like Mrs. Goodman after that . . . Since I moved to the South, I went through Illinois and had to 'set in the train with 'em. I didn't have to set right in the same seat but we was in the same car together. It embarrassed me. Yessum. I never had seen it done before and I jist though it was the terriblest thing I ever heard of . . . I've had some niggers be mighty nice to me . . . I think there's some niggers as good as white people, but you jest can't class yourself with 'em . . . I think the niggers oughta be sent back to where they come from or git a big plantation and make 'em stay on there. You take the old generation of niggers, they're not so bad, but these young 'uns comin' on, they're so biggety. I know people git along with those that are uneducated better than those educated . . . Another thing a nigger keeps the white men out of work. They'll work for cheaper wages. Look at Mr. Flore and Mr. Woodfin. They'll keep niggers on their place if they can git 'em . . . If niggers had the same chance as white people they'd be about the same. There's a bet-ter class of niggers just like there's a better class of white folks. Just like the little boy said, "There's a little bad in all of us." I don't know what it'd *be* you'd admire about 'em. The young generation jest think they're jest as good as white folks. You notice on the streets of Brinkley. They won't give you one inch to pass 'em. You take these *old* African niggers, they know their place, but 'chew jest take this young generation comin' up! . . . The younger generation hasn't any ambition, you can jest figger it any way you wanta. No'um, I don't think they're as clean as white people. You take Lillie, she's *clean*, and she's a good cook. Seems like niggers is more gifted in their music than white people are . . . A nigger can git work when a white man can't in the South . . . They're not as trustworthy as a white person. I jest think they're fitted for the plantation. You take *one nigger woman* can chop more cotton than *three* white women.

They're gifted with that hoe. No'um, they shouldn't be allowed to take all kinds of jobs. That's jest what's knocked out the white people. You take these porters on these trains, a white man could do that job jest as well. I don't think they should work together, but how you gonna help yourself down here? Jest like this WPA, niggers and whites work all together. I guess they have to live jest like the white people, but they oughta be separated. This WPA is the unfairest thing I ever heard of . . . I'm gonna tell you my honest opinion. I don't think they *should* vote, but they pay poll taxes and there's no way in the world to keep 'em from it. Some of 'em think they can't vote in the primary, but if it was taken to a test they could . . . I don't really think they have the same privileges as other citizens. We're in Arkansas now, that's all I'm speakin' for. As the boy said, "When you're in Rome do as Rome." No'um, I don't really think they *should* have the same privileges as white people.

These are specific reflections of the general frame of reference that Negroes are inferior and destined forever to play a servile role in a world primarily meant for white men. The popular stereotypes of the Negro are systematically, perhaps quite unconsciously, perpetuated. In the white man's vaudeville, radio programs, or joke books, the Negro appears as a happy-go-lucky, harmless, ignorant soul; in the white man's moving pictures or advertisements, the Negro is represented as the humble, faithful, God-fearing servant. And the Negro is popular and tolerated to the extent that he conforms to some similar stereotypes. Even the higher education that may be provided for him in the South has a strong vocational tinge—to teach him how to be a better shoemaker, servant, or mechanic for the white man. Other stereotypes, portraying the Negro as a potentially sensuous criminal, a danger to white womanhood, are sustained by the widespread, distorted publicity of rape as the cause of mob violence and by gossip concerning the Negro's sexual prowess.[30] All presuppose a lower standard of living for the colored man. Also, if one suggests that Negroes may not be happy the way they are, the answer is either a flat denial of the possibility or the retort that what they have is good enough for them.

The southerner who has this frame of reference toward the Negro as part of his mental context is likely to be extremely sensitive

[30] Cf. White, *op. cit.*, ch. 4 for a penetrating discussion of the reasons why the average southerner assumes that sexual crimes are the bases for most lynchings.

about it. He knows that the standards of judgment which he accepts as the basis of his point of view are not completely shared by the majority of the people in the whole nation. He is nostalgic for the days before the Civil War when his values were accepted as an intrinsic part of the whole culture. He realizes that he has been unable to defend his standards by force of arms, by law, or by ethical considerations. Yet because he feels that these standards still are a part of him, because they involve his personal pride and status, he is still very much on the defensive. And he must now defend himself in other than legal ways or in a second resort to civil war. He does this by his racial discrimination, the perpetuation of his standards from generation to generation, and, when necessary, by demonstrations of his dominance, demonstrations which are overt in local areas but covert from the point of view of the legally and ethically accepted standards of the national majority.

He will often assume, therefore, that, since the white man has almost unrestricted rights over the Negro, he must create a specific mechanism for the exercise of these rights when they have been violated and when they are not properly and promptly upheld by more generally accepted social mechanisms. The mechanism, psychologically, is the belief that it is his privilege and duty to engage in a man hunt and its death-dealing finale. Frequently, the man hunt will proceed with the knowledge and connivance of local law-enforcement officers. At such times, the man-hunters do not have to rationalize any discrepancy between personal and social standards for they are, after all, helping to enforce the law.[31] As would be expected, lynchings are most frequent in those areas where accepted ethical standards crystallized into law are least likely to be enforced. There is almost an exact inverse relationship between the density of population in the counties of the fourteen southern states and the number of lynchings recorded in those counties. A Negro in a southern county of less than 10,000 population is in sixty times as much danger of suffering at the hands of a mob as a Negro who lives in or near a large southern city.[32] Lynchings characteristically occur, then, in small towns or in rural areas below the economic

[31] Raper, *op. cit.,* 13 f.
[32] *Ibid.,* 28 f.

average where contacts with the law and with vehicles communicating ideas and information are meager.[33]

This deliberate perpetuation and enforcement of an accepted frame of reference which is strongly felt because of its ego involvement means that other frames of reference, with their consequently different attitudes, will encounter enormous difficulty. Divergent frames will be accepted gradually only by small minorities of the population who have somehow from education and experience interiorized different standards of judgment upon which they can base different frames of reference and attitudes. It means, furthermore, that since one psychological problem of southern whites is to maintain their status relative to the Negro, they cannot allow an improvement in the conditions and opportunities of Negroes unless their own conditions and opportunities are proportionately increased. And since the collapse of the economy based on slavery, the southern landowner has felt himself steadily sinking, while today he sees no bright and permanent prospects for rehabilitating himself to a commanding economic position.[34] The small landowner, the small merchant, and the white tenant farmer likewise see little chance for them to increase their economic and social positions. Hence, as the individual approaches closer to the Negro's cultural level, overt persecution remains the only available method of avoiding his own fear of inferiority.

The discrepancy between the status of the white and of the colored man can obviously be reduced not only by a decline in the position of the former but also by a rise in the position of the latter. Increased education and opportunity have enormously developed the latent talents so long submerged in the Negro race. The Negro is improving his position economically, politically, and culturally even in the face of great odds. This, too, often produces greater discrimination, segregation, and persecution. The Negro who dresses as well as a white man is an unwelcome person in most southern white communities; the able Negro doctor must be careful not to let his professional success beguile him into thinking that he can mix equally

[33] E. F. Young, The relation of lynching to the size of political areas, *Social & Soc. Res.,* **12,** 348.

[34] Cf. Odum, *op. cit.;* Charles and Mary Beard, *The Rise of American Civilization,* New York: Macmillan, 1927; Erskine Caldwell and Margaret Bourke-White, *You Have Seen Their Faces,* New York: Viking, 1937.

with his professional white colleagues or that his wife and children can live on the same plane as the wives and children of the white colleagues; the skilled or unskilled colored worker who has a job that a white man would like is, as we have seen above, a renegade. The situation is aggravated in many areas because of the fact that Negroes will work for lower wages largely because of the standards of living they are used to and, in some instances, because white workers are more conscious of the power of labor organization and hence refuse to undercut their fellows.

Since the position of the white southerner is so dependent upon the labor and status of the Negro, the more he keeps the colored man "in his place," the lower becomes his own cultural standard. He is forced by the logic of his own frames of reference to oppose general improvements in housing, methods of farming, and education. For, in the process, his position relative to the Negro might be threatened even though on an absolute and objective basis his condition might be improved.

The conditions which create a lynching mob are, therefore, deeply interwoven with the whole social context surrounding individual mob members. The norms of the culture and the possibilities the culture provides for the satisfaction of needs largely determine what things people take for granted, what obstacles cause their frustrations, what roles they regard as suitable for persons of their status. Just as an explanation of why a gun shoots a bullet is inadequate if one simply learns that it is because the trigger is pulled, so any explanation of mob action which begins merely with the commission of a specific crime and ends with the final gasp of the victim isolates the phenomenon and obscures understanding. Against the cultural background we have described, we may now examine specific lynchings in detail. Then we shall be in a better position to explain the psychology of the lynching mob and to compare it to the psychology of other types of mobs.

Two Lynchings

Two lynchings are described in detail. These particular lynchings are chosen not because they are especially interesting or unusual but because they are fairly representative of different types of lynchings and because the data on them are accessible. It is obviously impossible to select a "typical" lynching for discussion. Lynchings seem to vary in their "orderliness." On the basis of this characteristic, a distinction has been made between a *Bourbon* and a *proletariat* lynching.[35] The Bourbon type of lynching is relatively exclusive and well-regulated. It generally occurs in a Black-Belt area where there is a rigid demarcation between whites and blacks and where the leaders of the community believe that it is their duty to enforce community standards. Such lynchings are therefore often engineered by leading citizens with the knowledge of law-enforcement officers. The object is to punish a specific person for a specific crime. Other Negroes are protected. The mob is small and does not get out of hand. The fundamental motive is to assure white supremacy and maintain the accepted mores.

The proletariat type of lynching generally occurs in areas where Negroes are distinctly in the minority, where competition is keen between Negroes and poor whites, and where the object is to persecute the race, rather than an individual. Such lynchings are more brutal, more publicized. They are led by members of the poorer, less established classes and disapproved by the better citizens of the community. There is little interest in proving the guilt of the alleged victim or even getting the right victim. After the lynching, the mob frequently persecutes other Negroes by destroying their property, beating or killing them.

Both types are due basically to economic conditions: in one case the Negro is persecuted so that he can be used to advantage by an established white group; in the other he is persecuted because he is competing with an unestablished white group. In both types the problem of race, as such, is a secondary issue. Any rigid classification of lynchings on such a basis is difficult. Nevertheless, the distinction serves to point out the different social and personal functions of mob activity.

The first case described has more of the characteristics of the Bourbon lynching, the second case more of the proletariat variety.

A Black-Belt lynching.[36] On July 18, 1930, a seven-year-old white

---

[35] This distinction has been made by Raper and the characteristics of the two types cited are taken directly from his writings on the subject and from conversations with him. Cf. Raper, *op. cit.,* 55 ff., and *The Mob Still Rides,* 16.

[36] The description included here is a condensation and reordering of material given in Raper, *op. cit.,* 107-123.

girl, the daughter of a tobacco farmer, came home crying because Oliver Moore, Negro house boy had hurt her while playing a game with her and her younger sister in the barn. Because of the condition of the girl's clothes, the parents concluded that the Negro's game had been attempted rape. Moore ran away while the farmer and his wife were consulting. The county sheriff with a posse of excited citizens and a brace of bloodhounds set out in search of the Negro. The searches were fruitless, but Moore was at last apprehended by a single white man on August 16. A preliminary trial was held on August 19. The father and the girls told their story. The Negro was not allowed to say anything and no lawyers volunteered their services to defend Moore, who was then lodged in the county jail to await appearance in the superior court. Since no unusual excitement had accompanied the preliminary trial, both the sheriff and the judge felt the prisoner would be quite safe in the local jail.

About one o'clock the next morning, however, a deputy sheriff in charge of the jail opened the door when he heard a knock. A number of people were outside. Some of them were masked. The sheriff was quickly covered by guns, the keys to the jail were found by a mob member, the Negro taken out and tied in one of about twenty cars waiting outside. The whole abduction was efficiently handled and the orders of the mob leader quietly carried out. The mob was obviously well organized. Some time later the county sheriff was notified. He organized a posse to pursue the mob but did not know which way to go. About dawn the Negro's body was found hanging to a tree "riddled with bullets and buckshot." The lynching was staged as near as possible to the barn where the alleged crime had occurred.

Community setting. Edgecombe County, in which the lynching took place, has a long slaveholding tradition. It was settled in 1720 by Virginians who brought their slaves with them. In 1790 there were already thirty-seven families owning at least twenty slaves each. For over a hundred years the colored population has exceeded the white in the county. During the Reconstruction Period the Negroes had political power, but by 1900 their disfranchisement was almost complete. According to the 1930 census, Negroes constituted 57 per cent of the population in that year. Only about one-tenth of one per cent of all the people in the county in 1930 were foreign born.

With fertile soil and other natural advantages, the county has long been predominately agricultural. But while the per-acre crop value of the county is above the state average, the amount of money finally retained by the landlord or tenant is considerably below the state average. Since almost all crops consist of cotton or tobacco, it is necessary for the inhabitants to buy almost all their fertilizer and food. In 1930, the year of the lynching, over 83 per cent of the farmers were tenants. Discrimination against the Negroes is strikingly revealed in the differential expenditure for the education of white and colored children: the 1930 census showed that, whereas $22 per year was spent for each white child, only $3.40 was spent for each colored child.

Community reactions to the lynching. Although many of the larger papers in the state severely condemned the lynching, the smaller papers in the vicinity were not unduly perturbed. The local *Telegram* stated editorially that it did not condone the action of the massed men but added, "That the feeling of a people should be aroused is natural and we find ourselves, despite our views on lynching, not too greatly disturbed . . . We find ourselves calmly accepting the crime last night as inevitable." Local ministers and school teachers did not dare say anything against the lynching.

Unfortunately, no information is available concerning the personnel of the mob. However, the fact that the lynching was so efficiently conducted indicates that it had been well planned ahead of time. The judge in the preliminary trial was quite sure that many local citizens were involved.

The attitudes of some of the leading members of the community who were questioned are probably not very different from the attitudes of the actual mob members.[37] A court official said that, "From the standpoint of state and legality it's regrettable but, personally, I think it was a good thing." Another official said, "I hate that this thing occurred on account of the criticism it has brought. There's no question, however, of Moore's guilt, and personally I'm glad it happened." A newspaper man stated, "In principle, I'm against lynching, but this crime was so horrible. I think it was all right."

[37] All quotations taken directly from Raper, *op. cit.,* 117 f.

A policeman's reaction was, "The black son of a b—— got what he deserved. If the crime had been committed against the lowest white woman in the world he should have been killed; if I had been there I would not have interfered, for them folks would a-killed a good man to get that nigger."

In general the white people of the community are proud of their particular Negroes: "We've got the best Negroes of any county in the state; they are good workers, and they know their place." But what this "place" is can be seen from an article published in one of the county's papers the day after the lynching.

> If some white people were not so prone to be familiar with Negroes and socialize with them, allowing them reasons to suppose their presence among white people is acceptable, there would still live in the heart and soul of the Negro the fear and dread of swift and sure punishment in case of his wrongdoing.
>
> Oftentimes we have thought of this very thing. We have seen white boys and Negroes socializing right here in this community—pitching horseshoes together and engaging in many other pastimes—a practice that will inculcate in the mind of the Negro that he is acceptable company in white society. There is a way to treat Negroes and yet be kind to them. They should be given all that rightfully belongs to them—in material things as well as in rights and privileges. With that the border line should be drawn and they should be sternly schooled in the laws of segregation. We fear that the Edgecombe tragedy was brought about by lack of enforcement of this law.[38]

The Leeville Lynching.[39] One Saturday morning in the spring of 1930, a Negro laborer on a white man's farm, near Leeville, Texas,[40] came to his employer's house to collect the $6 in wages due him. The farmer's wife told him that her husband had gone to town and

[38] *Lillington News,* Aug. 21, 1930, quoted in Raper, *op. cit.,* 113 f.

[39] This report is taken almost verbatim from an article by Durward Pruden, A sociological study of a Texas lynching, *Studies in Sociology,* 1936, 1, 3-9, published by the Department of Sociology at Southern Methodist University. The article is a condensation of an M.A. thesis on file at the Southern Methodist University library. The thesis is the most complete account of a lynching and the lynching mob that has come to the writer's attention. The present writer has freely inserted passages from the thesis in the description included here and has reordered it to make it more appropriate for his purposes. He is greatly indebted to Mr. Pruden and to the editors of Studies in Sociology for permission to use this material.

[40] All names of places and people are fictitious.

had not left the wages. The Negro was disgruntled, left the house, but entered the kitchen door a few minutes later with a shotgun and again demanded the money. The woman backed away from him through a hall into a bedroom where he assaulted her several times. Fearing that the woman's five-year-old son in the backyard might give an alarm, the Negro, after tying his victim to the bed, went to look for him. She broke loose and fled across a field to a neighbor's house, where the sheriff was telephoned. Meanwhile, some men came walking along the road, and the Negro fled toward a creek bottom. One deputy sheriff came to the scene and arrested the Negro who, it is claimed, fired at him. The Negro confessed, agreed to plead guilty, waived all rights, and was secreted in a jail in a town some miles from Leeville.

This is the commonly accepted version of the crime and the arrest. But, as is frequently true in charges of this nature, other versions were heard. Most of the Negro newspapers and the local Negroes believed that the whole charge was a frame-up to cheat the Negro out of the money owed him. A number of white farmers, discussing the case later in private, said that they believed the woman wanted illicit intercourse with the Negro and invited him into the house. After the woman was satisfied, according to this version, she became frightened and angry. A county officer who knew the case thoroughly stated that he believed the woman encouraged the Negro and that the five-year-old child interrupted the pair, thus frightening the mother. The officer reported that he had once "pulled an aunt of hers out of the bed with a nigger." The accepted version of the arrest has it that the Negro shot twice at the sheriff just before he had come out of his car to make the arrest. But Negroes and a prominent white physician, who said they saw the sheriff's car later, maintained that there was only one bullet hole through the windshield and that it was directly in front of the driver's seat. This could not have been made by the Negro's shotgun, and their theory is that the sheriff shot at the Negro.

A medical record showed that the illicit relationship had occurred, and the Southern Commission on the Study of Lynching holds that this was one of the eight lynchings of the year (there were twenty-one in all) where the lynched person seemed most likely to be guilty of the accused crime.

The next Monday night a small group of men and boys loitered near the Leeville jail. By Tuesday, many exaggerated versions of the details of the assault were being repeated on the street. Tuesday night a large group of boys and men appeared at the jail and demanded the Negro. They refused to leave until the sheriff allowed some of their leaders to go through the jail and see that the Negro was not there. There were no further attempts at mob action until the next Friday, the date set for the trial.

On the morning of the trial, many people came to the Leeville business center—both local residents and others from farms and small communities of the adjacent trading area. The judge refused to have the trial held elsewhere but had four Texas Rangers present to guard the court. The Rangers took the Negro into the courthouse early in the morning before the crowd gathered. All morning, as the jury was being selected, the crowd around the courtyard and in the courthouse halls grew larger and more belligerent. Just as the situation was hanging in the balance between an orderly trial and a riot, a rumor was circulated that the governor of the state had telegraphed the Rangers not to shoot anyone when trying to protect the Negro. Although the rumor was untrue, it was accepted by the mob and so encouraged its members that the Rangers were practically helpless unless they caused extensive bloodshed. The precipitating event, which changed the huge, curious crowd into a vicious and active mob, was the bringing of the woman from the hospital to the courthouse in an ambulance and carrying her on a stretcher through the crowd into the courtroom. This was about one o'clock. After that the mob went wild. It broke into the courtroom and was repeatedly driven back by the Rangers, with drawn guns and tear gas. Men and boys on the stairs were yelling, "Come on, let's get him!" Men out on the lawn were excitedly calling to the officers in the second-floor windows, "Throw him out, you blue-bellied, nigger-lovin' sons of b——s." An old man sitting in a courtroom window cried, "Come on in and git him, boys." There were yells of "let's get the nigger now." The assaulted woman was brought back out of the courthouse on the stretcher. Some of the mob thought it was a ruse, and that the sheet across the stretcher hid the accused Negro. Accordingly the sheet was jerked back and they found the woman suffering from the effects of the tear gas. Her condition was immediately interpreted by the mob as being the result of hysteria induced by her having been brought face to face with "the nigger brute" in the courtroom. The judge at last decided to have the trial held in another town, and the Negro was hurried into a fireproof vault room on the second floor of the courthouse.

When the mob saw that the Rangers were determined to hold the courthouse, some of the members decided to burn it. A group of teen-aged boys, led by an excited and vociferous woman dressed in red, broke the courthouse windows with rocks, threw gasoline in, and fired the building about 2:30 P.M. The fire department used its ladders to carry the people from the second-floor courtroom. There was some objection to the rescuing of the judge, county attorney, sheriff, and Rangers. "Let the bastards burn up with the nigger," was the cry. But finally all were removed except the Negro in the vault. As the fireman tried to fight the blaze during the afternoon, the mob cut the fire hose as fast as it could be connected. Sometimes the firemen were attacked.

By this time the local daily was on the streets and in the rural byways with the story of the attempt at trial. Nearby metropolitan papers printed extras and a powerful radio station in a city seventy miles away broadcast a play-by-play account of the activity sent by a special announcer over leased wires. Several thousand people had already gathered. Everybody came, as they said, "Just to see what was happening." Many citizens were shocked to see their courthouse burning. Some members of the mob claimed that as citizens they had a right to burn their courthouse if they wanted to: "Let 'er burn down; the tax payers'll put 'er back."

The tension of the mob is reflected by the description of an automobile mechanic present, like everyone else, only as a "spectator":

> I was standing on a corner of the square watching the courthouse burn and talking to two policemen. I heard a man right behind me remark of the fire, "Now, ain't that a shame?" No sooner had the words left his mouth than someone knocked him down with a pop bottle. He was hit in the mouth and had several teeth broken.

The Rangers, who had left the courthouse, telephoned the governor for assistance, and about 4 P.M. a small detachment of National Guards arrived from a neighboring town. They marched around the falling ruins of the courthouse, saw they were too far outnumbered to restore order, and returned home. About 6 P.M. a larger unit of fifty-two soldiers arrived from a nearby city. Leaving a detachment to garrison their headquarters at the county jail three blocks west of the courthouse, they remained deployed around the smoldering courthouse ruins to push the crowd back from the hanging walls. As darkness fell, the spirit of the mob became uglier. They reasoned that if the governor would not let the Rangers shoot at them, he surely would not let soldiers shoot either. They began to abuse the soldiers, and soon a pitched battle ensued in which the troops were forced to retreat the three blocks back to the jail, followed by the angry mob which was throwing bricks, rocks, pieces of timber, chunks of concrete, broken bottles, sticks of dynamite. Several soldiers were badly cut and beaten, others had their rifles taken from them, and some of the mobsters received minor bullet wounds. Reinforced by their comrades at the jail, the troops made a determined stand there and started shooting into the air. The mob then withdrew and returned to the courthouse square to open the vault and get the Negro, about whose condition there was much speculation.

From about 8 P.M. to midnight, various efforts were made to open the upper room of the great two-story, steel-and-cement vault. A gigantic crowd packed the entire square and side streets. Dynamite was stolen from a hardware-store cache and from the highway department. A few charges were set off around the standing walls near the vault to see if it would crumble easily. But substantial citizens with business places around the square stopped the intended plan to blow the whole vault to pieces. Finally the mob leaders confiscated an acetylene torch.

By this time the members of the crowd seemed confident that they would soon have their victim. A feeling of good-natured camaraderie developed. A justice of the peace reported that a man you had never seen before, or one that you had seen but never met, would walk up, offer you a cigarette, smile good naturedly, and say in a most agreeable voice, "Well, friend, I believe we're gonna' get him pretty soon."

Working from the top of the ladder, the leaders were able to open a hole large enough to insert dynamite and blow a hole which the mob leader entered. He threw out the dead body, shouting "Here he is!"

"Everybody was crazy to see the nigger," said a spectator. So the corpse was drawn up on a limb of an elm tree in the courthouse yard.

Then the leader, still on top of the ladder and after drinking from a pint bottle, hollered, "Take him to niggertown, take him to niggertown."

So the body was fastened behind a Ford roadster whose spotlight had furnished the light for the opening of the vault. The car contained two boys and two girls, and other people struggled to get on it. About five thousand howling, yelling people fell into a midnight parade behind the corpse. Someone struck up the strains of "Happy days are here again," and soon hundreds joined in with "Let us sing a song of cheer again, happy days are here again." Motorists tooted their horns. The city police tried to direct traffic.

At an important corner in the Negro section of town, the body was drawn up to the limb of a cottonwood tree in front of a Negro drugstore. The store was forcibly entered and ransacked, the money and valuables pocketed, the confections passed around to the crowd, and the furniture and furnishings piled under the Negro's body for fuel. Some versions have it that the mob leader unsexed the Negro in the presence of the crowd of men, women, and children before lighting the fire. Others deny this. But those who claim that it was done were very specific in their descriptions of what had happened, although the descriptions vary. The crowd gave a mighty cheer as flames enveloped the Negro's body. Little boys pointed to the Negro and made suggestive comments as the trousers burned off. Men whispered to each other and laughed aloud. The body was still in its semi-crouched position as it dangled from the chain. The heat caused great blisters and welts to rise upon the flesh as it began to burn. The air was filled with the acrid odor of burning meat.

After the burning of the body some of the crowd—the onlookers —went home. But the more active elements continued ransacking and burning with gasoline the Negro business places, including a hotel, drugstore, two cafés, two barber shops, two dentists' offices, a doctor's office, two undertaking establishments, an Odd Fellows' hall, a Knights of Pythias building, a theater, a lawyer's office, a life-insurance office, a cleaning and pressing shop, and several residences.

They swore that they would "run all the damn niggers out of Leeville" and that they would "git rid of the damn niggers for good." Many members of the mob were very drunk. The fire department was not permitted to put any water on the fires except on nearby property owned by whites.

Meanwhile, all Leeville's two thousand Negro inhabitants were under cover. Some were given refuge by white friends and employers in Leeville; the others, with their old people, their sick, their babies and children, hurried away in old automobiles, wagons, buggies, on mules, and by foot. Some reached Negro friends in adjacent cities; less fortunate individuals spent a harrowing night in ditches, ravines, clumps of bushes, under houses or bridges.

About one o'clock Saturday morning, 150 more National Guards arrived with machine guns, rifles, side arms, and tear gas. They, together with the previously mentioned soldiers at the jail, were at last able to break the mob and disperse it. At 3 A.M. more troops arrived. At dawn the soldiers had the town under control with machine guns mounted at strategic points. Martial law was declared and arrests began. During the next few days there were continual rumors that the mob would reassemble on the outskirts of town at dark, make a new march against the soldiers, and complete their avowed job of burning all Negro dwellings and of driving their occupants out of town permanently. The armed force was increased to 419 men and more arms were brought in, but nothing more of importance occurred. A notice was found tacked on a white employer's office door, warning him to fire his Negro workers and engage whites. Warnings to leave town were discovered on some Negro dwellings.

A military court of investigation turned over 29 persons and 600 typewritten pages of confidential evidence to the civil authorities, who indicted 14 men and boys. They were removed to jail in the large city nearby. A citizens' committee to maintain order was organized and the troops left Leeville, after being there nine days. Finally the rioters were brought to trial in the city. But the judge found that he was unable to obtain a jury panel of urban men who would agree to convict the defendants even if they were proved guilty. The trial was moved to the state capital and one young man was finally given a two-year term for arson. This was more than a year after the lynching, when the defendant was already at odds with the law on other charges. But before ending his sentence, he was released by the governor on petition of Leeville citizens. The other 13 men were never tried.

Race relations in Leeville continued to be very strained for many months. The Negro citizens (most of whom returned) were never compensated for the loss of their property and were abused and severely persecuted. One Negro, for example, told this story:

> One Sunday afternoon about a month or so after the lynching, my family and I had dinner over at my mother's. As we were returning home in our wagon, a group of almost-grown white boys passed by, and one of them threw a rock at us. My wife was sitting on the seat beside me, nursing our youngest baby. With the baby in her arms she was unable to dodge readily. The rock hit her on the breast just above the baby's head. It hurt her terribly, and she cried and cried from the pain. I never felt so sorry for anybody in my life. I got the truck's license number and reported it to the law. They found the owner of the truck, but he claimed that some other fellows had borrowed his truck and that he wasn't with them. That was the last of it.

At last the situation became normal again.

Institutional reactions. The official reactions of the *churches* in the community were largely determined by the economic status of the members. The pastors of the four largest churches in Leeville, which are attended principally by the wealthier and the middle income groups, condemned the lawlessness. But ministers of the outlying churches in the poorer districts around the cotton mill and the railroad shops avoided discussion of the lynching because they knew that many of their members were in sympathy with it. One pastor in a small church was bold enough to censure the mob from his pulpit. But he was immediately waited upon by a committee of his members and advised to refrain from further mention of the subject if he expected to retain his position.

The *press* in Leeville undoubtedly contributed to the rise of the mob by carrying detailed stories of the crime and by publishing the rumor that the Rangers had been ordered not to shoot. This effect seems to have been inadvertent, arising merely from the usual newspaper practices. After the lynching, the editor of the Leeville paper caustically condemned the mob. However, the small weeklies in the nearby villages confined themselves for the most part to reports of news items about the lynching.

The *law-enforcement officers* did not all conduct themselves as their oaths and duties presumably required. The Rangers and National Guardsmen did their best to protect the prisoner, to avoid bloodshed, and to ferret out the mob members. The county attorney, however, seemed primarily interested in another death penalty for his record. And he did not dislike the publicity the case received. It seems that it was not necessary for him to have the woman brought to court to get a conviction because the death penalty was, in his own words, "a cinch." Had the trial been completed, there is no doubt that it would have been a "legal lynching." In talking about the Negro, the county attorney referred to him as a "damn black son of a b——." The city firemen at first made an effort to extinguish the courthouse fire but, after the riot, almost unanimously failed to help identify the mob members who had cut their hose and attacked them. The city police made practically no effort either during or after the lynching to help uphold law and order. During the lynching they confined most of their activity to directing traffic. The assaulted woman was a relative of one of the most popular policemen.

All *public-spirited citizens* were invited to give the military authorities information in the court investigation. They were promised secrecy. Practically none of the real community leaders, such as pastors, teachers, attorneys, college alumni, bankers, and big-business men, took advantage of this opportunity to help punish the mob members. Practically all the 64 people who testified before the court and who were not suspected of complicity had to be given specific orders to appear. A few had to be brought in forcibly by the officers. The majority of these people were uncooperative or plainly evasive, either because of sympathy for the mob or fear of retribution from mob members. Witness after witness answered under oath that he had been in the crowd all day, that he had lived all his life in and around Leeville, that he knew most of the inhabitants, and yet could not remember having recognized anyone among the thousands of people present during the day. "I don't think I seen a man I knew," "To save my life, I can't remember," "I wouldn't dare to say that," were some of their comments before the court.

Community setting. Texas ranks third as a lynching state. Only Georgia and Alabama exceed her in the number of lynchings recorded since 1899. That this is not due merely to the size of the state is demonstrated by the fact that practically all the lynchings have occurred in the eastern half of the state. At the time of this lynching, about 10 per cent of the county population was colored. Along with the Negroes at the foot of the economic ladder, there was a large element of propertyless whites in both urban and rural Wick county. More than two-thirds of the 5,169 farmers of the county were tenants. During the decade preceding the lynching, the county population decreased by 8,322, although the state as a whole showed an increase of nearly 25 per cent. Railroad shops in the county had moved away and two small colleges in Leeville had closed. The community was drastically feeling the pinch of economic decadence.

Negroes have not been allowed to live in six of the small towns of Wick county. "Nigger don't let the sun go down on you here" has been the tradition rigidly enforced. In Leeville the Negroes have been excluded from work in most industries and must content themselves with what money trickles down from the wealthier whites for such odd jobs as car washing, lawn moving, shoe shining, and day labor on the farms. In spite of this situation, the more ambitious Negroes had managed to accumulate some property and several had become quite prosperous. A number of them owned their own homes and had well-kept lawns, flower beds, and houses well-furnished and in excellent repair. Meanwhile, many of the poor Whites were getting poorer.

Mob personnel. Some distinction should be made between the various types of participants who gathered in the huge crowd. Not all were technically members of the "mob," those who were determined to lynch the victim. A compilation of the data, revealed by private investigation, on the men and boys charged or suspected by the military authorities and others gives a fairly accurate sample of the active mob.

The people who participated may be roughly placed into three groups, according to their economic status. (1) Many of the better citizens who opposed the lawlessness, but dared not do anything about it. They were mainly of the upper economic group. (2) Others who did not participate, but who were either indifferent or in favor of the lynching. These people were chiefly middle class. (3) The active mob, essentially people in the lowest economic bracket who, in general, had to compete with the Negro. Table II classifies 58 of these individuals by occupational status.

Table II

ACTUAL MOB MEMBERS CLASSIFIED BY OCCUPATIONS

Do not work or do odd jobs	8		
Unemployed teen-aged boys	6	Total unemployed	19
High-school boys	5		
Mill workers	5		
Road workers	4		
Factory workers	2	Total common laborers	13
Truck driver	1		
Nursery shrubbery worker	1		
Farmers and farmhands	8	Total farmers	8
Mechanics	4		
Welder-plumber	1		
Cement worker	1	Total skilled laborers	8
Bricklayer	1		
Railroad switchman	1		
Bank clerk (a youth)	1		
Advertising manager of a department store	1	Total salaried people	3
Gin manager	1		
Grocery-store operators	2		
Filling-station operator	1	Total owners of businesses	4
Dry-goods store operator	1		
Insurance agent	1		
Fruit peddler	1	Total miscellaneous	3
Banjo player and singer	1		

At least 11 of the active participants in the riot are known to have had previous police records. Nine had been in the hands of the law for stealing, fighting, or bootlegging. Two were under suspended sentence for stealing, and one, a hobo, had spent 12 years as an inmate of an insane asylum.

The acknowledged leader of the mob, Lank Smith, was a man 40 years old who could neither read nor write. He had no particular profession but occasionally did a little cattle trading and "bronc bustin'" in rodeos. He drank a great deal and was described by officers as "a rough-and-ready bully." He had been before the courts several times as a bootlegger. With his wife and little daughter, he lived in a shabby part of town near some Negro shanties. He owned no property and belonged to no church. The wife provided most of the family's support by taking in washing. His attitude at the opening of the vault was described as that of a great benefactor—a protector of white womanhood—doing his duty in a brave and dramatic manner. A few years after the lynching he was killed in a drunken brawl on a South Texas sheep ranch.

Percy, the boy who was given the two-year prison term, was 17 years old. His father was dead and his mother was a low-paid worker in a shirt factory. At an early age he began skipping school, stealing chickens, and coming into the hands of the police. The welder-plumber was the only one in the mob who owned any taxable property and the only person indicted who could put up a bond. He was sensitive about being indicted and claimed to have been practically conscripted to operate the acetylene torch in cutting through the vault. Among the other members of the mob were: a man who later had trouble with a farmer because he raped the farmer's wife; five overgrown and maladjusted high school boys, one of whom had a prostitute for a mother; a poor fruit peddler with several children; a road worker who testified that he had been out to get the Negro "for the sake of the honor of the white woman who had been mistreated"; an unemployed inebriate well known for his maltreatment of his wife and children; two boys from upper middle-class homes.

Attitudes of participants. The Negro in Wick County is regarded as an inferior by all classes of people in all walks of life. On the whole, the people in the upper economic groups disapproved of the lynching. They preferred to have law and order and they hated to see their town receive such adverse publicity. Since they do not compete with the Negro but merely use him, their own interests were not advanced by mob action.

A local college president stated, "I believe the best people were against it, but they dared not say so."

Persons in the middle economic class seem in general to have disapproved because they opposed the destruction of property. They believed almost all the rumors about the Negro's brutality. Their indifference toward the issue involved is shown by the fact that they were equally amused when the mob chased the soldiers away from the square and when the soldiers later chased the mob out of 'niggertown." A few of this group participated in the riot. In various ways they lent moral support to the mob members and frequently made remarks about "what ought to be done to the nigger." Almost without exception they blamed the judge for not ordering the sheriff to take the Negro back to jail so that the mob could have taken him without burning the courthouse.

An elderly farmer held, "The officers was to blame. When they seen the mob at the trial, they should of started back to jail with the nigger. Then the mob could of lynched him." The local barber felt the same way: "There wasn't any use in burning all that property. The judge should have changed venue. It was an awful thing to go through." So felt the wife of the owner of a small cafe: "We did a grand business that day. The officers should have started to the jail with the Negro. Then the mob could have got him without burning the courthouse."

Some other attitudes of middle-class people are reflected in their statements. A typewriter salesman reported, "Believe me, those damned niggers were sure good after that. They just bowed and scraped around. You got to do something occasionally to keep them in their place or they'll get too smart." A member of the Parent-Teachers organization said, "Only one man was sentenced for burning that courthouse, and he shouldn't have been." A photographer reported, "Before the troops stopped us from selling them, we made about $300 on our flashlight picture of the burned nigger." The opinion of the county physician, who was the family doctor of the assaulted woman, was that "the deputy sheriff should have just shot the bastard without ever arresting him."

The attitudes of those in the lower economic bracket who participated most actively in the lynching are reflected by a waitress who felt that "the Negro deserved to die and burning was too good for him." A tenant farmer when questioned about the burning of the Negro property, said "The town is better off without it." A shoe repairman about 35 years old believed, too, that "the nigger got what he deserved." He said, "They will get a little smart if you don't keep them in their place." The attitude is further illustrated by a Negro truck driver's remark that white laborers had been friendly to him until he got his job and then they persistently abused him.

Summary. The lynching was the result of an assault of an ignorant Negro on the wife of a tenant farmer. It is not entirely clear that the Negro was guilty, and the issue involved is one of race rather than sex.[41] This lynching occurred in an economically backward county. The intensity of the racial prejudice which pervades the entire social structure of the county varies with different economic levels. The most intensely biased groups are those nearest the Negro in their standards of living, those who have to compete with him. Almost everyone in the community participated in the lynching in some way or other. Although the members of the actual mob seem to have been drawn largely from the lower income groups, other citizens were implicated because they either sanctioned the behavior of the mob or refused to reveal information which would help local and state officials enforce the law.

WHY LYNCHING MOBS?

These descriptions of mob behavior and the review of the social context within which lynchings occur must now be translated into psychological terms. What we want is an understanding of why, from the point of view of the individual involved, certain objective conditions give rise to mob behavior. What are the psychological counterparts of this social environment and what are the motives which lead to mob behavior?

Defense of status. It is obvious that the traditional social values of the particular milieu in which the individual mob member lives have become interiorized to form personal standards of judgment He takes for granted certain evaluations of the Negro: the colored man is relatively unintelligent, lazy, superstitious, sensuous, carefree and the like. The particular assumptions regarding the characteristics of the race will vary with different individuals depending upon the particular values of their restricted environments, their own training and experience. But whatever patterns of specific values are accepted as standards of judgment, by and large the individual presupposes that the Negro is inferior and must be kept in his place. Just what this "place" is will vary with different individuals. But this frame

[41] That racial antagonism rather than punishment for sexual impropriety is the case is illustrated by the fact that in Leeville, shortly before the lynching, a Negro man pled guilty of attacking a Negro woman. He was fined $12.50 and released.

of reference is sufficiently general to determine rather consistently the way in which the individual will react to the Negro in a variety of situations, whether or not he has ever faced those particular situations before or "learned" to conduct himself in a particular way. In other words, the general frame of reference will determine what attitudes the individual will have when a given stimulus—whether it is a legislative proposal, a petty theft, or the performance of a gifted singer—is related to this basis of interpretation.

A correlative standard of judgment is, of course, that the white man is superior, which means, of course, that the white man must keep *his* place. Analysis of this reverse side of the story, so seldom stated but so inevitably implied by those who have accepted the pervading values of the South, reveals the particular mental context prerequisite to participation in a lynching mob. For these more positive counterparts of the values as ordinarily verbalized have become a part of the ego. A person will feel that *he* is insulted if someone ascribes to him the alleged characteristics of a Negro or if someone even calls him a "nigger-lover." Since these assumptions are part of the individual's ego, they determine the particular status that he will regard as proper for himself. He, as a white man, is "above" the colored man and therefore deserves certain rights and privileges that the Negro should not have.

The particular status which an individual will believe is proper for him will vary enormously according to his background. The wealthy white landowner may regard himself as so far above the colored people who work for him that he can subjectively afford to look down on them paternally and benevolently, perhaps be seen with them frequently because his status is so clearly differentiated and recognized by all in the community. The well-established middle-class business or professional man may regard himself as definitely superior, yet feel that the Negro deserves more opportunity. He may, therefore, work aggressively for certain educational or housing improvements which will raise the Negroes' standard of living but still keep them as a class economically and culturally below his own. The poor-white tenant farmer may also regard his color as a mark of superiority but realize it is one of the few remaining signs of his own status and thus object to any kind treatment of the Negro, any improvement of the Negro's condition, or any association with him.[42]

However, this relative status of the white man is not always maintained. At times he finds it threatened. A discrepancy arises between what he believes his status should be and what his status actually is. Since he cannot "lower" his status without relinquishing those values which he has accepted and which have become a part of his ego, he is motivated to preserve his status by removing what he regards as the circumstances threatening it.

Lynching as a "solution." But the conditions that jeopardize the status of the white man, are, as we have seen, extremely complex. A whole host of events have given rise to economic conditions which make it difficult for the white man to maintain whatever superior standards of living he believes are due him; public opinion, outside the world which he calls his, has impinged on that world and made it seem likely that the Negro would someday have greater political and cultural equality. But these more basic causes of the discrepancies experienced are by no means clearly understood, and their relationships to the concrete life of a single individual are obscured by his self-interest and lack of perspective. He will know that a drought or a fall in the price of cotton affects his living conditions adversely

---

[42] In this discussion we are by no means presupposing that *all* white people in the South behave in the alternate ways described or that all of them are potential mob members. Our analysis is of those people who, for one reason or another, participate in or condone lynchings. In any explanation of a phenomenon that occurs within a particular culture, one must always be on guard to avoid the generalization that *all* people in the culture have accepted uncritically and completely certain social values which are traditionally found in the culture, that is, which have been previously held by a large proportion of the persons constituting that culture. At the present time, there are many organizations in the South composed primarily of southerners working for the complete equality of the Negro. The persons composing such organizations have obviously not accepted uncritically all traditional values. Their education and other experience have made them question these older assumptions. These persons and the organizations they represent are, of course, bitterly attacked by certain more established groups and vested interests.

In a poll of the population made in July 1940, by the American Institute of Public Opinion, the question was asked: "Do you think that the same amount of tax money should be spent in this state for the education of a Negro child as for a white child?" Eighty-seven per cent of the northerners answered in the affirmative while 55 per cent of all southern whites sampled said "yes." The fact that at least half the people in the South express their willingness to spend equal amounts on the education of Negro youths indicates a considerable break from the old norms.

but just how inventions, industrial changes, more universal education, population migrations, reciprocal trade treaties, and the like are
related to his everyday life is but little comprehended. The more
remote and fundamental causes of his conditions and their relationship to the whole social context are vague in his mind, if they ever
enter it. He seeks a simpler meaning for his troubles and an object
against which he can act. The Negro, both as a race and as an individual, fulfills both requirements. The Negro—not a decrease in the
demand for cotton, soil exhaustion, or government regulations, or
taxes—is the "reason" why his income is low, his position insecure.
And the Negro is obviously a concrete symbol that he can attack.

The motivation of an individual's participation in a lynching
mob is often further obscured because of the psychological effects
of the restricted world in which he lives. This is, of course, particularly true of mob members who are in the lower economic-
cultural levels. Not only are they geographically isolated but they
are psychologically isolated from many of the pleasures and recreations of life. Poverty, ignorance, and tradition may insulate them
from the entertainment and knowledge provided by books, magazines, newspapers, and trips to town. Frequently a primitive religious
background forbids card playing, dancing, attendance at theaters
and moving picture shows. The sacredness of sex, the guilt of some
white men because of their own escapades with colored women, and
their possible fear that the Negro may, occasionally, be attractive to
white women are further causes of complication.

As his status becomes more and more threatened and as he becomes
more and more frustrated, the potential mob member also becomes
increasingly suggestible to any stimulus which fits his preexisting
frame of reference that Negroes must be made to keep their place.
Almost any event can serve, under these circumstances, as the immediate stimulus to arouse action which the individual believes will
preserve his status. The unquestioned acceptance of his frame of
reference will lead him to believe all suggestions regarding the
alleged details of a Negro's crime and to rationalize without hesitation or evidence the guilt of a particular Negro who has been caught,
perhaps merely because a few bloodhounds hesitated by a particular
Negro shanty. Since the frame of reference of a single individual is
so similar to that of other individuals in the community and since

so many experience comparable psychological consequences as the result of objective conditions, all these individuals group together when some pretext is found for taking overt action against a distinguishable common enemy.

New norms. The separate desire of each individual to defend his status and all the values which constitute his world is coincidental with the desires of the other individuals around him. Hence, his values are identical with those of others in his temporary immediate environment. The usual ethical values of the whole community or nation which conflict with these uniform, personal values are absent. A microcosm exists where restraints of law and of public opinion are lacking and where individual activity is valued in so far as the common purpose of the group is carried out. Hence, an ordinarily obscure and uninfluential person may become, like the Admirable Crichton, a hero or a leader if he can express the common values of the group and satisfy its desire to kill an offender. Likewise, because of the pervasiveness of the common value in the microcosm, the more usual distinctions between participants are ignored. Social or psychological barriers which separate bankers from day laborers, housemaids from mistresses, and policemen from criminals evaporate for the time being.

When the great majority of community members are alike in condoning punishment for Negroes or when it is generally known that the "law" is not rigidly enforced, then the whole community may be regarded as a temporary macrocosm in the larger state, sectional, or national macrocosm. But when attempts are made to enforce the law or when the standards of judgment of a large number of persons or of certain influential citizens would not lead them to accept the extra-legal punishment of a Negro, then the individuals comprising a mob must be more secretive and more efficient. In such instances, the mob members may be regarded as constituting a small microcosm within the macrocosm of the community.

In either case, for the members of a mob, their action is meaningful and satisfying and will, they feel, safeguard their status. An observer at one lynching reports, for example, that a ten-year-old colored boy was brought close to the burning body of a victim and told, "Take a good look, boy. We want you to remember this the longest day you live. This is what happens to niggers who molest white people."[43]

The point is further illustrated in the words of one member of a Georgia mob:

I reckon folks from the north think we're hard on niggers, but they just don't know what would happen to the white people if the niggers ran wild like they would if we didn't show them who's boss. If I was you, I wouldn't go back up north and say you saw us down here trying to catch a nigger to lynch. It just wouldn't sound right saying it up there, because people would get the idea that we're just naturally hard on all niggers all the time. There's a lot of fine ones in this country, but they're the ones who know how to keep their place, and they don't make trouble. This nigger that raped that white girl is a mean one. Of course, that girl is a whore, and everybody knows it, and for all I know she led him on, but just the same she was a white girl, and he was a nigger, and it just wouldn't do to let him go. That's why we're out here trying to jump him in the woods. Maybe the sheriff will get him before we do, but it's going to be a race, and whoever gets him first is going to keep him. I reckon you understand how it is now, and if I was you I wouldn't go back up north and say you came down here and saw us trying to lynch a nigger. If you say something like that, people will think we're hard on niggers. I've got niggers working for me, and I get along the best way with them, because they know how to keep their place. If that nigger out there in the woods gets jumped before the sheriff finds him, it will all be over and done with by sundown, and everybody will be satisfied.[44]

If an outsider questions the legality or ethics of the mob's actions, he will be told that he is not a red-blooded American, or that he doesn't know how to handle colored people. The pervading frame of reference of mob members finds ready justification for their actions.

The unspeakable brutality that often accompanies a lynching is sometimes explained as a form of sexual perversion. There is no

[43] James Weldon Johnson, *The Burning of Ell Peron at Memphis,* publication, New York: National Association for the Advancement of Colored People.

[44] Caldwell and Bourke-White, *op. cit.,* 159.

doubt that some of the torture could be adequately accounted for only by appeal to the concepts of psychiatry or psychoanalysis. But a survey of the lynchings where acts of aggression have been most violent clearly indicates that there are other important reasons for brutality besides the release of sexual prohibition and frustration.[45] Of particular importance to the social psychologist is the fact that when a mob is composed of a large number of people, it is impossible for everyone to fire the fatal shot, jerk the rope that will break the victim's neck, or light the faggots that will burn him to death. Yet because many people have gathered to "lynch a nigger," they feel thwarted if they cannot in some small way have a hand in the affair. Their own action in the drama gives them a sense of closure and a feeling that they have vindicated their status.

Hence, the torture will often be deliberately prolonged so that everyone interested can have his chance at the victim. For example, one observer reports that "on the way to the scene of the burning people all around took a hand in showing their feelings in the matter by striking the Negro with anything obtainable; some struck him with shovels, bricks, clubs, and others stabbed him and cut him until when he was strung up his body was a solid color of red, the blood of the many wounds inflicted covering him from head to foot."[46]

Or the victim's body will be mutilated after his death. For example, at another lynching: "Firearms were popping on all sides. Even women were seen to shoot revolvers . . . Finally the leader asked 'Have you had enough fun, boys?' 'Yes, cut him down,' came the answer."[47]

A good deal of the brutality, then, is the result of this mass participation rather than the action of a few perverted individuals. When a few mob leaders torture their victims in front of large crowds of people, there is undoubtedly a perversion in the self-appointed executioners which may be present in milder form in the spectators whose chief satisfaction in the lynching, however, is their prolonged feeling of participation.

[45] For a discussion of this problem in broad psychoanalytic terms, see J. Dollard, L. Doob, et al., Frustration and Aggression, New Haven: Yale University Press, 1939.
[46] The Waco Horror. Supplement to The Crisis, July 1916.
[47] Burning at the Stake, a publication, New York: National Association for the Advancement of Colored People, June 1919, 7.

The lynching mob contrasted to other mobs. The psychological conditions giving rise to lynching mobs are essentially the same as those giving rise to other mobs bent on persecution. The victim may be a Jew, a "foreigner," a "Red," a labor organizer, or any one who acts as a symbolic threat to the status of a particular group. A primary condition of such mob formation is a discrepancy between the status people feel is rightfully theirs and the status they have or fear they will soon have if something is not done to prevent the collapse of the values which they hold. The prolonged or intense threat to their ego values motivates them to some action which has meaning for them and which gives them temporary satisfaction. The need for meaning, or for an understandable interpretation of their situation, increases with the need to preserve or enhance status. They become highly suggestible in this situation and readily find a "cause" of their conditions in the activity or presence of some previously disparaged group whom they believe is threatening their values.

But not all mobs follow this general pattern of the *persecutory mob*. Other mobs might be called *revolutionary*. They take essentially an offensive, rather than a defensive, position. The mobs involved in certain social upheavals or labor disputes are examples.[48] Their overt behavior is similar to that of the persecutory mob, but their psychological motives differ. What the members of these mobs desire is a change in the pervading norms of the culture, because the norms no longer accommodate their needs. They are not defending an insecure status, but trying to force a redefinition of status onto the culture as a whole. Their victims are, therefore, people not below but above them in the "accepted" social hierarchy. The object is to overthrow those already in power who perpetuate the norms with which they are dissatisfied, rather than to prevent the acquisition of more power by minority or disparaged groups. Psychologically, members of both types of mobs are satisfying their needs and taking meaningful action against what they regard as the source of their discontent. Both are motivated by their feeling of self-regard, but the expression of self-regard for the persecutory mob assumes the cruder form of defending status. The self-regard of the revolutionary mob may take the form of

[48] These mobs and the social context giving rise to them are treated more in detail in chs. 8 and 9.

maintaining self-integrity and seeking action which will change norms to fit a new conception of status.

The "mob mind." Much has been written about the "mind" of the crowd and the mob. Authors have frequently endowed the crowd itself with a mystical mind—something over and above, independent of the individuals who composed it. "The fact that men are put into a crowd puts them in possession of a sort of collective mind," wrote LeBon in 1895.[49] Such a notion is no longer tenable. Whatever characteristics the crowd or the mob exhibit must be owing solely to the mental processes and the reactions of congregate individuals. And these individuals obviously do display characteristic thought and behavior.

We have shown what conditions structure an individual's mental context and motivate him to participate in mob behavior. To make our story complete, a word should be added about the characteristic mental processes of individuals who are members of a mob. These characteristics will generally emerge, however, only under the conditions we have described. An outline of these characteristics is found by following the discussion in Chapter 2, where we noted some reasons for the variations in individual egos.[50]

1. Members of a mob are likely to confuse causal relationships. We have seen how the mob member, dissatisfied with his lot in life, and often unequipped by training or experience to distinguish a cause from an effect, jumps at oversimplified explanations offered him. Once an interpretation is provided and a solution in terms of direct action is proposed, there is little further thought of examining the explanation or altering the course of action. What a person hears as a rumor may become a firm belief; an emotional impulse may be acted upon as a reasoned judgment; a bit of phantasy may be taken as the perception of an external event; pain may become pleasure. Because of this fusion, this lability of meaning, the individual will react inconsistently to a stimulus. Its meaning will depend upon its context, upon the interpretation given it by a leader or by the conditions of the moment.

2. The individual world of the mob member becomes circumscribed and confined. The "impression of universality," so frequently

---

[49] G. LeBon, *The Crowd*, London: Unwin, 2nd ed., 1897.
[50] Cf. pp. 37-41 of this book.

referred to by social psychologists as a characteristic of the crowd or mob mind, may be a misleading concept unless it is remembered that the universe, at least for the moment, is for the individual a highly restricted one—a microcosm in his normally more extended world. In the microcosm, thought and behavior are judged in terms of the temporary, limited values, without reference to outside cultural norms. Hence, there is greater immediacy of action: the inhibiting effects of the norms and values of the culture are no longer operative.

3. For the mob member, there is comparatively little distinction between the self and the material objects which are included in his restricted world. He identifies himself with these material objects rather completely. We have seen how, if he is a member of a lynching mob, he will try to carry off with him some stick of wood, some stone that has been used in the lynching process. The protection and reverence offered by crowd members to objects or possessions of the leader or the total membership is notorious. Objects become sacrosanct because they have great personal significance, because any violation of them violates the ego.

The mob member also makes comparatively little distinction between the self and the social environment. The individual characteristically "loses himself" in the crowd or mob. The acceptance of common values, the disregard for usual social distinctions, and the collapse of usual barriers to social intercourse are bound to have a leveling effect on status and individuality. A premium is put on submission to the norms of the microcosm, not on individual stability or accomplishment. The individual's ego is composed, for the time being, largely of the surrounding values.

These characteristics are at least some essential components of what has been called the *mob mind*. However, it should not be assumed that all these characteristics are discernible in members of every crowd or every mob or that they are, when found, exhibited to the same degree. As we have already pointed out, mobs and crowds will differ in their nature and purposes. The leaders of mobs will vary enormously, for example, in their ability to seek valid causal relationships. It would be difficult to compare Lank Smith, the leader of the Leeville lynching, to Lenin, the leader of a St. Petersburg mob. Yet, while mobs may differ widely in their characteristics from the point of view of the outside observer, from the point of view of the participating member the actual mental processes may not be quite so unlike one another.

In general, the individual mob member is inclined to display the characteristics, mentioned in Chapter 2, of an "immature" person. The type of ego involvement that he exhibits is comparatively crass and direct. The refinement and sublimation generally esteemed by society are not easily found. For this reason, mobs and crowds are usually condemned by those who write about them. LeBon holds that crowds are characteristic of the lower, inferior classes;[51] Martin implies that crowd members are vulgar and commonplace.[52]

But it must be remembered that what is an "immature" or "crass," "inferior" or "vulgar" person for one society may be a model or saint for another. Judgments such as these are themselves relative to whatever values happen to hold in a given culture at a given time. Mobs are "good" or "bad," depending upon the observer's own standards of judgment. A man named Horst Wessel, who was a member of what democratic people would term a "mob riot," was made into a hero by the Nazis and had a national anthem named after him. The Loyalists in the days of the American War of Independence described the rank and file who composed the revolutionary mobs as "half savages," "insects vile that merge to light," "rats who nestle in the lion's den"; the leaders they termed "bankrupt shopkeepers, outlawed smugglers, wretched banditti, the refuse and dregs of mankind."[53] Moreover, George Washington, acknowledged as the leader of the mob, inspired a Tory poet to write:[54]

> Thou hast supported an atrocious cause
> Against thy king, thy country, and the laws;
> Committed perjury, encouraged lies,
> Forced conscience, broken the most sacred ties;
> Myriads of wives and fathers at thy hand
> Their slaughtered husbands, slaughtered sons, demand;
> That pastures hear no more the lowing kine,
> That towns are desolate, all—all is thine.

[51] LeBon, op. cit.
[52] E. D. Martin. The Behavior of Crowds, New York: Harper, 1920.
[53] Charles and Mary Beard, op. cit., 269 f.
[54] Ibid.

The "goodness" or "badness" of mobs can only be evaluated, therefore, when the objectives of the mob are considered in relation to the whole social context within which they arise. Glib generalizations condemning all mob behavior may frequently be made by persons who themselves are enjoying certain rights or liberties achieved by "mobs" of an earlier day. For people in our present-day American culture, various actions by specific groups that may have had some of the characteristics of mobs and that were affiliated with great social movements were certainly instrumental in providing the particular culture we now have. Examples are some of the overt activity of groups associated with the Reformation, the English Revolution, the settlement of the Western Hemisphere, and the Civil War, in addition to the American Revolution.

Furthermore, the characteristics of the "mob mind" cannot be loosely applied to all mobs since these characteristics will be determined in part by the particular relationship the mob leader or the mob member believes his goals have to the existing social structure. Thus the members of a revolutionary mob will in all probability have a much more systematic, more highly rationalized, more penetrating, and less specific crede than will the members of a persecutory mob. The social values the revolutionary mob wants to change will be more inclusive so that the mob may rapidly expand into a social movement with representatives and "cells" scattered over wide geographical areas, but still all focused on common objectives.

The wastefulness, cruelty, and "irrationality" of the mob mechanism as such are characteristics which most people most of the time obviously abhor. But, like the larger and somewhat comparable phenomenon called war, the great majority of individuals will finally resort to such a mechanism if it proves to be the only solution for the difficulties or threats which face them. Sometimes the mechanisms of mobs or wars are unhesitatingly accepted by participating members without any apparent consciousness that their actions are wasteful, cruel, and irrational. The individual does not ask himself whether the end in view justifies the means of accomplishment. This condition is perhaps most clearly shown in the proletariat lynching mob we have described. The hysteria associated with the first World War presents a somewhat parallel case. At other times, however, people will hesitate to take such anti-social action until they are convinced that the ends do justify the means, that there is no other alternative. At least a small minority of some persecutory and revolutionary mobs only grudgingly participates in actions uncongenial to them. There is ample evidence in the second World War that the masses of people in all the belligerent nations accepted the action unenthusiastically. The second World War is not accompanied voluntarily by the traditional military songs and flag-waving.

The specific conditions giving rise to mob behavior will vary enormously with the economic, political, racial, and religious characteristics of particular cultures at different times and in different places. However, the psychological effects of these various conditions will be more uniform and explicable with common conceptual denominators such as those we have used in describing only one particular set of conditions relatively localized in space and time. Certainly mob behavior is not an inherent characteristic of any race, any type of person, any geographical section of the world. Mobs arise as "solutions" for particular circumstances and can only be prevented when such circumstances are not allowed to arise.

CHAPTER 5

THE KINGDOM OF FATHER DIVINE[1]

Father Divine's kingdom serves as a prototype of those social movements we know as "cults"—organized actions, generally rather restricted and temporary, in which the individual zealously devotes himself to some leader or ideal. The fact that we shall be concerned with Negroes is merely accidental. It just happened that the writer had an opportunity to study this particular cult; it just happened that this cult had Negroes as members. Cults are found among individuals of various colors, nations, and classes, and within almost every society. No one "race" as such is more prone to join a cult than any other. As we shall see in this and later chapters, Father Divine's movement is somewhat similar to, and serves the same psychological functions as, the Oxford Group, the Townsend Plan, the Nazi Revolution.

In our analysis of mob behavior, the scene was the South, the villains were black, the heroes white. The scene now shifts to the North; the villains are white, the heroes black.

THE KINGDOM AS A MICROCOSM

"Father Divine is God!"

Whether whispered, spoken, sung, or shouted hysterically, these words are believed by hundreds, even thousands, of people. They may be heard almost any afternoon or evening at the main kingdom of heaven, which forms part of a crowded street in New York's Harlem. During the past few years the street has been more crowded than ever, for now Father Divine's cars and busses with their placards

[1] This chapter was written in collaboration with Muzafer Sherif and appeared under joint authorship in the *J. Abn. Soc. Psychol.*, 1938, **33**, 147-167. The original article is reprinted here almost verbatim. Father Divine is still as important a figure as he was when the investigation was made. To be sure, he has added some new heavens to his universe; there has been some turnover of followers; some angels have fallen from grace and been replaced by new ones. New encounters with the law have been reported. But neither the conditions that give rise to the movement nor the psychological functions it serves have changed in any appreciable way.

of "Peace," "We thank you, Father," and "Father Divine's peace mission" are lined along the curbing. Nearby laundries, cafeterias, and small shops, otherwise like most of their kind, display signs of "Peace," "Special attention given to FATHER DIVINE children," "I thank you." On Saturday and Sunday afternoons and evenings moving crowds fill the sidewalk in front of kingdom headquarters. Sooner or later most of the people are inside.[2]

The doors of the kingdom are always open. In the small corridor, leading to the upstairs assembly hall, we face a brightly colored sign: "The relation of your conscious mentalities is but the reconception of God's omniscience." The hall itself is filled with believers, sitting on simple wooden benches. Most of them are Negroes, with a sprinkling of whites. White visitors are easily recognized. They are given seats or ushered to the platform at the front of the hall.

The room is filled with crude banners. High overhead is stretched in silver letters: "Father Divine Is Dean of the Universe." The followers (or "children," as they call themselves) are singing the verse:

> Father Divine is the captain
> Coming around the bend
> And the steering wheel's in his hand.

The song has five verses. Singing is accompanied by a small brass band. No one officially leads the "children." It is unnecessary. A few already know the song, and the rest soon catch the simple rhythm. The crescendo increases with each verse.

At the end of this song, a large, middle-aged colored woman testifies how Father cured her bad knee, which specialists had been unable to help. Some listen; others close their eyes and moan. Shouts of "Isn't it wonderful!" "He's so sweet!" and "We thank you, Father!" are frequent. One or two hysterical Negroes walk around dazed and shouting, occasionally falling. The testimony ends with the first line of another song, sung with great feeling by the testifier. It is immediately picked up by others. The band catches the tune. Soon all are singing:

[2] More complete biographical accounts of the Rev. M. J. Divine and of both historical and descriptive accounts of his movement may be found in R. A. Parker, *The Incredible Messiah*, Boston: Little, Brown, 1937; John Hosher, *God in a Rolls Royce*, New York: Hillman-Curl, 1936; and S. McKelway and A. J. Liebling, *Who is this King of Glory? New Yorker*, June 13, 20, and 27, 1936.

> One million blessings,
> Blessings flowing free,
> Blessings flowing free,
> There are so many blessings,
> Blessings flowing free for you.

As the song continues (substituting "billion" and "trillion" for "million"), some begin to sway, shouting becomes more frequent, a white man jumps up and down praising Father, the rhythm is emphasized by the clapping of the children. Still no one is leading them. This song ended, there is another testimonial. A man castigates himself for his former sins. He was an adulterer. He had stolen food and money. He had been a drunkard. Someone told him about Father. He came to hear him and was immediately cured of his evil ways. He intersperses his testimony with "I do thank you, Father. You are so wonderful." Other children confirm his belief. They listen intently to his confession. He talks about ten minutes, exhausting himself with the vitality of his speech. He sits down, wipes his face, puts his head on his knees. Someone begins to sing:

> Now don't let me say it, unless I mean it.
> Oh! Don't let me say it, unless I mean it.
> For I know it will manifest just as I've seen it,
> Since you are here, Sweet Father.

It has eleven verses and a chorus. The last verse is sung loudly, with clapping and many outbursts, some of the children tap dancing, some crying, some laughing.

This spontaneous flow of songs and testimonials continues for hours on end. There is perfect freedom to do what one wants—to sing, shout, cry, sway, jump, meditate, testify, or dance. Frequently the eyes turn to the many banners on the wall where homemade signs tell us:

Father Divine is God Almighty. The same one that John said, "There would come one greater yet and I will baptize you with the holy ghost and fire."

Out of one people Father Divine made all men, therefore races, colors, creeds, distinction, divisions, nationalities, groups, segregation, nicknames, classes, and all such abominations must come to an end. All these things are the flesh and no flesh shall glorify itself in the presence of the almighty Father Divine. Man's work is done. God alone shall reign. This is his day of reign. Thank you Father.

Our justice and truth is called in the expression of the Father. Peace.

Peace, peace, peace! Father Divine is the wonderful counsellor, Prince of Peace. At his name all war shall cease.

We turn to our colored neighbor and ask him when Father Divine is coming. He looks at us blissfully and says, "He's here." "Where?" He points at random: "He's there, there, everywhere. He's in your heart." Another follower notices our dilemma and advises us to go downstairs to the banquet table. Father speaks there, if he speaks at all. Many have already gone down. It is about 11 P.M.

The banquet hall is filled. A large, horseshoe table takes up most of the space, and around it are seated about a hundred children. Another hundred or more are standing in the crowded spaces nearby. There is one place conspicuously vacant at the head of the table, near which sit several well-dressed Negroes and one white. We are told they are Angels. They seem more self-possessed, more patient, more intelligently alert than the rest. On the table, in front of the Angels, are great platters of turkey, chicken, cold cuts, fruit, and bread. The air is close and sticky.

This room, too, is lined with banners, proclaiming such sentiments as: "Father Divine is the only redemption of man"; "Father Divine is God and a little child shall lead them."

In general the group downstairs is more orderly, more unified than it was upstairs. Still there is no leader present. Yet here is a self-contained microcosm, bound together by a common set of norms.

FACTORS CREATING AND SUSTAINING THE MICROCOSM

The testimonials which continue show that, within the microcosm, basic needs are satisfied. Children who live outside the kingdom also tell how Father has provided for them.

One woman says:

I thank you, Father Divine, God almighty, for what you have done for us since coming in contact with the Peace Mission. Thank you, Father. My brother was ill and suffering pain and covered with sores. In two weeks' time he was able to work without pain or sores. Truly there is nothing to do but to thank you, Father.

Another ends her testimonial in song:

> Father I thank thee, Father I thank thee,
> Father I thank thee, for what You've done for me.

The testimony of Live Dove, a pretty young Negress, is received enthusiastically:

> People have been talking about God for many years, but today, a God whom you can't see or never have any personal contact with just doesn't fill the bill. A promise of some home far beyond the clouds, with milk and honey flowing freely, really isn't what it takes to keep going down here, on terra firma. If God can't take care of me here and now, then how can I know or even believe He'll do so very much after I'm dead and gone . . . Now, all in all, I ask you, what more of a God do you want than one who'll give you shelter, food to eat, clothes to wear, and freedom from sickness, worry, and fear? Now isn't that wonderful![3]

In return for the benefits they receive, supposedly everything the children have is Father's—their money, their services, their thought, their love. Those who come to live in one of the numerous kingdoms give Father their property, their insurance, their extra clothes, their savings—everything. Most of those who live outside the kingdoms give him something, after providing minimum needs for themselves.

Even more important for the unity of the microcosm is the common "positive attitude" Father has inculcated in them. They are told constantly "to visualize Him, so they can realize Him, so they can materialize Him."

> If you concentrate your thoughts and your energy and your mentality in the Positive direction you must produce and receive the results of the POSITIVENESS, which will be SUCCESS and PROSPERITY and HARMONY, where the negative direction will cause the result to be the expression of negation with all of its expressions and from all of its angles. You see, that is the Mystery.[4]

[3] The *Spoken Word*, Aug. 18, 1936, 21. This is a semi-weekly publication of the Peace Mission. Weekly magazines are the *World-Herald* and the *New Day*. The kingdom's newspaper, the *New York News*, is published each Saturday.

[4] Hosher, *op. cit.*, 167 f.

The effect of the positive attitude—constantly thinking of Father and thanking him—is to cause the thought to enter:

> . . . the sub-conscious mentality so that your very sub-consciousness got it, then and there, you had it. Now isn't that wonderful? As you had it, so you have it. By this, you can speak the Words into "tangibilization" or outer expression "visibilated" and cause mankind to observe that which you have been thinking. This is a beautiful thought, is it not—the great Universal Brotherhood of man and the conscious recognition of the FATHERHOOD OF GOD, and the realization of the PRESENCE of both it and them—of both HIM or HE and them.[5]

To protect the "positive attitude" and to make it easier to cultivate, Father has strictly forbidden his children to have any direct outer contact with possible sources of "negative attitudes"—those which would shift concentration from him to something else. The children are forbidden to read any newspapers or magazines, except those published by Father. They must read only the books Father or his Angels recommend. They must listen to no radio programs, except when Father broadcasts. They are not allowed to attend moving picture shows. Their senses, as well as their services and thoughts, are Father's.

The unity of the microcosm is further preserved and emphasized by the almost complete break most of the children in the kingdom have made with the outer world. For one thing, all dates appearing in any publications are followed by the letters ADFD: "Anno Domini Father Divine," although some of the followers interpret the letters more simply as: "Always Divine Father Divine." The new frame of reference is further established by the rebirth of the follower. Since he is "reborn" when he enters the kingdom, his age is reckoned from that date. He gives up, furthermore, his former name and identity, receiving another name by revelation and thereby severing a whole host of past associations, personal and social values. The new name is a "kingdom" name which fits the pattern of the new world: "Quiet Devotion," "Glorious Illumination," "Crystal Star," "Job Patience," "Celestial Virgin," "Fineness Fidelity," "Flying Angel," "Rolling Stone," "Quiet Love," "Wonderful Devotion."

[5] The *New Day*, July 9, 1936, 4 f.

With the disappearance of the old identity goes all thought of race, color, or vocation: "All God's children are equal"; "In God's sight there is no difference in color." No one is allowed to use the words "black," "white," or "Negro" in the kingdom. One speaks of "a person of the darker (or lighter) complexion."

A new vocabulary has been created to express the wonderfulness of Father. Father sets the pace in coining words and phrases; the children imitate him. Another extract from one of Father's messages shows some typical "kingdom" words:

> It is a privilege to realize GOD AS INFINITE, EVER-PRESENT and OMNIPOTENT, and yet INCARNATABLE and REPRODUCIBLE and RE-PER-SONIFIABLE, AS HE has been PERSONIFIED. GOD would not be OMNIPOTENT, the same today, yesterday and forever, if HE were not REINCARNATABLE. GOD would not be the same today, yesterday, and forever, if HE were not RE-PERSONIFIABLE. Now isn't that wonderful?

("Truly wonderful!" assert the children.)

Parents who join the kingdom are separated as man and wife. They generally leave their children behind in the outer world to fend for themselves. More frequently a single parent (usually the mother) enters the kingdom, forgetting and giving up completely children and spouse. Worldly habits, such as smoking and drinking, are taboo. There is no cohabitation in the kingdoms. The general, positive attitude is sufficiently dynamic to overcome these specific, worldly behavior patterns. All signs of bodily afflictions, such as glasses, trusses, or crutches, are thrown away. Ailments are forgotten. No medical or dental attention is allowed.

The isolation achieved by the follower, when he breaks thus from the outer world in his change of name, his reckoning of time, his contacts, his habits, his thoughts, and his close personal associations, makes it possible for him to form a new frame of reference very similar to that of the other children around him. The deliberate cultivation of the "positive attitude" keeps the children psychologically united. During the meetings they are kept overtly together by the simple words of the songs, the simple melodies of their particular variety of spirituals, and, above all, by the simple rhythms which instill the behavioral accompaniments of clapping and swaying and often lead to a more exaggerated physical activity.

INDIVIDUAL DIFFERENCES AND CONFLICTS WITHIN MICROCOSM

But within the boundaries of this small world are still found differences and conflicts characteristic of any group of people. An observer will notice the differential enthusiasms of the followers: a few are hysterical, many are excited, some are calm and deliberate. Inquiry reveals that there are differential sacrifices: although most of the children give all they possess and earn, some withhold a small portion, while others keep their material things to themselves. The testimonials, too, reflect varying degrees of enthusiasm and sacrifice. Father's rewards are meted out unequally because of his realization that different children have different values for his purposes. One finds, within the kingdoms, individuals who seemingly possess no more personality traits in common than one would expect from any group of similar size chosen at random. A high degree of intelligence is displayed by some of the followers; a few are obviously below the average. In short, we may hazard the guess that within the microcosm the psychologist would probably find an almost normal distribution curve for any measurable trait or capacity.

Rivalries and schisms develop in heaven as they do elsewhere. Jealousy is often shown by those who are not so close to Father as some others. An Angel, sitting at the right hand of God, is envied by all. Father's alleged sexual intrigues with certain Angels create friction among those intimately acquainted with the machinations of the kingdoms. More obvious rivalries and potential schisms develop in some of the meetings when a controversy ensues over the interpretation of Father's words. One follower may preach Father's gospel in a way which is inconsistent with the meaning another follower has derived. If a quarrel seems imminent, an Angel will intervene and point out, "Father wants only praise. Preaching is His exclusive right"; or, "It is Spirit that makes you praise Father this way or that way." Hereupon, the controversy stops; all seem satisfied with the explanation and the Angel sings, "Father writes on the wall," temporarily dissolving dissension.

To avoid sectarianism within the kingdoms, Father teaches his children to tell all their secrets to him alone. His chief Angels spread the doctrine of peace and serve as spies. For example, a possible rupture in the Los Angeles kingdom was prevented by Faithful

Mary ("Angel number one"), who went from New York as Father's personal missionary. To these western brethren she explained:

> Father says when you write something about his works and criticize, you are trying to knock him and he will expose you. Because whenever you have anything you want God to know personally, you will tell God alone. You may know when you are writing up something, and putting it in the paper you want every one to know about it. Now if you loved Father, in the mortal consciousness, and you had a sister who got pregnant, or broke a leg, as we called it in the South, don't you know you would not have it established in the paper, because you wouldn't want any one to know it?[6]

Father is well aware of the dangers of controversy, against which he warns his children. They must align themselves with "cosmic forces" or else the cosmic forces will destroy them.

> God will express dissatisfaction, or dissatisfaction in what you are doing, if you will reflect or manifest dissatisfaction. Now, isn't that Wonderful—for the reaction of your thoughts and actions may be manifested in the atmospheric conditions of the weather. It is indeed Wonderful! This has been the experience of all Religions. The Cosmic Forces of Nature through the Ages, worked according to the conscious mentality of the people. When their minds are antagonistic and conflicting one with the other, the atmospheric conditions would be exhibited from that angle of expression. Now isn't that Wonderful![7]

The cosmic forces are all on Father's side. He can turn them against dissenters, who thus are caused to sicken and to die.

> If man works inharmonious to Me we believe the Cosmic Forces of Nature will destroy him.[8]

These mysterious forces are the causes of wars, floods, tornadoes, race riots, storms, pain, and disease. They can be brought under the control of the individual to work for his personal satisfaction and happiness only when there is "harmony in his conscious mentality."

[6] Hosher, op. cit., 153 f.
[7] The Spoken Word, Aug. 11, 1936, 5.
[8] Hosher, op. cit., 121.

POLARIZATION AROUND CONCRETE SYMBOL

Father's children, then, are likely to quarrel individually or in groups during his absence. The "cosmic forces" may tend to catapult some children away from the kingdom's center of gravity. But as the time for Father's appearance approaches, all differences dissolve. The developing crescendo of the songs in the banquet hall downstairs and the general increase in excitement indicate that personal identity is being submerged in a common value. All thoughts are centered on Father. All eyes are searching for a concrete focal point—found in the empty chair at the head of the table. The songs themselves reflect the intense need for the symbol of this common feeling:

> Father, I love you, Father I do.
> Father, I love you, Father I do.
> Father, I trust you, Father I do.
> Father, I trust you, Father I do.
> Father, I need you, Father I do.
> Father, I need you, Father I do.

Father arrives. His entrance is greeted with an uproar. He is an unusually short, well-dressed Negro about sixty years old, though he looks younger. He sits down. Dishes of hot food are brought him which he blesses by starting on their way around the large table. Sometimes Father pours coffee. All the while there is more singing, interspersed with more testimonials. Father seems unmoved by all this turmoil. He pays absolutely no attention to the praises heaped upon him. The most glowing testimonial fails to excite him. He knows that it is unnecessary to respond to each song or testimonial. He knows that he is already the idol of the people, a symbol already created by their intense feeling. And since the idol is strong in the minds of the children, it needs no support from the outside. He eats and chats with his neighbor, though he may somewhat nervously drink many glasses of water while undergoing this bombardment of adoration. Those at the table eat heartily as Father has told them to do. When one person finishes his meal, another takes his place. After an hour or so of eating, most of the children are happily replete.

Now that Father has satisfied their hunger, the followers appear blissfully content. Satiety has further dulled all critical processes. The unity of their attitudes, their full stomachs, and their fatigue make them more suggestible than ever. Their testimonials and songs show that all ego identities have broken down. They are one with God.

Father rises to speak. His opening words sustain the identity in the minds of the children. "Peace, everyone." "Peace, Father," shout the children.

> Here you are and there I am, there I sit and here you stand, and yet I sit and stand as well as sit in the midst of the children of men. As you are so am I and as you may be, so am I that you might be partakers of the Nature and the Characteristics of Christ.[9]

Or,

> Here we all are again, just the way we should be, just as I am. When I say, "Here we all are again," it means nothing less than the consciousness of the Allness of God in the likeness of man, and the nothingness of man, where such a recognition stands. Now isn't that wonderful? A place wherein you can stand, where all the Allness of God and the nothingness of matter will be a reality to you.[10]

For several minutes he directly sustains their belief that he is God and that they are part of him:

> Oh, it is a privilege to live in the Land of the Living, where God Himself according to the Scripture, shall be with us, and shall be your God and you shall be His People, for the Mouth of Spirit is Speaking. Oh, it is a privilege to realize, every positive spoken word can and will be materialized if you will allow such to be, by the sacrifice of your life for that which you have spoken.[11]

There is no doubt in the minds of the children that they are face to face with God. "We believe every word you say, Father," they shout from time to time. Father reassures them in their belief, explaining that "by your intuition you know it is true."

The message may last an hour. The delivery of the message, like the testimonials and the singing, is dramatic. But Father's exit, like

[9] The *Spoken Word*, Aug. 18, 1936, 17.
[10] *Ibid.*, May 30, 1936, 17.
[11] *Ibid.*, July 7, 1936, 17.

his entrance, is businesslike, in spite of the praises which follow him to his car outside or to his office on the top floor of heaven.

Father's mysterious movements add to his divinity. He has a private airplane to speed him through the heavens. One never knows when or where he will appear. The statement that he was never born, but was "combusted" in Harlem about 1900, is generally known to the children.[12] His letters, which they read in their papers and magazines are the letters of no ordinary individual. All bear the same ending:

> This leaves ME as I hope you are and all who are concerned may also be, Well, Healthy, Joyful, Peaceful, Lively, Loving, Successful, Prosperous and Happy in Spirit, Body and Mind, and in every organ, muscle, sinew, vein and bone and even in every atom, fibre and cell of MY Bodily Form.

At the 1936 International Righteous Government Convention it was moved and passed that "Father Divine is God." There were no dissenting votes.[13]

Since he is God, all are under his power—city, state, and federal officials, kings, premiers, and popes. His publications reproduce his letters to Mayor LaGuardia, President Roosevelt, Pope Pius XII, Mahatma Gandhi, and other celebrities. Occasionally, city or state officials come to speak at his meetings, but Father, as would be expected, always steals the show. If Divine has not yet demonstrated his control of individuals outside his microcosm, at least those within it are acting under his direction. Before the 1936 presidential election, Father repeated in sermon after sermon that his followers should not vote until he had told them how to vote.

> Hold your HANDS. I say, STAY your HANDS, until you find the man that will stand for RIGHTEOUSNESS, TRUTH and JUSTICE for "He that waits upon the Lord shall renew his strength." Now isn't that wonderful! Now I know you are enthusiastic, and filled with the spirit of Politics for RIGHTEOUSNESS, yet I believe every one of you will HOLD your HAND; will stay your HAND, until you get the Command."[14]

"Yes, Father," cry the children. "Since," as Father said, "not one

[12] Hosher, *op. cit.,* 259.
[13] *Ibid.,* 238.
[14] The *Spoken Word,* June 20, 1936, 5.

of the major parties, officially and nationally, or conventionally, has come to me and accepted of my righteous government platform, we must stay our hands.[15] His command—repeated hundreds of times—was apparently effective, for the Harlem polls were virtually deserted on election day.[16]

IMPACT OF EXTERNAL WORLD ON MICROCOSM

The world that Reverend Divine has created, the world in which he is God, the world in which his commands are obeyed, is essentially a microcosm within a larger world organization. It has its own standards, its own norms. Yet, even in the moments of greatest frenzy, in the geographical center of the Kingdom of God, *the realities of the outside world may be seen to intrude.* One notices that the testimonials of white children are listened to more attentively than are those of the Negroes. When a white visitor enters, or wants to pass in the crowd, children of the darker complexion politely make way for him. The class consciousness and servility of the Negro have become so ingrained that they pervade a heaven where one of the strongest tenets is that there shall be no thought of race or color.

Because of the glaring discrepancies between the beliefs and standards of the kingdom and those of the harsher world outside, it would be expected that a follower's exit from the former world and his entrance into the latter would be fraught with difficulties. Most of the children spend their week days working in a society where Father Divine is not God, where there are rigid differentiations regarding color, race, and class. What happens when the devout follower leaves the kingdom on Sunday night?

Father is aware of the possible difficulties arising from the fact that he demands all a follower's love and thought and also commands him to do his work well. "Do your job conscientiously but think constantly of me." Both tasks can be accomplished simultaneously, says Father, "if you don't let your right hand know what your left hand is doing." Those who have menial or routine jobs are apparently quite able to think about one thing while doing another. The discrepancies between the two world orders are not seen by the more ignorant believers. But anyone in a responsible position requir-

[15] *New York Times,* Nov. 4, 1936.
[16] *Ibid.*

ing concentration and intelligence finds it almost impossible to visualize Father and, at the same time, to perform efficiently.

Happy Star, a trusted housekeeper in a family to which she is devoted, was completely unable to reconcile the two duties successfully. She reported:

> It drove me almost crazy to try to plan a dinner for the family and guests and at the same time relax my conscious mentality. And sometimes when Mr. Tepper (head of the house) would ask me something, I would say, "Peace; thank you, Father." This embarrassed me to death. I did not know what to do. I tried to resist Father's hypnotic powers and kicked myself for going to the kingdom and giving up my salary. But I kept going.

A responsible butler reported that he found it difficult to be alert in his duties and, at the same time, to think always of Father. Furthermore, his teeth were aching, his eyes were bad, and he was constantly constipated. Since Father had forbidden any medical or dental attention, as well as the use of drugs, and since the butler was giving Father all his monthly wages, he could do nothing to remedy his condition. And yet, though he became skeptical of the movement, he did not leave for several years.

Why is it difficult for intelligent children to escape Father's influence? They all give the same answer—"fear." Father is all-powerful. He has told them that the cosmic forces are on his side, that he has power of life and death. Several incidents have served to strengthen this belief. In June 1932, Judge Smith sentenced Father to jail. Three days later the judge died. When asked about this Father said, "I hated to do it." Will Rogers made some unfavorable remarks about Father in a radio broadcast. His airplane crash soon followed. Huey Long refused to see one of Father's Peace Mission delegations. A few days later he was assassinated.[17]

This fear of Father pervades the kingdom. Blessed Life, who finally left heaven, had been one of Father's most important Angels until Father got all his money. Then he was gradually moved from the head to the foot of the table. Soon he had a very menial position in the kingdom, and Father no longer paid attention to him. He grew skeptical. Sores developed on his legs. He was not able to speak

[17] Hosher, *op. cit.*, 177.

to his wife when they met at the meetings. Why could he not talk to her as to any other sister? He was lonesome and desperately unhappy. The bedmate, with whom Blessed Life had been sleeping for weeks, died of tuberculosis. His wife finally communicated with him secretly, helped him overcome his fear, and the two escaped. But many in the kingdoms have no outside connections, no money, no job, and remain in agony.

This condition may partially account for some of the psychopaths taken from the kingdoms to the Bellevue Hospital. It certainly accounts for the fact that one is likely to remain a follower, even with rapidly growing doubts. The only people who remain happy are the poor and the ignorant, who have lost nothing by the transfer of allegiance.

INCOMPATIBILITY OF THE TWO WORLDS

Some of the more courageous and intelligent children do leave the kingdoms. For them adjustment is difficult. Happy Star finally left, but admitted later that it was eighteen months before she realized that no harm would come to her. Although a conservative, refined Negress, she said it was hard to "hold myself in" when she was no longer under Father's spell. She wanted to do in excess all that Father had forbidden—smoke, drink, have sexual relations with her husband. Mrs. Hopkins is also a backslider. For Father she had given up her small savings, her family, her friends, her reputation as a reliable cook. When she left the kingdom she had nothing to depend on. Her husband would not take her back. Penniless and worried, she realized that she had "been a fool," and didn't know where to turn next. She must make a new life for herself. She does not like to talk about her days in the kingdom. She is filled with her hatred of Father. "Not for what he did to me," she says, "but for what he is doing to all the poor souls in there now."

These cases could be multiplied. They all illustrate the complete incompatibility of Father's microcosm and the world of reality. One collapses when the other is entered. Compromise is impossible. Behind this fact lies the explanation of Father Divine's following. His children are people who want to escape the world of reality, where their needs are not satisfied, and enter into a new world, where they will have material and psychological comfort.

Here are some typical biographical snatches gathered at random from conversations with children in the kingdom:[18]

(Mrs. Green, Negress about 35.) I'm happy now, but while I was down yonder in Alabama, I was bowded with trouble. My children give me so much trouble, I just liked to worry myself to death, but since I been living in this consciousness, I know that Father is God, and he takes care of his own. That wan't my children nohow; they was God's all the time, so I've give 'em up mentally, cause I know God will take care of 'em. Two boys and a girl. The boys by my first husband and the girl by my last. Them boys was all the time getting in trouble, and the white folks is so mean down there, 'til it kept me worried. But they ain't like that in the kingdom. It's jest wonderful. Everybody is the same . . . I didn't know about Father down there, that is not 'til I come to New York, but he caused me to come here to him. One day I just pitched down everything, and left, and I got work and a woman on the job told me about Father and I came and been coming ever since. I don't worry about nothing now. Thank you, Father.

(Mrs. Cushing, Negress about 40.) I made up my mind that I was going to New York, where I could see God in the flesh. I told Jim that I was going to leave California. He didn't want me to come, so I left him. He wan't no good nohow, but I had been living with him a long time. We was supposed to be married by the laws of the world, but according to God's law we was living in adultery . . . No, I don't miss him none. He wan't nothing but a worry all the time. When we left Florida with our white folks, I had to do most everything, then when I got sick, he acted like he was mad cause I had to stop working. Men don't mean you no good in this world, and the sooner you find that out the better off you are. Put your trust in God, and he will give you everything, or else he removes it from your consciousness.

Many of the songs suggest past or present troubles:

> Father's going to save this soul of mine:
>   Yes, He is, I know He is.
> Father's going to heal this body of mine:
>   Yes, He is, I know He is.
> Father's going to feed me all the time:
>   Yes, He is, I know He is.

[18] The writer is indebted to Miss Esther V. Brown, a colored student at Columbia University, who mixed freely with the "children" in the kingdom and gathered many case histories.

Others express conscious gratitude for the escape:

> I have found Heaven, Heaven at last.
> I leave behind me all of my past.
> I come to rest on his sacred breast.
> I thank you, Father.

REASONS FOR EXISTENCE OF MICROCOSM

1. *Escape from material hardships.* It is not difficult to see why Father Divine should flourish in Harlem, famous for its congestion, poverty, high rents, and general squalor.

In many tenements basic sanitary facilities are unknown. Open fireplaces are used to heat congested railroad flats. In 1931 the death rate from tuberculosis was three times as high in Harlem as in New York City as a whole. The infant mortality rate in central Harlem was the highest for any district in Manhattan. Other diseases were disproportionately high. The National Urban League reported in 1932 that in a single block in Harlem 70% of the tenants were jobless, 18% were ill, 33% were receiving either public or private aid and 60% were behind in their rent. There were practically no recreation facilities for the children, except on the streets. In 50 cases picked up at random only one was found to have contact with organized recreation. In three years the ownership of Harlem real estate by negroes had decreased from 35% of the total to 5% of the total.[19]

Bewildered and hopeless souls, living under these conditions, readily surrender to a god who literally provides them what they have always craved—food, shelter, peace, security. They are anxious to believe and to follow a god who says:

I am lifting you, and all humanity out of the ruts, the mirks, and mires, out of human superstition, out of lacks, wants and all human limitations, out of all the depressions and off of the welfares and other public charities into the reality of God's PRESENCE, where there is a FULL and a PLENTY for all of His Children.[20]

When they compare their days in the kingdom with their days outside, the contrast appears heavenly indeed. Father encourages the children to believe that heaven is on this earth, not on another one.

Men have used Religion to keep you in poverty! They used Re-

---

[19] Hosher, *op. cit.,* 88 f. See also, Parker, *op. cit.,* 34-59.
[20] The *Spoken Word,* Aug. 18, 1936, 29.

ligion to bind you in Slavery! But I have come to break their bands
and set the prisoner free . . . All that they have surmised and all
that they have striven to get you to visualize, I have brought down
from the sky. We are not studying about a God in a sky. We are
talking about a God here and now, a God that has been Personified
and Materialized, a God that will free you from the oppressions of
the oppressors and free you from the segregations of the segrega-
tors . . .[21]

To the poor, the oppressed, and the segregated, these words are an
answer to lifelong prayers and needs, momentarily bringing the individual's level of accomplishment and performance up to his level
of aspiration.

2. *Meaning provided*. The provision of a certain material comfort,
the promise of security, prosperity, and health, provides sufficient
explanation for the faith of many followers. One finds in the kingdoms, however, some children who, even before coming to him,
have had material comforts, security, health, and comparative freedom. The desires that Father satisfies in them are somewhat less
elemental, but none the less real. For one thing, Father gives meaning
to the environment in which they live. Complexity, confusion, hopelessness, and purposelessness are changed into simple understanding,
peace, happiness, and a faith in the abstract principles embodied in
the person of Father.

A middle-aged white fisherman from the coast of Oregon, Humble
by name, has crossed the continent several times to spend a few days
in the main kingdom. He had already had food, shelter, security, the
material comforts of the middle class. But the state of the world
troubled him. He could make nothing out of changing economic and
social conditions. Somehow he heard of Father. Now he says:

As you study this movement more and get to know Father better,
you will become convinced, as I am, that Father has the only solution
for all political, economic, and social problems of the present day.
I believe Father is God in the same sense that I would call a man,
who knew the laws of mathematics and was able to control mathe-
matical formulas and equations, a mathematician. Father knows the
laws of the universe and is able to control cosmic forces—something
that only God can do. Therefore, Father must be God.

[21] Hosher, *op. cit.,* 233.

For Humble and many others of his class, Father provides an escape from a tortuous mental confusion caused by complex, conflicting circumstances. He gives meaning to the individual life and to the world. It is perhaps largely for this reason that one finds in the movement so many "joiners"—people, many of them whites, who have been Baptists, Holy Rollers, Christian Scientists, and Theosophists before coming to Father. Their search for a solution to the meaning of life leads them from one formula to another.

3. *Status raised.* Even more important in explaining the adherence of many middle-class followers, especially Negroes, is the fact that in Father's movement they are given a status which they have always craved and which has always been denied them in spite of their comparatively large bank accounts.

A well-paid, healthy cook of the darker complexion related how Mother Divine[22] called for her with her big car and chauffeur and how Father called for her husband with his Rolls Royce and chauffeur. "We felt like we were big shots," the wife confessed. Their status was raised from that of servant to that of their employer or anyone else who might ride behind a chauffeur. They were, furthermore, riding with God and the wife of God.

The Reverend M. J. Divine is sincere and aggressive in his fight for Negro equality. He and his followers not only want to raise their status as now regarded but they also want to change the "criteria" for status. His "righteous government" platform demands legislation in every state, "making it a crime to discriminate in any public place against any individual on account of race, creed, or color, abolishing all segregated neighborhoods in Cities and Towns, making it a crime for landlords or hotels to refuse tenants on such grounds; abolishing all segregated schools and colleges, and all segregated areas in Churches, Theatres, public conveyances, and other public places." It further demands "legislation making it a crime for any newspaper, magazine, or other publication to use segregated or slang words referring to race, creed, or color.[23]

This reformation of social status, even if temporary, is a sufficient

[22] Mother Divine occasionally appeared with Father as his wife, although she was generally kept in the background. She recently died in a charity hospital, apparently forsaken by Divine, who will not admit that sickness and death can come to a real follower.

[23] The *Spoken Word*, June 20, 1936, 11 ff.

reason for many people to follow Father's movement. For where else can the servile Negro or the outcast white so easily find a real democracy? Who else is so openly fighting for Negro equality?—only the Communists, for whom Father directed his followers to vote in 1932, but from whom he has now severed all relations.

Father encourages self-respect by familiar devices. He makes good use of *prestige suggestion*. For example, in the *World Herald* we read:

> FRENCH COUNTESS VISITS FATHER DIVINE. Joining the *ever increasing* list of *celebrities* and *important figures* from *every* walk of life that have visited FATHER DIVINE since HE has made HIS Head-quarters in New York is the "Comtesse Roberte de Quelen." The tall, stately, *blond* Countess, on an extended vacation from her Chateau Historique de Sûrville in Montereau, France, was one of FATHER DIVINE'S guests, Monday night. Finally overcome by the Wonderful SPIRIT of FATHER, and the beautiful singing and enthusiastic testimonies of the Angels, plus the sumptuous banquet, the Countess arose and literally beaming, said "I love this place, and I love you all!"[24]

Such words from foreign, white nobility obviously enhance the egos of followers with circumscribed environments and limited opportunities.

The *impression of universality* is maintained in sermons, publications, and slogans. On the back cover of every *Spoken Word* (a semi-weekly publication) the Kingdom Peace Missions are listed. We find that there are 13 in Harlem, 25 throughout the rest of New York state, 90 others scattered over the United States, and 22 in other parts of the world, including Australia, the British West Indies, Canada, and Switzerland. Significantly enough, at the end of the list we read, "Because of the unknown number of FATHER DIVINE connections throughout the world, the above is but a partial list for reference." A banner in the banquet hall assures the children—"20,000,000 people can't be wrong. We thank you Father." In a parade held in January 1936, a large banner informed spectators that there were 22,000,000 people in the movement. Already by September of the same year, the number had increased to 31,000,000. The actual number of the following is almost impossible to ascertain. Estimates range from 3,000 to 25,000.

Whatever the exact membership of the group may be, there is no

[24] The *World Herald*, Jan. 7, 1939. Italics the writer's.

doubt that the norms of the kingdom are accepted by thousands of individuals. An official investigation of the movement, ordered by a New Jersey judge, summarized as follows the reasons for its growth:[25]

1. Search for economic security.
2. Desire to escape from the realities of life and impoverished conditions.
3. Search for social status.
4. Instinctive search for God and assurance of a life hereafter.

The first three of these conclusions are similar to those outlined above as basic causes for the movement's appeal. The committee's fourth conclusion, however, will not withstand psychological scrutiny. It would be more accurate to substitute, for the phrase "instinctive search for God," the idea that individuals are constantly seeking to give meaning to their environment and that, when a meaning rooted in the realities of the world cannot be found, the individual either creates and reifies for himself a symbol that will satisfactorily resolve his conflicts or accepts from his culture some preestablished symbol around which to relate his environment meaningfully.[26] The last phrase of the committee's conclusions— "assurance of a life hereafter"—does not seem to square with actual facts. Father Divine, as we have seen, preaches that the Kingdom of Heaven is on this earth, not beyond it, and that those who completely align themselves with cosmic forces will have everlasting life.

The disparities between the microcosm and the larger world macrocosm become more acute as the discrepancies increase between basic and derived needs satisfied in the two worlds. We noted the collapse of Father Divine's microcosm when a follower reenters the world of reality. Frictions between microcosm and macrocosm will continue until one of two things occurs. Either the microcosm itself must be patterned to fit the needs of an individual, living in our modern world, or the conditions in the larger macrocosm must be changed to provide the satisfactions and meanings now artificially derived in the microcosm.

[25] Committee report to the Hon. Richard Hartshorne, Judge, Court of Common Pleas, Essex County Court House, Newark, N. J., Dec. 11, 1933, 35.

[26] Cf. C. K. Ogden, *Bentham's Theory of Fictions*, New York: Harcourt, Brace, 1932; H. Vaihinger, *The Philosophy of "As If"*, New York: Harcourt, Brace, 1925; T. W. Arnold, *Symbols of Government*, New Haven: Yale University Press, 1935.

CHAPTER 6

THE OXFORD GROUP

From time to time in our culture there emerge religious sects composed of people who, for one reason or another, cannot find satisfaction in the traditional, well-established churches. Most of these sects are derivatives of Christianity. Some have eschatological creeds that distinguish them from other faiths; some have their special prophets; some, their distinctive social philosophies.[1] If any religious movement, whether ancient or modern, is to spread and to survive, it must somehow fill the needs of individuals.[2] An understanding of any religious movement, therefore, must place its genesis in its proper historical setting and pay close attention to the particular troubles that burdened early followers. Then the intricate processes of institutionalization, which perpetuate beliefs and authorities and adapt the movement to exigencies arising in the course of time, may be viewed with more perspective.

A recent and widely publicized religious development of our own day has been what is variously known as Buchmanism, the Oxford Group, or Moral Rearmament (MRA). Although this new credo has not been institutionalized, has no organization, and therefore has no "members," analysis of its developmental history, its appeals, and its followers should give us some insight into the psychological processes likely to be involved in many other religious movements. And, because the story of Buchmanism really begins in the 1920's, we should be able to place it in our own social context and understand

[1] For a discussion of the rise and history of the most widely accepted religions, see G. F. Moore, *History of Religions,* New York: Scribner's, 1919-1927. For a popular account of some more modern religions, localized in the United States, see C. W. Ferguson, *Confusion of Tongues,* Grand Rapids: Doubleday, Doran, 1936. For a discussion of the many sidedness of religious appeals, see W. James, *Varieties of Religious Experience,* New York: Modern Library, 1936; J. H. Leuba, *The Psychology of Religious Mysticism,* New York: Harcourt, Brace, 1925.

[2] For a discussion of the continued appeal of Christianity, see J. M. Mecklin, *The Survival Value of Christianity,* New York: Harcourt, Brace, 1926.

more precisely the relationships between the individual participants
and the cultural conditions surrounding them.

Brief history. Buchmanism, or the Oxford Group Movement,
centers around the person of Dr. Frank N. Buchman, a former
Pennsylvania Lutheran minister.[3] It was in 1908, while visiting
England, that Buchman received a vision in a small Keswick church.
He was "changed." He realized that he had been selfish, dishonest,
and filled with grudges against certain people. These faults he confessed to his former antagonists, asking their forgiveness. He returned
to the United States in 1909, and set out to change others. For several
years he was at Pennsylvania State College as a YMCA secretary.
In 1915, he traveled to the Far East with Sherwood Eddy. In 1916,
he went to the Hartford Seminary to carry on his work. Until 1920,
his followers were comparatively few and his efforts not widely
known. It was in 1920, that he went to Cambridge University and
began his conversion of undergraduates. In 1921, he was at Oxford
quietly gathering students around him. In both these universities
he seems to have been especially eager to mix with sons of well-
known families. At Oxford he concentrated on Corpus Christi and
Christ's Colleges, both known for their aristocratic, rather than
their intellectual, traditions. Until this time his gospel and methods
were known as Buchmanism or the Group Movement. The name,
"Oxford Group," which caused so much misunderstanding and ill
feeling because of its confusion with the earlier Oxford Movement of
Cardinal Newman and because of its implication that Oxford University was somehow officially involved, became attached to the
movement about 1921, when Buchman took with him to South
Africa and other distant points some "teams" of Oxford converts
to help him "change" more people.[4] It appears, however, that Buch-

[3] More complete accounts of the history of the movement will be found in the
writings of zealous supporters of the movement, such as H. Begbie, *More Twice-
born Men,* New York: Putnam's, 1923; A. J. Russell, *For sinners only,* reported
in *New Republic,* Mar. 8, 1933; Samuel M. Shoemaker, *National Awakening,* New
York and London: Harper, 1936. Non-partisan accounts are in Ferguson, *op. cit.;*
J. C. Brown, *The Oxford Group Movement,* London: Pickering & Inglis. All these
reports are in substantial agreement.

[4] For a reflection of the attitude of people who felt that Buchman had no right
to allow the movement to be called the Oxford Group and for the legal complications involved, see the letters in the *London Times,* June 3, 5, 6, 7, and 8, 1939.

man was not reluctant to let the misnomer spread because of it
obvious prestige value.

In 1924, Buchman was in the United States getting the confes
sions of undergraduates in America's counterparts to Oxford anc
Cambridge, namely Harvard, Yale, and Princeton. Most of his inter
est here, as in England, seemed to be to have boys and young mer
reveal to him their sinful, erotic thoughts and their sinful autoerotic
practices. This mission ended dramatically when President Hibber
of Princeton denied Buchman the right to speak on the university
campus. Then the Oxford *Isis*, in 1928, demanded his expulsior
from Oxford—Buchman's adopted alma mater. The emotional ex
citement and exaggerated emphasis on the sexual sins of under
graduates was felt by the authorities to be anything but a healthy
influence.

It became obvious then, that the movement must seek a wider
base. So Buchman returned to England and urged some distin
guished adults to do some dignified soul-searching. He met with
such success that, by the time he returned to the United States ir
1933, with a team of sixty converts, he was well-enough established
to make the Waldorf-Astoria Hotel the group headquarters and tc
convince Bishop Manning and other highly respectable clergymen
in this country that his movement was worthy of their following.
He had become so important that he was received by the Archbishop
of Canterbury and the Lord Mayor of London on his next trip tc
England. On May 28, 1938, in a speech in London, Buchman
launched his doctrine of Moral Rearmament, a program to cure all
national and class hostilities. From this time on, the movement
gained new impetus, especially in England, Canada, United States,
Denmark, and Holland. Since Buchmanism transcends creeds and
churches, since it has no established organization of its own, and
since its converts keep in direct contact with God without any
earthly intermediaries, no figures are available from which to give
an accurate estimate of the extent of the movement. Probably at least
50,000 people throughout the world would acknowledge Buchman
as the man who had shown them a new way of life.

Even his followers admit that Frank Buchman is not a particularly
impressive individual. A widely quoted description of him reports
that "in appearance he is a youngish-looking man, tall, upright,

stoutish, clean-shaven, spectacled, with that mien of scrupulous, shampooed, and almost medical cleanness, or freshness, which is so characteristic of the hygienic American."[5] Buchman is not an outstanding orator, a great intellect, a magnetic personality, or a self-appointed prophet. He is essentially a man with a method and mission. Both method and mission are old-fashioned. But both have sufficiently new characteristics to fit them to a modern tempo. And, above all, both are used astutely by Frank Buchman to change certain groups of people whom he accurately predicts will be susceptible to them.

The aims. The Oxford Group has been defined as *"a name for a group of people who, from every rank, profession, and trade, in many countries, have surrendered their lives to God and who are endeavouring to lead a spiritual quality of life under the guidance of the Holy Spirit* . . . This means living as near as we can, by God's help, to the life He has mapped out for us. When we diverge from His plan for us we can, by surrendering our lives to Him, get back to that plan again."[6] The essential tenet is to surrender one's life to God, who will then communicate to the individual directly and inform him how he should conduct himself. The movement is thus highly individualistic. Each member becomes "changed"; each is bound only by the dictates of God.

The movement, furthermore, is highly anti-intellectualistic and non-sectarian. "Questions of definition, of logic or psychological analysis, of scientific explanation are subordinate to the facts of actual experience," writes a follower.[7] The basic assumptions are: (1) men are sinners; (2) men can be changed; (3) confession is prerequisite to change; (4) the changed soul has direct access to God; (5) The Age of Miracles has returned; and (6) those who

---

[5] Begbie, *op. cit.,* 34. No attempt is made here to analyze the personality or motivation of the group leader. Such analysis would undoubtedly be highly significant as a case study but it is not so pertinent for our understanding of the movement as such. It is not the particular characteristics of the leader alone which make him successful but also the social and personal *relationship* between the leader and his doctrines, on the one hand, and the followers and their background, on the other.

[6] *What Is the Oxford Group?* by A layman with a notebook, New York: Oxford University Press, 1933, 3 f.

[7] P. M. Brown, *The Venture of Belief,* New York: Revell, 1937, 54.

have been "changed" must "change" others.[8] Somewhat more spe
cifically, the aim of each Grouper is to achieve the Four Absolute
laid down by the founder: Absolute Purity, Absolute Honesty, Abso
lute Love, and Absolute Unselfishness. How is this to be done?

There are essentially five procedures involved.[9] The first pre
requisite is *to give in to God*. One gives in to God during a "quiet
time," a practice undoubtedly adopted by the Pennsylvanian Buch
man from the Quakers. Here one "waits on God" who will almost
inevitably have some communication to transmit. "The place to
begin this," said Dr. Buchman in a world-wide broadcast, "is to take
fifteen minutes a day to listen to your God. By a miracle of science,
many millions of people are listening unitedly at this time to
human voices. By a miracle of the spirit, God is always broadcasting
to the world. Just get quiet, early in the morning, before the doorbell
or the telephone rings, and ask God what he wants you to do."[10]

The second duty is *to listen to God's directions*. "You don't have
to be very bright to listen," Dr. Buchman assures his followers,
"because God does all the talking. Wherever you are and whoever
you are, God can talk right down your street. He can talk in every
language. Honesty, purity, unselfishness, and love make sense from
Arkansas to Timbuktoo. Just ask God to make you different and
where he wants you to start."[11] It is recommended that, while re
ceiving directions, one have a notebook and a pencil so that noth
ing God suggests is forgotten. The neophyte is told that during
this period "you probably won't hear any voice or anything unusual.
But a quiet, insistent thought may come into your mind. Something
you did wrong and have never yet put right. Something you forgot.
The name of someone you ought to help. Something to do. A new
kind of love begins to move in your heart. A new sort of firmness
gets into your will. And you have a plan for the day."[12]

[8] These six "central assumptions" are quoted directly from the report of the Com
mittee of Thirty, *The Challenge of the Oxford Group Movement—An Attempt
at Appaisal*, Toronto: Ryerson Press.

[9] For more elaborate discussions of the technique, see the Rev. S. M. Shoemaker,
National Awakening, New York: Harper, 1936, chs. 5 and 6. The Rev. Shoe
maker of the Calvary Episcopal Church in New York City is the acknowledged
leader of the movement in the United States.

[10] *New York Times*, Dec. 4, 1939, 10.

[11] *Ibid.*

[12] *Ibid.* Described by a follower, Mr. Twitchell.

God's directions will vary, of course, with the individual's own problems. Thus, a cook at an Oxford Group camp meeting reported, "We have our Quiet Times in the morning so that through guidance we may make our menus." Employees who are changed may be admonished for "cheating in expense accounts; stealing the firm's notepaper, indiarubber, or pencils; arriving late in the morning; reading novels concealed in the desk; slipping out for a drink at odd times during the day."[13] A young man will be told to give up his sexual sins. A bootlegger will be shown the folly of his ways. The literature of the movement is saturated with accounts of God's directions. Here is one selected almost at random:

A short time ago a young fellow came to consult me about the question of his career. All the family are changed, but the mother and father are out in Africa, and for some reason the youngster had always taken his career for granted. He was studying to be a doctor, but had not yet actually embarked on the medical course. He told me all the facts, and together we listened to God. The thoughts that came to him were:

(a) That there had been certain times in the past when he had had qualms as to whether it was the right thing for him to be a doctor.

(b) That one of the reasons that was urging him toward the medical profession was a desire for security. He felt that as a doctor he would always be sure of earning a living.

(c) That there was a good opportunity for farming waiting him in Africa.

(d) That there was a great need of life-changing in the neighborhood where his father lived, and they would be able to work together as a team.

The thoughts that came to me were:

(a) The difference in the tone of voice in which he spoke of farming showed clearly that this was what he was really keen on.

(b) The fact that, in my experience, if a boy was keen on becoming a doctor, he was nearly always *very* keen and prepared to stand out against everybody to maintain his choice.[14]

A third step has rather recently been introduced by the leader

[13] Stephen Foot, *Life Began Yesterday*, New York: Harper, 1935, 63.
[14] *Ibid.*, 110.

and is known essentially as *checking guidance*. Dr. Buchman advocates that people do just what God tells them. But sometimes they may mistake their own thoughts for God's directions and indulge in what is really selfishly motivated behavior, which they have attributed to God's will. Hence the Grouper, especially if he is a newcomer, should show the directions God has given him for the day to another Grouper who will help him verify his instructions. "Consult a trustworthy friend, who believes in the guidance of the Holy Spirit." Occasionally what has been accepted as God's guidance will turn out, on examination, to be something apparently ungodly or something that seems to have been inaccurately recorded as it passed through the Grouper's mind. If any "error" is noted, the Grouper is assured that God will soon make his directions clearer.[15]

The fourth step is to carry out God's directions, *restitution, to get straight with others*. To cite some of the American leaders' examples, this may mean that one has to write a letter long overdue, pay some bills, adjust income tax figures, or apologize to a neighbor or the cook.[16]

A final requirement to attain the ideals and spread the movement is the process known as *sharing*. This means the sharing of one's sins.[17]

> In plain language it is telling, or talking over, our sins with another whose life has already been surrendered to God or, if we have already surrendered, assisting others to surrender by opening—as we are

[15] Hugh O'Connor, The Oxford Group reaches out, *New York Times Magazine*, July 19, 1936; H. J. Rose, *The Quiet Time,* pamphlet issued by the Oxford Group, New York City.

[16] Shoemaker, *op. cit.,* ch. 6.

[17] The essential difference between the confessions of the Buchmanites and the Catholics is that the former share in the presence of other group members, sometimes before thousands of people. Indeed, Group meetings consist largely of the confessions of various members. Group confession of sin was a very common practice in most early forms of Christianity. It still persists, of course, in some of the more primitive varieties of Christianity in this country.

The Catholic Church long ago banned such public confessions. In the fifth century, Leo I ordained that no public confession would be permitted that was not first approved by a priest. In 1215, the Catholic Church abolished any form of public confessional and substituted the ritual of private confessional. The reasons for the abolition of the group confessional was that people were so apt to exaggerate their sins for various personal reasons that the occasions became more scandalous than edifying.

guided—laying our past sins or present temptations alongside theirs, so that they may be able better to recognize and bring to light those sins which have stood between them and God![18]

After the acknowledged Grouper has recited some of his own all-too-human actions, a newcomer may divulge his sins. If he does, a new convert has been made, another life has been changed. The initiate then gives in to God, gets his guidance, has it checked, makes the proper "restitution" for his past, and himself goes out to change other lives. So the process goes on.[19]

And the whole procedure moves rapidly as the need for life-changing becomes more apparent. The individual Grouper must do *his* part if the world is to be saved from utter destruction. Life-changing is taken as God's solution for all crises.

> I am painfully impressed in this time of bewilderment, discouragement, demoralization, and despair, by the extreme urgency of life-changing on a colossal scale. If you and I do not do our part it is clear that chaos is ahead, and even near at hand. I believe that we are in the midst of actual revolution and that God is preparing a new social order . . .

writes one of the leaders.[20]

Since the duty of carrying out God's plan rests solely with the individual it is therefore particularly essential that the Group contain as many key people as possible. Buchman believes the church has horribly neglected what he **calls the** *up-and-outers*—the wealthy people who represent the vested interests.

> Think what might happen (says the Reverend Shoemaker) if we had that quality of God-controlled life in the City Hall of New York, in the Capitol at Washington, in the League of Nations at Geneva.

[18] *What Is the Oxford Group, op. cit.,* 27.

[19] There are not infrequent reports by backsliders who claim to feel silly and embarrassed when they think of their past performances. Others just can't see that it ever did them any good. Some observers report that Buchman's followers are often narrowminded, uncooperative, or spiritually snobbish. Ministers who have been changed and who rely entirely on God's guidance, rather than on study and preparation for their sermons, are accused of becoming bores. For such criticisms, see D. E. Silcox, The Oxford Group in Canada, *Christian Century,* Sept. 12, 1934, 1137-1140; D. J. Wilson, A critique of Buchmanism, *Christian Century,* Aug. 23, 1933, 1059 f.

[20] P. M. Brown, *op. cit.,* 64.

Think of the nations confessing their sins, instead of the sins of other nations. Think of national repentance and restitution, of national conversion and salvation, of the governments of this world deciding the issues of the world on the basis of God's direction. And pray, why not?[21]

Buchman himself carries the doctrine to its logical conclusion when he states:

I thank heaven for a man like Adolf Hitler, who built a front line of defense against the anti-Christ of Communism. Think what it would mean to the world if Hitler surrendered to the control of God. Or Mussolini. Or any dictator. Through such a man God could control a nation overnight and solve every last, bewildering problem. The world needs the dictatorship of the spirit of God. They (social problems) could be solved within a God-controlled democracy, or perhaps I should say theocracy, and they could be solved through a God-controlled fascist dictatorship.[22]

If one could only get the leaders, particularly the dictators, to listen to God the millennium would appear. This would obviously be the most efficient procedure. Instead of changing millions of citizens, the only requisite would be to change the relatively few people who run governments. For there is a plan to guide them. What is it?

It lies in a faith in God which includes an experiment. It lies in believing that God is, that He has a plan, and that He will reveal that plan to us. It lies in fitting in with that plan ourselves, and finding that God will take care of us when we dare to make that experiment.[23]

God also has a plan for industry which will be revealed to any industrialist or worker who is sufficiently willing to give in to God and listen to His plan. Economic depressions and consequent unemployment are due essentially to sin.[24] Therefore:

Thoughtful people are realizing more and more that there is a much costlier price which must be paid for a decent world than the mere rearrangement of its economics. No reformation from without, through political or economic instrumentalities, can bring about the thing we most need. We need a mighty awakening . . . a spiritual

[21] Shoemaker, op. cit., 76.
[22] New York World-Telegram, Aug. 26, 1936.
[23] Shoemaker, op. cit., 40.
[24] Stephen Foot, op. cit., 66.

reformation on wide and deep lines that will lift the world off its hinges. That is what we need. It will solve our problems and nothing else will.[25]

There is ample evidence that business men have turned to God for guidance and that he has not failed to advise them. A west-coast manufacturer reported that his employees now gather in his office before work "to get God's direction for the day." This practice, he reports, has solved all his labor troubles. Another convert called together the local chamber of commerce and "openly admitted his false aggressiveness and his garrulous piousity"; a "new unity came to his life."[26] A successful business man, under the influence of the Group, confessed to a competitor, "I want to own up to you I've overreached you twice in a business deal."[27]

The Group has widely advertised its solution of strikes which, it says, "have no place in a Christian world."[28] The Group claimed to have settled the Pacific-coast maritime strike of 1934, by lifting the whole dispute "to a higher plane. The effect of bringing God into the dispute was miraculous. The atmosphere cleared overnight and the leaders began to understand the new principles. The strike on the Pacific coast was the first strike in history in which Christ was called upon to act as arbiter."[29] Apparently, in this dispute two followers represented the Lord and made their report to an Oxford Group assembly. But the strike continued for some time after the manifesto was issued. However, the manifesto at least temporarily showed the assembled followers that God was not powerless in capital-labor controversies.

The accompanying problem of unemployment automatically disappears if one accepts the Buchman solution. For, since "everybody who is not working for God is unemployed," all one has to do to become employed is to work for God. "Unemployment on this basis ceases to become a problem and becomes an opportunity." An

[25] Shoemaker, op. cit., 99.

[26] Russell, op. cit., 263.

[27] Ibid., 265.

[28] C. S. Williams, Buchmanism "settled" the coast strike, Christian Century, July 25, 1934, 969 f. This article quotes from a manifesto of the Oxford Group issued at Banff, Canada on June 8, 1934.

[29] Ibid.

unemployed man who is an Oxford Grouper reveals the effect of
Buchmanism in his life:

> I know from my own experience how long-continued unemploy-
> ment destroys ambition, aspiration, self-respect, and produces a sense of
> frustration and hopelessness. To my mind, the most pressing problem
> today is not merely to get men back to work, but to help them to
> use their leisure in the most constructive way. The Oxford Group has
> declared a spiritual world war which offers to every man and woman
> instant enlistment and full-time employment. For myself I know that
> surrender to Jesus Christ solves the personal problem of frustration;
> my change enabled me to recapture a belief in the existence of God,
> it cleaned up my life . . . The introduction of the Spirit of Jesus
> Christ into social and economic problems is the only hope the unem-
> ployed man has . . . Unemployment is more than a social disease,
> it is an expression of spiritual poverty as it may be a cause of spiritual
> decay.[30]

An unemployed Londoner reports that "full-time employment can
be found when God is guiding, because all the hours you are awake
you are looking for someone to help."[31]

Such, in brief, are the aims of the Oxford Group and the manner
in which the aims are instrumented into action. It is impossible to
describe them more specifically or more concretely. They become
specific and concrete only for the individual who has two-way communication with God. And their specificity is always in terms of the
behavior and purposes of a single individual.

The followers. Because Buchmanism is essentially a rugged, if
spiritual, individualism and because its founder deliberately concen-
trates on changing important people, the followers are, in large
measure, people who would normally avoid a social gospel which
pointed out the responsibilities they should have for their less fortunate fellow men.

An observer of an Oxford Group assembly meeting, held at Stockbridge, Massachusetts, in 1936, writes that the Groupers "represent
a tolerant, easy-going citizenry—and what is unusual in.religious
meetings—most are men. The majority are well-to-do; many are
prosperous, if not wealthy. The groups include leaders. Not only

[30] Stephen Foot, *op. cit.*
[31] *Ibid.*, 74.

bishops in the service of God, but surgeons repairing the human viscera . . . A British lord, a French baroness, a Scottish Communist, and a noted English horseman—all of them insisted that their daily lives had been completely surrendered to an immediate and divine authority. There were undergraduates whose most exacting effort had been, probably, a search for a plan of life."[32] Many socialites, financiers, or nobility were to be seen.[33]

Another indication of the interest Buchman has aroused among the up-and-outers was the party tendered him in the House of Commons by more than one hundred of its members on the occasion of his sixtieth birthday. The Duke of Windsor wired him at the time, "Through your responsibility our nation is becoming conscious that God alone can steer the ship of state."[34]

The greatest roundup to date of persons of power, wealth, prominence, or noble birth appeared in a little booklet edited by H.W. (Bunny) Austin, former member of the British Davis Cup team and now an aggressive life-changer. The booklet, *Moral Re-Armament: The Battle for Peace,*[35] appeared, significantly enough, in the fall of 1938, when war was threatening. It contains a series of manifestoes, most of them reprinted from the *London Times,* endorsing moral rearmament or advocating something of the kind.[36] Among the names attached are those of 33 members of Parliament, 25 peers in high government positions, 12 baronets, 37 well-known athletes, 21 journalists, a large number of industrialists, 17 trade-union heads, and some distinguished academicians. Among the names are those of Earl Baldwin of Bewdley, Field Marshall Lord

[32] O'Connor, *op. cit.*

[33] Dr. Buchman himself stays at the best hotels and travels only first-class on ocean liners. When questioned about his luxurious habits, Buchman replied, "Why shouldn't we stay in 'posh' hotels? Isn't God a millionaire?" One of his epigrams is that "good food and good Christianity go together." Among those present at the Stockbridge meeting were Mr. and Mrs. Cleveland Dodge, Mrs. Harry Guggenheim, W. Farrar Vickers, Sir Philip Dundas, and Mrs. Henry Ford. *Time,* June 15, 1936, 35-38.

[34] Stanley High, What is moral rearmament? *Saturday Evening Post,* Aug. 12, 1939, 212-223.

[35] London: Heinemann, 1938.

[36] It should be pointed out that a person's signature on a manifesto does not mean, however, that for either personal or political reasons he has lent his name to the general principles of the movement as they apply to international affairs.

Birdwood, Sir William Bragg, the Earl of Clarendon, Lord Milne, the Earl of Lytton, the Viscount Trenchard, Lord Stamp, the Duke of Beaufort, and a host of others who represent the traditional British ruling class. On December 1, 1939, "a call to our citizens," urging the need for "that new force of Moral Re-Armament," was issued and signed by 650 Lord Mayors, Lord Provosts, Mayors, Provosts, and Chairmen of City Councils in England.[37]

Against such a background, it is not surprising that the writings and testimonials of the Groupers frequently show an air of condescension and smug complacency. One advocate writes, for example:

> One of my pleasantest recollections of last year was a Quiet Time with a couple of stewards and some stokers in the baggage room of S.S.Europa at 6:30 A.M. together with some other members of the Oxford Group team on our voyage out to Canada. Thousands of other people have had similar experiences since being changed and in many households now it is the usual thing for the staff to join with the master and mistress in a Quiet Time every morning. On one occasion recently while I was staying with some friends the Quiet Time was led by a young housemaid who did it most naturally. Why not? There are some households where the first person to be changed was the cook, and as a result of that the whole of the family and staff have been changed also.[38]

And Lord Addington in one of his testimonials reflected the same hauteur when he said, "A conservative aristocrat, I am proud to stand on the same platform with a Dutch socialist."[39]

Techniques. In spite of the fact that the changed individual is supposed to go out and change others, Buchman does not rely entirely on God-inspired personal initiative to increase his numerical strength. The worldly devices of the advertiser, the public-relations counsel, and the propagandist are used by the leader in the service of God.

Buchmanites do not indulge in rough-and-tumble revival meetings and in sudden emotional conversions. Such an approach would be far too crude to attract sophisticated college students, business men, statesmen, or labor leaders whom the movement would like to gather into the fold. Nor is Buchman himself at his best when speaking

---

[37] *The Rise of a New Spirit*, publication of the Oxford Group, New York, 16 f.
[38] Stephen Foot, *op. cit.*, 85.
[39] *Time*, June 15, 1936, 37.

before a large group: he is neither on orator nor a showman. The approach of the Buchmanites is more refined and dignified. Every attempt is made to turn the acquaintanceship of a potential follower into a friendship. Congeniality and cordiality are cultivated. The process may take months, even years. But a feeling of intimacy and a sense of mutual confidence are essential if life-changing is to be engineered successfully.

One of the favorite mechanisms for producing the sociability and informality needed to nurse these friendships is the house party. An undergraduate, a newly married couple prominent in the social world, or a business man will be invited somewhere to spend the week-end. They find several other guests present. The other guests mingle with the relative strangers in all the social activities the hostess has planned. They play tennis together, walk together, swim together, and in general build up a sense of camaraderie. Religion and problems of the soul are tactfully avoided at first by the companions. Then, perhaps on the last evening of the week-end, when all guests feel rather intimate, the newcomer finds himself surrounded by people who are talking about the question of a personal God, about God's will as it is related to individual lives, about what God has done for them, about their own rather intimate problems. As one member put it, "We just get together and chat about Christ." There is no feeling of shyness or shame in the discussion. The guest feels rather obligated to participate after the kindnesses of the week-end. Self-revelation is indirectly encouraged, for it is the topic of conversation. The more dramatic the revelation, the more intense the audience, and the more glorified is the interlocutor. The famous "painless soul-surgery" has begun. The guest now or at a later house party may find himself confessing completely to one or more members whose confidence and insight he values. After his confession he feels "cleansed" and finds that his self-surrender enables him to hear God's commands in the Quiet Hour. He is now "God-controlled."[40]

Occasionally large assemblies are held. These attract the attention of the general public. After much underground publicity the meet-

---

[40] For firsthand accounts of people who have attended house parties, see O'Connor, *op. cit.;* K. Brown, Religious houseparty, *Outlook,* June 7, 1925, 27-29. An agnostic's confession, *Outlook,* May 22, 1929, 128 f.; *Life,* Feb. 15, 1937.

ings are elaborately staged, and as often as possible the names of prominent people are obtained as "sponsors" of the meeting. One such meeting was held in Madison Square Garden in the spring of 1939. Twelve thousand people attended. Among the sponsors of the assemblage were Joe DiMaggio, known to all lovers of America's favorite game, Henry Ford, and Mayor LaGuardia.[41] The meeting was an event of such proportions that it inevitably received wide publicity.

Buchman capitalizes on the prestige of "big names," as does almost every propagandist, only to a greater degree than the average: revered figures in our national history are linked to the movement.

> George Washington Listened at a Time of Conflict
>   And gave a nation Freedom,
> Benjamin Franklin Listened at a Time of Chaos
>   And brought a nation Order,
> Abraham Lincoln Listened at a Time of Crisis
>   And preserved a nation's Unity.[42]

A prominent senator spoke on the same radio program with Buchman in Washington; Mrs. M. Edison Hughes, who was the wife of Thomas A. Edison, spoke with him on a New York broadcast. A booklet issued by the group in this country contains excerpts from speeches by the late Speaker William B. Bankhead, Senator Arthur Capper, Rear Admiral Richard E. Byrd, former Secretary of War Harry H. Woodring, Senator H. S. Truman, and Mr. Henry Ford, all of whom endorsed moral rearmament.[43] Famous athletes are asked to spread special messages. For example, at one time a famous racing driver, a heavyweight boxer, a tennis player, and various football players distributed posters, window displays, and more than 5,000,000 milk bottle caps in England, urging peace through moral rearmament;[44] and statesmen or financiers were asked to endorse some program, as we have seen. Some critics have accused the move-

[41] MRA Week, *The Nation*, May 21, 1939, 575.

[42] *One Hundred Million Listening,* publication of the Oxford Group, New York City.

[43] *The Rise of a New Spirit, op. cit.*

[44] "Famous scientists" are said to agree that God has a plan. *Newsweek,* May 22, 1939, 21.

ment for not living up to its standard of Absolute Honesty in the freedom with which it uses such names. The contention is that anyone who says a good word for the movement or who admits that "something must be done" to better conditions in the world is represented, if his name is important, as an ardent supporter. Also, many prominent people have undoubtedly found themselves in the same position as Congressman Joe Martin who said, "Sure, I'm for MRA whatever it is. It's just like being against sin."[45]

The Oxford Group does not want to be known as snobbish, however. Recently Buchman has taken great care to emphasize its democratic nature. "Statesmen, labor leaders, businessmen, sportsmen and workers, men of vision, united in a common purpose for a common cause," said the leader in a world-wide broadcast where others on the same program included (in addition to a countess and a brigadier general), a Jewish housepainter, a Catholic nurse, a member of the British Labor Party, and a cowboy who sang to his own mandolin accompaniment.[46]

These large meetings also undoubtedly help to create for the outsider the impression that the movement is highly important, that it is growing, that it is something to be taken seriously; while the follower is consoled to see that the mental world within which he lives is shared by thousands of people. Leaders constantly reiterate the international scope of the movement. In the parade at the Stockbridge gathering, the flags of 18 nations were carried as well as those of all 48 states. It is perhaps significant that the swastika, but not the hammer and sickle, was among them. The movement claims to have teams in 60 countries. In a world-wide broadcast Buchman stated:

> We now move from a hundred people listening to a hundred million people enlisting. A world-wide family. You cannot pick and choose who will be rearmed. Every one should be rearmed. When we listen and enlist we shall learn to share and care. This will bring us nearer to the solution of that vexed problem of unemployment. If every one cared enough, and every one shared enough, wouldn't every one have enough?[47]

[45] MRA in Washington, *Time*, June 12, 1939, 54.
[46] *New York Times*, Dec. 3, 1939.
[47] *New York Times*, Dec. 4, 1939.

Buchman is famous for his *slogans* and for his twisting of popular phrases. Like a good advertiser, he knows that slogans will catch attention, be more easily remembered, and more readily repeated. Some of the slogans that have come to him in his Quiet Times are:

Sin Blinds and Sin Binds.
Jesus Christ still suits, saves, and satisfies.
PRAY stands for Powerful Radiograms Always Yours.
A Supernatural Network Over Live Wires.
A Spiritual Radiophone in Every Home.
There is enough in the world for everyone's need, but not enough for
    everyone's greed.
Constipated Christians.
Come Clean.
JESUS Just Exactly Suits Us Sinners.

Nor are symbols forgotten. Moral rearmament is represented in blue and white by four vertical lines (the four Absolutes) with MRA printed horizontally over them to form a cross.

WHY AN OXFORD GROUP?

The movement centering around Frank Buchman has already had a checkered and diverse history. Its earliest appeals, and its clientele in the 1920's are not strictly comparable to its appeals and clientele in its later years of soul-surgery and moral rearmament. Thus the satisfactions Buchmanism has provided its followers have somewhat varied through the years. And at any one period of its history, the needs of followers with different personalities and backgrounds would be rather diversified. It is impossible to give any simple psychological formula to explain the movement as a whole. Nevertheless, Buchmanism does have certain outstanding characteristics and does seem to attract certain groups of people. What are the particular needs of the followers and why does the teaching of Buchman seem peculiarly satisfying to them? To answer this question we may roughly distinguish between the earlier and later forms of the movement.

Earlier years. From the point of view of the social psychologist, the first few years of Buchmanism are the least interesting and important. His work did not assume any large proportion; it attracted attention and followers only in the restricted college areas within which he operated. Since his appeal was successful chiefly because of the guilt a number of young men and boys suffered from what they considered their own immoral, abnormal sexual behavior (masturbation), the explanation for his success belongs properly in the domain of the psychoanalyst or some other branch of psychotherapy. But the techniques he used and certain of the psychological characteristics of the early meetings with undergraduates were developed in this period and provided the same personal satisfactions they did later when more mature persons were involved and when less primitive needs were the source of individual anxieties.

The confessions made by the young men to Buchman and to each other brought the customary "relief" or "catharsis" so vividly experienced by sinners throughout the ages and so well known to the mental healer, whether he is a physician, a parent, a sympathetic friend, a priest, or a professional psychotherapist. There are various possible explanations for the relief obtained by Buchman's young followers and for their subsequent devotion to him and to his methods. For some individuals, "relief" consisted perhaps of several component relationships, for other individuals perhaps only a single one was operative.

In the first place, the technique of "sharing" in a small group immediately creates around the individual a closed microcosm, a little mental world with its own norms and values. Hence the discrepancy he has felt between his own needs and practices and the standards of the larger world disappear. In the microcosm, all people are sinners. Like himself, no one is suppressing his guilty feelings. Status and membership in the microcosm are obtained because one has been a sinner, not a saint, in the recent past. Hence the feeling of inferiority and the emotional security that so often result when an individual cannot honestly and completely identify himself with the prevailing moral code disappear completely. When a person has "given in to God" in this situation, he has expressed overtly the practices he has secretly guarded. The standards of the new microcosm, initiated by Buchman, implicitly sanction his past behavior, as past behavior, and make him feel that a new stage of life has been reached where a new beginning can be made with a new self-confidence resulting from the disappearance of thoughts of inferiority and shame. The new status achieved by becoming a respectable member of the group encourages self-justification through self-assertion.

Furthermore, the individual is now an "in-group" member of a rather highly selected gathering. He has knowledge that others do not possess. The mutual confessions reveal his secrets to others and theirs to him. As an insider, the individual himself now qualifies as a soul-surgeon and life-changer. His status is enhanced and is recognized by other members of the group and perhaps by a few outsiders whom he begins to interest by his sympathy and apparent insight. Thus, persons who may be social misfits or who are, for various reasons, psychologically isolated may achieve a sense of fellowship and social participation they have long sought. The encouragement of informality and congeniality by the leader, the use of first names, and the close companionship between members of the same group or team further break down social barriers. The individual can maintain his position by repeating his confession in some form on different group occasions. Psychologically, the repetition of confession may be a form of substitute gratification for the sin itself, thus giving the individual a mild erotic pleasure at the same time it provides relief and status.

There is likewise an undoubted excitement and thrill involved in the act of sharing. Listening to the anti-social escapades or practices of one's fellows seems, for many people, to have a particular fascination. One may vicariously enjoy the vice portrayed and at the same time justify the interest as a part of God's work, thus gaining a new satisfaction, since to carry on God's work is the most highly accepted value in the ego of the individual Groupers. Lurid confessions become hallowed and sanctified under the accepted religious norms. Even the leader himself seems sometimes thrilled by confessions. A follower reports:

> After one of the meetings at the last Cambridge houseparty Frank (Buchman) burst into my room exclaiming: "You should have heard Loudon Hamilton's talk on Sin! Great! Never heard anything so revealing. That's what you should get for your book!"[48]

Sometimes the meetings may have a purely entertainment value.

[48] Russell, *For Sinners Only*, reported in *New Republic*, Mar. 8, 1933.

Thus a physician reports that he heard a young man trying to decide whether he should take his girl to a theater or to an Oxford Group meeting for their prospective date.[49] And one Grouper, an Oxford student, felt that attendance at group meeting "is more fun than running about to cocktail parties."[50] One visitor was asked after a meeting, "Isn't Jesus jolly"?

Probably more important than the element of excitement for young people in the Group is the fact that many of them find in Buchman's leadership and in his principles an ideal or a common goal with which they can identify themselves. The values upon which the ideal is based become the values of the individual members. The process of striving to achieve these values (a process which involves restitution for one's faults, getting others to come clean or to confess) gives the adolescent or bewildered young person a genuine purpose at a time in life when he is becoming conscious of his own responsibilities and potentialities. "I was having a very good time in my life," said one Grouper, "but I did not have any purpose. The Oxford Group taught me how to find God."

The characteristic "relief" experienced by young people who confessed to Buchman and affiliated themselves with his movement in its early years is a particular variety of "relief" commonly needed by college or preparatory school men, although by no means limited to them. Various autoerotic practices are known to be indulged in, at times, by the vast majority of young men. For many of them, the subjective consequence is a feeling of guilt, inferiority, or lack of self-control. Certainly, many young people who have recently left home and community ties are still rather unsatisfactorily adjusted socially. Certainly, many of them miss parental guidance and authority in a new environment where emotional immaturity and sentimentality are frowned upon by schoolmates who are anxious to show or to affect the independence and sophistication so highly valued by undergraduate tradition. Dr. Buchman, therefore, chose a fertile field in which to begin his new adventure. But his methods and his aims so radically conflicted, as we have seen, with the estab-

[49] Dr. F. H. Dodd, A physician's criticism, in F. A. M. Spencer, *The Meaning of the Groups*, London: Methuen, 1934, 57.

[50] The Oxford Groups—genuine or a mockery, *Literary Digest*, Jan. 28, 1933, 118.

lished, institutionalized way of life that he was forbidden to carry on in this circumscribed field.

There are obviously many personal and social complications involved in the unequivocal surrender of youths to Buchman and to God. A few of them should be mentioned now, since they are especially relevant to the practices of the early years and the predominantly young clientele the leader gathered around him. Other results of the movement as a whole will be discussed shortly.

It is apparent that many of the confessions and restitutions center around trivial matters. By confessing something essentially unimportant and by the self-imposed obligation of rectifying an oversight or minor injustice, the individual feels exonerated for all his shortcomings. Even if major faults are confessed, it is hardly likely that most members, especially young ones, would have sufficient insight to know whether the faults were genuine. Furthermore, even if we grant that the individual has an insight into his symptoms, the superficial act of admitting the trouble to himself or to others by no means discloses the real root of his difficulty. He may alter some specific habit or behavior without understanding the cause of that behavior; he may change a very specific attitude without changing any of the basic values from which it derives. The sources of motivation are likely to be completely obscured, thus making any general adjustment or understanding impossible. The reliance on a vague conscious or unconscious feeling for guidance will be considered, by some, a poor substitute for a more intellectual appraisal of the most satisfactory orientation to the environment. A morbid introspectionism and egocentrism may be encouraged by the constant emphasis on sin. This may lead, at times, to an unwarranted feeling of superiority or intolerance. In extreme cases, the practice of listening to voices and the emotional exhaustion that can follow ceaseless testifying may lead to mental unbalance.

Later phase. The social psychologist is primarily interested in the later period of the Oxford Group movement. For only after it broadened its base and began to attract people of all ages in large numbers did it really become a significant social phenomenon. In order to enlarge its following in the way we have described, it must have appealed to more highly derived drives than before. What were the troubles that Buchman solved for so many people and why did they turn to his doctrines rather than to those of established churches, political parties, or social ideologies?

It is probably not accidental that Buchmanism flourished to its fullest extent in the depth of the depression which began in 1929. The early 1930's were hard years, not only for those suffering material want and seeking jobs, but for many well-to-do people who were discovering that the depression was not a temporary thing and that perhaps some rather drastic changes were necessary if general prosperity was to be restored. Just what the solution could be few people seemed to know. And it became more and more dubious that any final solution could be reached that would preserve the powers and privileges of those who were used to them. "I often think that if Christ were here He would be equally concerned for the rich," writes the American leader of the movement.[51]

Buchmanism took another spurt in the fall of 1938, just before and after the Munich agreement, when war was narrowly and temporarily averted by ceding to Hitler's demands. Again some solution short of war was sought by all people and again many members of the traditional ruling classes, especially in England, wondered vaguely if any peaceful solution could be found that would not jeopardize their positions. If data were available on the fluctuation in Oxford Group membership, they would almost certainly show that, during periods of unusual social crisis or indecision, the movement received new followers in large numbers and that, as relative social stability was restored, fewer newcomers entered the ranks and older followers became less zealous.

As we saw in earlier chapters, there are two highly derived and important motivations involved in these critical periods. First, there is the desire for meaning or interpretation of events and, second, the desire for security, not simply material security but psychological security involving security of status, of self-integrity, of associations, of institutional and personal ways of life. These desires are often rather directly stated by leaders of the movement. Reverend Shoemaker writes, for example:

> We should not be so much disturbed about much that is going on around us today, if our minds were not primarily fixed on security, and if we did not read outward events so largely in terms of what

[51] Shoemaker, *op. cit.*, 32.

they do to personal security. People are asking more feverishly than ever where their security lies.[52]

The same follower, in a published prayer, asked:

O God, Who hast made us for Thyself, and *without Whom our life is wanting both in meaning and in light*: *Grant us the vision* of Thy will for the world and for our own lives, that *knowing Thy plan for us*, we may both please Thee and renew the face of the earth by the might of Thy Spirit.[53]

And the letter to the *London Times*, signed by Earl Baldwin and other British notables, implicitly approving moral rearmament, begins by stating: "Today all are anxiously asking, To what is the world heading? What is the future of civilization?"[54]

The essential secret of Buchman's more recent success is that he provided for many people a meaningful interpretation of events which, at the same time, implicitly preserved their security and their self-regard. The Four Absolutes and the method of attaining them gave certain people a new frame of reference which conformed to their basic values and was itself so general that almost every situation could be judged in terms of it. By increasing their range of acquaintances, mixing freely with other believers, and doing good deeds that they thought important, many followers found a place for themselves in a new social world, their behavior became more directed and purposeful. By keeping the doctrines highly individualistic and by assuming that nations and institutions would be good only when the individuals who composed them were good, Buchman and his followers were able to avoid taking an explicit stand on any controversial social or economic issue. The greater concern of men, rather than of women, in everyday political and economic questions and the Buchman solution to these problems probably account for the observation that the movement, unlike most religious bodies, is composed largely of men.

Since members of the upper and upper middle classes, more than other classes, are threatened by loss of prestige, power, or influence by any positive program of social amelioration, they are especially attracted to the movement. Such persons solve social problems by escaping completely from any reference to the social context within

[52] *Ibid.*, 34.
[53] *Ibid.*, 77. Italics the author's.
[54] *London Times*, Sept. 10, 1938.

which the problems arise and persist. "There are other forces than the economic ones," says one follower, for example. "We are beginning to reckon with God. We have gone as far as we possibly can by political means. Now it is high time that we put the control into God's hands."[55] Specific social crises are lifted from their normal setting and their more earthly practical solutions are ignored. In 1933, Dr. Buchman stated that the following of God's plan "was the only solution to the Danzig problem." He also noted:

> The President's social-trends report indicates there will surely be a revolution in this country. We are going to make it a spiritual revolution. What hunger marchers need is to be changed.[56]

Whether the problem is one of war or peace, starvation or plenty, employment or unemployment it is transferred to God, thus relieving the individual Buchmanite of any social responsibility.

This transference and the whole Group doctrine of guidance could not function if Buchman had not recreated the idea of an omniscient, omnipotent God. And part of the success of his movement lies in the fact that he reified the symbol of God at a time when conditions were critical and when many established religions were beginning to think of God in a less formalistic way. By reestablishing God as an entity entirely outside the individual, the Buchmanite is able to get external sanctions for his own wishes. He attributes to God directions and commands that are essentially his own fancies and desires. He ascribes to God, as one of His attributes, a "plan," a plan which is all embracing. Hence all the individual has to do is listen to God's plan. And when the individual listens, the specific directions he obtains in his Quiet Time are inevitably based on his own standards of judgment and his own wishes no matter how unconscious they may be. In this way God, who exists outside the individual, gives him sanction and authority to do as he wants. God's values become his values because he has himself projected them into the symbol of God.

Since Buchman himself never specifies what God's plan is in any concrete situation, the appeal is sufficiently general and vague to satisfy all tastes. "Never in my long experience in Washington have I found anything on which all parties in both Senate and House

[55] From a testimonial quoted in Foot, *op. cit.*, 76.
[56] *Literary Digest*, Jan. 28, 1933, 18 f.

have so thoroughly agreed as on America's need, and our own need, for this new spirit," is the dubious tribute paid moral rearmament by the late Speaker Bankhead.[57] At times these tastes seem horribly irreconcilable. For example, the leaders of two warring nations both sent messages simultaneously to Buchman advocating moral rearmament. Cabled Generalissimo Chiang Kai-shek, "Glad focusing world attention on this all important question of moral rearmament"; cabled the Japanese Prime Minister, "Believing necessity of moral rearmament for solution of world problems, sincerely hope for every success of your noble movement." But neither Generalissimo nor Prime Minister laid down his arms. In the petty details of everyday life, God's plan provides comfort and approval. "Our budget is God-controlled," said a socialite. "There is a real thrill and purpose in teas and dinner parties."[58] And the illusion of working for God gives people with leisure and a lack of personal resourcefulness a more purposive existence. "I knew everybody worth knowing and I had done everything worth doing, and it became monotonous," reported a wealthy young woman. "I met this group and then I found that cocktail parties were not as interesting as their gatherings. I found that Jesus Christ had work for me to do."[59]

Buchmanism has gathered momentum, therefore, essentially because it shows certain bewildered people a way to interpret their personal troubles and the larger social problems of their world without endangering their status. It provides a psychological mechanism whereby they can escape the responsibility of dealing directly with conditions which they realize are not right and just. It attracts to itself people who want to improve these conditions without injuring their own positions and who want to avoid any alignment with existing institutions or ideologies which assume that individual problems cannot be solved without collective action. Its lack of any well-formulated program makes it highly opportunistic; its resignation to "God's" plan forces it to abandon reason as an instrument to be used in the solution of all problems; its individualism and refusal to consider the social context that gives rise to social problems makes it inevitably anti-democratic.

[57] *The Rise of a New Spirit, op. cit.,* 4.
[58] *Time,* June 15, 1936, 38.
[59] *Literary Digest,* Jan. 28, 1933.

CHAPTER 7

THE TOWNSEND PLAN

One characteristic of man is his capacity to dream and scheme when all is not so perfect as it might be in what he regards as his world. Sometimes the dreams drive him to the ruthless conquest of his neighbors, sometimes they send him across oceans in search of unknown treasure, sometimes they lead him to revolt and to set up a new social order. Sometimes man knows his schemes are only imaginative creations impossible of realization; sometimes they are carefully calculated to meet the contingencies of contemporary life; sometimes they are uncritically accepted as immediate panaceas. The United States in its short history has had its greenbackism, its populism, its 16 to 1 silver platform.

The Townsend Plan is just another one of a long procession of schemes. It has arisen at a certain point of time. It has had a phenomenal growth. If the plan were ever put into effect it would profoundly alter our whole economy. The problems it hopes to solve and the appeals it has are specific to the American culture in the depression years of the 1930's. A psychological analysis of the scheme should, then, help us understand further the man of our particular era. At the same time, if our examination is adequate, it should give us some insight into the reasons why other schemes, whether historical or contemporary, seem to catch hold and carry with them for longer or shorter time the enthusiasm and devotion of thousands of people.

THE PLAN IS BORN

In the 1920's, California was crowded with middle-western farmers, retired business men, and gray-haired people from all walks of life. Some of these had come to the land of sunshine and opportunity to begin again lives that had elsewhere proved hard and hopeless. Some had come with their small savings to spend a quiet,

secure old age.[1] When the depression of 1929 finally crept westward, it caught these people who were without deep roots in native
soil. The inertia of Herbert Hoover, then President of the United
States, was no comfort to their sudden despair; the platform of
Franklin D. Roosevelt as presidential candidate in 1932 was not
abundant with immediate promises. Something more was needed.

During the early 1930's, California was filled to overflowing with
economic, social, and religious blueprints. In 1932, technocracy was
born. Everyone should have a $5,000 standard of living said the
technocrats. It was possible. All we needed was a change in our
methods of production and distribution. Then the Utopian Society
was founded in 1933, urging a cooperative state. Upton Sinclair's
more realistic EPIC plan (End Poverty in California) capitalized
on discontent, taught a modified socialism, and got him the democratic nomination for governor. But technocracy was complicated
and seemed distant; Utopia was educational and not immediate;
EPIC sounded strange, was labeled communistic and atheistic, and
was beaten by a systematically organized campaign of the vested
interests.[2]

One of the immigrants who lived through all this was Dr. Francis
E. Townsend. His boyhood home had been a log cabin in Illinois.
He had taught school in Kansas, worked his way through a medical
college, and carried on a horse-and-buggy practice in the Black Hills
of North Dakota. His life had not been an easy or a highly successful
one. So he, too, went to southern California in search of the ease and
success that so far had evaded him. In 1931, he tried to organize a
Dry Ice manufacturing plant. Then he got a job in the Long Beach
City Health Department. This terminated in 1933, leaving him in
his sixties, unemployed, with a family to support, and with only
a few hundred dollars in the bank. So he tried to sell real estate for
a friend, Robert Earl Clements.

In this period of hopelessness and worry, so the story goes, Dr.
Townsend looked out his bathroom window one morning to see

[1] For a description of California in the 1930's and an account of the various movements that started in the state from 1932 to 1936, including the Townsend movement, see L. Whiteman and S. L. Lewis, *Glory Roads: The Psychological State of
California*, New York: Crowell, 1936.

[2] See Upton Sinclair's *I, Candidate for Governor, and How I Got Licked*, Pasadena,
California: 1934.

three old women picking usable scraps out of garbage cans. Shifting his eyes not far from this scene, he saw store windows filled with food. He became enraged at the injustice of it all. His wife tried to calm him but he wouldn't be calmed. He said he wanted people to hear his shouting about the horrible conditions that vexed him. He wanted God Almighty to hear him. He wanted the whole nation to hear him.[3]

What could be done to relieve the suffering of humanity? Townsend thought and read. From his "random readings" he wrote the first draft of the now famous Townsend Plan.[4] He rushed the plan to his friend Clements, who was skeptical, but said he would study it. Clements spent several weeks of reading in the library and was then convinced the plan was good. He added one point and became a co-founder of the movement.

The plan is simplicity itself.[5] It has only three essential parts: (1) All citizens of the United States, 60 years old or over, shall receive a monthly pension of $200. (2) Every person accepting this monthly pension shall agree under oath to spend it within the boundaries of the United States within 30 days. (3) The pensions will be financed by a 2 per cent tax on all business transactions.

This is the proposal offered to "provide an adequate plan of recovery from the devastating financial depression which has so dreadfully afflicted us as a people." Among other things the plan will, according to its founders, "restore national prosperity without inflation . . . provide immediate employment for all . . . reduce crime . . . reduce taxes . . . balance the budget."[6] Or, as Dr. Townsend said in one of his speeches, our plan will "restore prosperity through supplying the people with purchasing power so that the wheels of industry will again turn; frankly face the fact of a permanent army of unemployed because of machine efficiency and solve this unemployment problem in a clean and rational manner

[3] R. G. Swing, Dr. Townsend solves it all, *Nation*, 140, 1935, 268-270.

[4] The "original" of the Townsend Plan is variously said to be an ironical suggestion by Bruce Barton, published in *Vanity Fair*, August 1931, or an adaptation of technocracy, written by Steward McCord.

[5] The official statement of the plan and the arguments for it are contained in the official booklet by Francis E. Townsend and Robert E. Clements, *The Townsend Plan*, Washington, D. C.: National Headquarters, 1935.

[6] *Ibid.*, 5.

and finally assure every person that he will be provided for by a grateful government in his old age."[7]

The figure of $200 a month was set because "it has been shown by statisticians that an investment of $2,000 to $2,500 in commercial production is required to make possible the permanent employment of one worker,"[8] and because "a standard of living measured by anything less than $200 per month does not permit the enjoyment of enough of the spiritual, educational and artistic features of life to bring out the really valuable traits of human character and make the most of our citizenship. Since the manufactured wealth of the nation for the single year of 1929 was almost one thousand dollars for each man, woman, and child in the nation, to say nothing of the unmanufactured wealth produced in that year, it is apparent that we can afford a minimum standard of living for adults measured by $200 per month. This amount is not in excess of the amount earned on the average by people above the age of sixty years since each generation of people above the age of sixty produces over and over the entire wealth of the nation. Practically all wealth must be renewed every forty years or so."[9]

This is no place to discuss the practicability of the Plan itself. The figures are loose and often vary with the occasion. The founders believe, for example, that "it will only be a few years until we shall be compelled to drop the retirement age to 55 or, perhaps, 50."[10] Suffice it to say that the plan is thoroughly condemned by all economists of any standing, whether they are of a conservative or a liberal brand. They have issued special reports to indicate the catastrophe that would result if the plan were adopted.[11] They point out, among other things, that the transactions tax proposed would not begin to yield the amount of money necessary to finance pensions; that the plan would enormously increase prices, reduce farm incomes and real wages, increase unemployment; that the administration of the collection and supervision of the transactions tax would be

[7] Nicholas Roosevelt, *The Townsend Plan*, New York: Doubleday, Doran, 1936, 7.

[8] Townsend and Clements, *op. cit.*, 8.

[9] *Ibid.*, 29.

[10] *Ibid.*, 30.

[11] *The Economic Meaning of the Townsend Plan*, report of twenty-two social scientists of the University of Chicago (edited by Harry D. Gideonse), Public Policy Pamphlet No. 20, Chicago: University of Chicago Press, 1936; *Report of the Committee on Old Age Security*, New York: Twentieth Century Fund, 1936; *The Townsend Scheme*, New York: National Industrial Conference Board, 1936.

tupendous and costly; that the plan would not distribute money
on the basis of need and that, even if the proposal is only talked
about and not adopted, it "distracts attention from more reasonable
pension plans."

But the Plan was conceived and was officially announced by its
founders on New Year's Day of 1934. Why did it spread like wild-
fire? Why did it become the backbone of a national political party
in 1936? Why did it become both the hope of millions and the
bête noire of serious political leaders, social scientists, and laymen?
Before we continue the story of the movement's development, we
must pause briefly to examine the social context within which the
plan was let loose.

Social Setting

It is both unnecessary and impossible to review here the familiar
picture of economic and social discontent that has been part of the
American scene since the depression of 1929. The Townsend Plan
came at a time when there was a growing recognition of the problem of technological unemployment and of the rise in the age level
of the population. Furthermore, the idea was spreading that the
country could provide people with more consumable goods, if production and distribution were somehow better arranged. Moreover,
the question of more equal distributions of wealth was discussed
and publicized everywhere. A few facts regarding the economic
framework of our culture at this time and some poll data regarding
the needs and opinions of the population must suffice to outline some
characteristics of the social context into which the Townsend Plan
so swiftly penetrated.

Income distribution and needs. The distribution of incomes in the
United States is by now an old story to any student of the social
sciences. But it must be repeated again since its implications, which
for the social psychologist explain any economic panacea, are so
important. The chart on page 174, taken from the report of the National Resources Committee dealing with consumer incomes in the
United States,[12] summarizes the distribution of incomes of the 29
million families in this country for 1935-36.

[12] National Resources Committee, *Consumer Incomes in the United States: Their
Distribution in 1935-36,* Washington: United States Government Printing Office,
1938, 3.
There is no completely reliable information on income distribution by age groups.

As summarized in the Committee's report, the chart indicates tha[t]
"14 per cent of all families received less than $500 during the yea[r]
studied, 42 per cent received less than $1,000, 65 per cent less tha[n]
$1,500, and 87 per cent less than $2,500." When the proportion o[f]

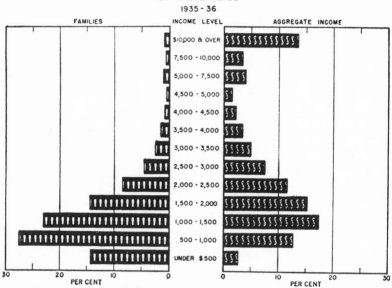

DISTRIBUTION OF FAMILY INCOME IN THE UNITED STATES
BY INCOME LEVEL
1935 - 36

the aggregate income of families in various economic brackets i[s]
analyzed, we find that "42 per cent of families with incomes under
$1,000 received less than 16 per cent of the aggregate, while 3 per cen[t]
with incomes of $5,000 and over received 21 per cent of the total.
The incomes of the top 1 per cent accounted for a little over 13 per
cent of the aggregate."

These statistics may be humanized by comparing them to the
answers given by a representative population to the question asked
by the American Institute of Public Opinion (AIPO), "How much
income a year do you think the average family of four needs for
health and comfort?" The median amount indicated was $38 a
week or $1,950 a year.[13] In other words, the income Americans think

---

Some of the difficulties encountered in the search for such data are reported by Marjorie Shearon in *Soc. Sec. Bull.*, March 1938, 1, 5-16.

[13] American Institute of Public Opinion, release July 18, 1937.

a family of four *should* have is an income that exceeds the income which approximately three-fourths of such families actually *do* have.[14] The *Fortune* poll asked its population: "What do you really think would be a perfectly satisfactory income for you?" All people did not say a million dollars. About 60 per cent of them would find an income of less than $3,000 "perfectly satisfactory."[15] This is an income which only 7 per cent of the population was actually receiving in 1936.[16]

Just what people would probably do with an increased income has been carefully analyzed in another report of the National Resources Committee.[17] This prediction clearly indicates that increased incomes would by no means go entirely for the purchase of "luxury" goods. If, for example, the total possible expenditure increased by two-thirds, there would probably be a 44 per cent increase in the purchase of food. "Undoubtedly part of the increased food expenditure would go into an improvement in quality—more milk, meat, and fresh vegetables—and only part into an increase in quantity."[18] The amount spent for housing would go up 57 per cent, for clothing 88 per cent, for medical care 88 per cent, for recreation 122 per cent, for education 134 per cent. Such figures clearly reflect the fact that people want and are in need of better food, better housing, more medical care, more education, and the like. This is further illustrated by answers to an AIPO question, "Have you ever put off going to the doctor because of the cost?" Forty-two per cent answered yes. *Fortune* asked, "How much money has your household spent during the last year for dental bills?" Seventy-two per cent answered either nothing or less than $25.[19] This is certainly not because all these people had perfect teeth.

Some derived drives. In addition to the satisfaction of physical needs is the equally important satisfaction of more highly derived motives stemming from civilized life in a complicated, interdepend-

[14] National Resources Committee, *op. cit.*, 36.

[15] *Fortune*, February 1940.

[16] National Resources Committee, *op. cit.*, 6.

[17] National Resources Committee, *Structures of the American Economy*, pt. I: *Basic Characteristics*, Washington: United States Government Printing Office, 1939, 14 f.

[18] *Ibid.*, 15.

[19] *Fortune*, Oc ,er 1936.

ent society. As we have already pointed out,[20] these derived drives from the point of view of the individual, can be just as demanding as more primitive needs. One such need is that for economic security. How well is it satisfied? The AIPO asked the question, "If you lost your job and couldn't find other work, about how long could you hold out before you had to apply for relief?" Over 50 per cent of the population not already on relief reported that they could last less than six months.[21] Another general derived need is for the maintenance of one's status. How is this satisfied?

The AIPO asked people to what *social* class in this country they felt they belonged and also of what *economic* group they thought they were a member. The results in per cent are contained in Table III.[22]

Table III

	Social-Class Identification	Economic-Group Identification
Upper	6	1
Upper middle	14	6
Middle	63	41
Lower middle	11	21
Lower	6	31

At least a third of the people, then, seem to feel that they belong in a social group that their economic status does not properly fit. And what chance do people feel they have to improve their positions? *Fortune* asked, "Do you think that the years ahead hold for you, personally, a good chance for advancement or the probability of no improvement over your present position?" A third of the people saw no probability of improvement; a larger percentage of those in the older age groups and the lower income groups were pessimistic.[23]

The desire for congenial work must be satisfied in this age of specialization if people are to feel properly adjusted. But over 40 per cent of the population would choose a different career or occupation

[20] Ch. 3.
[21] American Institute of Public Opinion, release, Aug. 24, 1938.
[22] *Ibid.*, release, Apr. 2, 1939.
[23] *Fortune*, February 1940.

f they could start life over again and do as they pleased. Only about
:o per cent of factory laborers would *not* care to change their occu-
)ations; only 30 per cent of people in the poor economic group
vould *not* want to change their jobs.[24] And with so many people
loing things they dislike to earn a living, how many of them can
xpect some vacation from their routine? When *Fortune* asked,
'How many days' vacation do you expect to have this year?" 45 per
ent of the population answered, "None."[25]

This story of discontent as reflected in the wishes and opinions
)f the American people could be amplified with dozens of illustra-
ions comparable to the few we have given.[26] They all point to the
onclusion that most people do not have the economic security, the
ducation, the work, or the leisure they desire. There is more than
)oetry, then, in the phrases of the Townsend Plan founders when
hey talk of the present "dark clouds of distrust and gloom and
lespair," and of "the bleak and fearful winter" that lies ahead for
ging people.

Ignorance of current events and possible solutions. How can these
lark clouds be dissipated? Solutions to the problem of satisfying
t least some of the needs of the people have been proposed by
xperts; some solutions have been attempted through state and
ederal legislation; some have been widely publicized. But there is
mple evidence that a large proportion of the population, particularly
he lower cultural groups with the greatest need, is either unaware
f possible remedies offered or, being aware of them, knows little
bout them or is disinterested. For the federal, state, or other institu-
ionalized action, either planned or in operation, apparently appears
) the single individual as comparatively impersonal and remote.
t is not easy for a busy, worried, uneducated person, already
arassed with pressing problems of his own that demand immediate
)lution, to see the significance in his life of a certain foreign policy,
 certain agricultural subsidy, or a certain regulation of the stock
xchange. To be sure, more people do have opinions on issues that
re apparently less remote to their interests or that fall within the

[24] *Ibid.*, January 1938.
[25] *Fortune*, July 1936.
[26] The complete published results of the American Institute of Public Opinion and
ortune polls are regularly contained in the *Publ. Opin. Quart.*

scope of existing frames of reference.[27] But, with government's grow
ing more complex and more impersonal, it is not rare to find a sig
nificant proportion of people baffled. This ignorance and bewilde
ment of the people may also be illustrated if we select a few issue
which the public opinion polls have posed to representative citizen
and if we note the size of the "no opinion" vote—the percentage c
people who, for one reason or another, just have not made up thei
minds on the issue at hand.[28]

QUESTION	No Opinion	DA
If you were assured complete medical and hospital care for yourself in case of accident or illness how much a month would you be willing to pay for this service?	34	6/
In general, do you approve or disapprove of what Father Coughlin says?	47	4/
If you had to choose between Fascism and Communism, which would you choose?	52	6/
Have you an opinion on the National Labor Relations Board?	63	2/
Do you think the Wagner Labor Act is fair?	54	4/
Do you approve of the TVA?	52	4/
Do you think that government regulation of the stock exchanges has helped investors?	42	9/
Which labor leader do you like better: Green of the AF of L, or Lewis of the CIO?	43	9/
Which type of labor union do you favor: one single union for all workers in an industry (the CIO) or separate unions for each craft in an industry (like carpenters, masons, etc.)	30	3/
Would you like to see the Republican Party be more liberal or more conservative than it was in the presidential campaign of 1936?	31	10/
In politics, do you regard yourself as a radical, a liberal or a conservative?	26	3/
Have you heard about Secretary Hull's efforts to make trade treaties with other countries? (No.)	51	2/

Intolerance. In spite of the apparent need for a serious examinatic
of the political, economic, and social presuppositions and of th
traditions, systems, and specific legislation that have so far failed t
produce a more perfect society, the people who compose that societ
and who suffer from its maladjustments are not anxious to have

[27] Daniel Katz, Three criteria: knowledge, conviction, and significance, *Pub
Opin. Quart.*, 1940.
[28] All data taken from the American Institute of Public Opinion.

horoughly discussed. Freedom of speech is frequently restricted to reedom for those essentially on one's own side of the fence or for hose who want to talk about trivial things. Again, a few examples rom the polls will illustrate the state of affairs (figures in per cent).

Do you think that in America anybody should be allowed to speak on any subject any time he wants to, or do you think there are times when free speech should be prohibited or certain subjects or speakers prohibited?[29]

Anybody, any subject, any time	49%
Prohibit some	44
Don't know	7

(If prohibit some) What subjects?

Socialism, Communism, Nazism, and other isms	40%
Subjects against our Constitution or form of government	39
War, foreign, or other propaganda	11
Subjects concerning religions and morals	9
Un-American subjects	8
Subjects concerning labor, strikes, likely to cause riot	5
Politics	2
Subjects against the President	2
Other	4

Should college teachers be free to express their views on all subjects, including government and religion, in class rooms?[30]

Yes	50%
No	45
No opinion	5

Are you in favor of legislation requiring teachers in your state to take a special oath of loyalty?[31]

Yes	47%
No	34
No opinion	19

Do you think Congress should provide money to continue the Dies Committee another year?[32]

Yes	63%
No	23
No opinion	14

Regarding the distribution of income, the inability of people to atisfy certain basic needs, the latent or overt discontent resulting rom economic insecurity and thwarted hopes, the ignorance or be-vilderment of many people in search of possible ways to alleviate nwanted conditions, and the rigidity of frames of reference up-

[29] *Fortune*, February 1940.
[30] American Institute of Public Opinion, April 1936.
[31] *Ibid.*, September 1936.
[32] *Ibid.*, November 1939.

holding the "American way," these bits of data shed some ligh
on the social context into which the Townsend Plan plunged. I
such a plan had been proposed in 1928, or during some other perio
of the nation's history when relative prosperity reigned, or whe
there were still new frontiers to which the dissatisfied might migrat
in search of a more abundant life, the chances are that such a pla
would have had a stillbirth. Or, if such a plan had been proposed i
a more closely knit culture where individual differences in oppor
tunity were not so great, where people were less dependent on cir
cumstances beyond their control, where they could more easil
comprehend the mechanisms of government and project into thei
own lives the probable results of government activity, the plan woul
again, undoubtedly, have been rather short lived. But Dr. Townsen
was an aging, sympathetic American, himself suffering from th
maladjustments of the culture, himself ignorant of the complexitie
of modern government. Both he and his plan were symptoms of th
times. We must remember this as we return to the story of th
Townsend movement itself.

Growth of the Movement

After Robert E. Clements decided to back Dr. Townsend's brai
child, the idea was in the hands of an aggressive young real-estat
agent who saw clearly the need for an organization and the poss
bilities ahead if the plan were efficiently promoted. He and Townsen
rented a small office in a store building in Long Beach, California
repaired and painted it themselves, hired a stenographer, and bega
to send out leaflets to people whose names they obtained from di
ferent sources.[33] After five weeks, they were receiving about 10
replies a day, after eight weeks, 200 a day. It became apparent tha
the original office and staff were inadequate. The headquarters wer
moved to Los Angeles and 95 people were hired to handle the mai
which in September, nine months after the initiation of Old Age Re
volving Pensions, Limited, amounted to 2,000 replies a day.[34]

[33] This description of the development of the organization is merely a sketch. I
purposely omits the names of many of the people prominent in the organization a
one time or another and is not concerned with the internal politics of the movemen
These details are interesting in themselves, to show the jealousies that arose an
the way in which the plan was used by clever manipulators for their own advantag
The detailed story is told in Whiteman and Lewis, op. cit., chs. 7-14.

[34] H. Harris, Dr. Townsend's marching soldiers, Current History, February 193
43, 155-162.

The organization was financed by a membership fee of 25 cents per year, in return for which the member was sent an eighteen-page pamphlet describing the plan. The pamphlet also urged the new member to form a Townsend Club in his neighborhood. These Clubs not only would ease the administrative burden of headquarters but would also create the machinery to exert pressure on Congress. The single purpose of the Townsend Clubs, according to the pamphlet, is that "of planning uniform action to bring the Townsend Plan of old age revolving pensions to a successful conclusion by an act of Congress." This purpose is to be effected by having members circulate petitions which are sent to the Clubs from national headquarters. The petitions urge Congress at the "earliest opportunity" to adopt two bills that would put the plan into immediate operation: the first bill provides for the $200 pension for those over 60 with the provision that the money be spent in 30 days; the second bill provides for a national transactions sales tax.

As Dr. Townsend said later, these petitions were zealously distributed and eagerly signed.

> A wonderful transformation had come over the people who had taken the petition out. Hope was in their faces; a new gleam was in their eyes. These people saw that there was still a ray of sunshine for them, that they might still win a modicum of comfort in old age. So, like typical Americans, they began a battle for human rights, armed with a do-or-die spirit. The original handful of people has multiplied, first by the hundred, then by the thousands, then by the hundred thousands, and now by the millions. Between twenty and thirty million American citizens have affixed their names to these petitions to the Congress of the United States.[35]

It is difficult to check the doctor's figures. By November 1935, there were said to be 4,000 Townsend Clubs throughout the country with an average membership of 500 each. Petitions "weighing thousands of pounds" were sent to Congress. Certainly the movement spread much more quickly than even the founders had dreamed it would. In San Diego, for example, 80 Townsend Clubs were soon established with 30,000 members or almost one-fifth of the population of the town.[36] Old folks, vacationing in California, took the message home with them to the East and Middle-west.

[35] Roosevelt, *op. cit.*, 7 f.
[36] R. L. Neuberger and K. Loe, Old people's crusade, *Harper's*, 1936, **172**, 426-438.

Although the movement extended its base, control was still highl
centralized. Clements saw to it that all state managers were appointe
by national headquarters and not elected by local vote. The consti
tutions presented to the Clubs for adoption provided no opportunit
for deviation from the national program. The headquarters reserve
the right to revoke, without trial, the charter, funds, and records o
any local Club. Late in 1934, national headquarters were moved t
Washington in order to facilitate political activity. With the founder
and their staff went a new corps of statisticians and economists
And in January 1935—only one year after the inauguration of th
plan—a bill to make the Townsend Plan a law was introduced int
the House by a California representative who had been elected or
the basis of a platform which contained nothing but the advocac
of the Townsend idea.

The national treasury continued to receive the dues of the mem
bers. It was also swelled by the formation of the Townsend Nationa
Legion, a special organization in which membership could be ob
tained by paying dues of one dollar a month. The sale of Townsend
buttons, bearing the motto, "Youth for work—age for leisure," and
of papers and other advertising matter, sent out by headquarters
helped both the national treasury and local clubs, which wer
allowed to keep a percentage of the returns on such material but wer
not allowed to keep any of the regular membership dues.

It was almost inevitable that an idea that had proved to be suc
a "natural," that was corralling so many people who had money t
support it, should also attract certain individuals or vested interest
whose motives were less sincere and honest than those of the goo
doctor. A well-known San Francisco public-relations counsel o
dubious reputation was soon a power behind the throne; chai
stores, which would profit by the plan since they would only hav
to pay one transactions tax, publicized the plan and advertised in it
literature; organized opponents of public ownership, unions, and
"radicals" tried to use the new machinery for their own devices
Hence, to the ingenuity of the founders was added the professiona
advice of experienced organizers and promoters.

Speakers were sent all over the country to ask old people how the
would like to have $200 a month "to do with as you want—provide
you spend it." Mass picnics were organized with elaborately decorate

platforms, bands, microphones, and picked orators. Dr. Townsend himself was the star performer at many of these. Traveling by airplane he was able to address thousands of people all over the country in a short space of time. One day, for example, he talked to 5,000 people at a picnic in northern California, flew south and addressed another picnic with 50,000 in the audience.

In order to keep the increased number of geographically scattered followers informed of developments and united in efforts, a paper—the *National Townsend Weekly*—was started, early in 1935. And in order to widen the appeal of the movement and increase its political strength, a vigorous campaign was begun about the same time to attract young and middle-aged people. It is not difficult to imagine the many reasons why young people would become enthusiastic about a plan which gave each of their elders $200 a month. It would remove the burden of support from their shoulders; the indulgence of parents and grandparents would undoubtedly augment the coffers of younger family members; the removal of older people from business and professional life would create more jobs for youth. And, as the founders were quick to point out, youth deserves an opportunity.

> Each year (they say) the schools and colleges are turning out many thousands of young men and women prepared to take their place in life. These must be provided with opportunity to work out their ideas and purposes. They are the foundation of today upon which is built a greater tomorrow. They must have security on which to establish an occupation, a business, a home, and to rear a family to carry on after them. They must be given a chance. There must be work for them to do, the work of building a greater America. They must be able to look forward into the future with assurance that they will receive just consideration for their years of service.

Few people, no matter what their age, could object to this.

In the fall of 1935, the Townsend movement was sufficiently organized to launch a national political convention. Thousands of faithful followers trekked to Chicago, stayed in cheap hotels and rooming houses, heard dozens of speeches extolling the plan, outlining responsibilities, urging the listeners to give more money and to carry on. The demonstration was of such magnitude and such fervor that it was news all over the country. People everywhere learned from their daily papers what the plan was and how enthusiastically thousands of people were sacrificing for it.

Political leaders began to get worried. When Congress convened in 1936, it found several members and bills urging adoption of the plan. The wild claims of the founders might hoodwink thousands of innocent people but they could not hoodwink the majority of Congress. An investigation of both the plan and the leadership was voted in the House by a majority of 240 to 4. The financial returns of the movement to the founders was laid bare; the shady pasts of certain organizers and managers were exposed. Dr. Townsend walked out of committee hearings and instructed his lieutenants to refuse testimony. Aside from changes in the internal politics of the movement, the investigation accomplished no concrete purpose. The public had been enlightened. But, for the followers, Dr. Townsend became a martyr who was being persecuted by one-sided, prejudiced un-Americans. The *Weekly* urged that the whole investigation had been arranged by the Liberty League and its millionaire backers who were staging an unprecedented Roman holiday to dishonor a man whose only interest was to help the common people. Any arguments or figures uncovered by the inquiring congressmen were branded as untrustworthy by the *Weekly* which, the followers were told, was the only source of information telling the truth.

That the movement had not suffered appreciably from the inquiry was amply demonstrated by the attendance at the second national convention held in Cleveland in July 1936. It is estimated that 12,000 people came. Clements told them that the movement now had 5,000,000 members and 25,000,000 supporters. In addition to the co-founders and the usual Townsend speakers, two new men were seen and heard at the convention. The Reverend Gerald Smith, who wore the mantle of Huey Long and his Share the Wealth movement, was a principal speaker. He took a Bible from his pocket, condemned Roosevelt and all radicals, and, after divesting himself of coat and collar, outdid even himself in rabble-rousing. The Reverend Charles E. Coughlin continued the Roosevelt attack in his own oratorical tradition. Congressman William Lemke endorsed the idea of providing old people with $200 a month and won Townsend's personal support for his Union Party. All speakers were lustily cheered except Norman Thomas, socialist, who reminded his listeners

hat Father Coughlin himself had formerly called the Plan "economic insanity."

The movement continued as a political power. In 1938, Townsend
instructed his adherents to vote against the New Deal. He explained
that its Social Security program was a snare and a delusion. "No New
Dealers can be full-bodied Townsendites," he said. Compromise was
not possible. It was an all or none affair.[37] In the election of 1940,
Townsend himself worked for the Republican candidate, believing
that the Republicans endorsed pensions. However, some of his
lieutenants worked for the Democrats, hence the votes of the followers were undoubtedly more divided than usual.

SUSTAINING THE MICROCOSM

In accepting the scheme of Dr. Townsend, his followers have
obtained new standards of judgment. These standards of judgment
provide a general frame of reference that directs their specific opinions. People who have in common these standards of judgment and
this frame of reference may be conveniently conceptualized as
members of a microcosm—a common subjective world composed
of social values that are not held by the majority of people in the
larger culture. If the microcosm is to be held together, if it is to
grow and sometime replace with its values the accepted values of
the outside world, it must be carefully nurtured. This process may
be facilitated by various devices. Some of them may arise quite spontaneously from the followers themselves; some may be consciously
planned by the organizers. They all serve to preserve the values of
the microcosm.

The leader. An important feature of the Townsend movement is
the marked submission of the followers to the leader, Dr. Townsend.
It is especially easy for old people to identify themselves with him.
He is like them. He understands their worries and their needs.
Although he often rides in chartered planes, he is careful to preserve
his "folksy" manner. It would probably be rather difficult for him
to do otherwise. When on the platform in the summer months, he
may be seen with his coat off, his suspenders much in evidence.
During the Cleveland convention he received reporters in his hotel

[37] R. L. Neuberger, Townsend racket, new phase, *The Nation*, 1938, **147**, 259-260.

room with his shoes off. Such episodes from his public life remind his followers that he is still one of them.

It was almost inevitable that a man who could create a plan that gives benefits so immediately and who could put his energy so completely into his self-appointed task should be hailed as a modern Messiah. In club meetings he is constantly referred to as "that great humanitarian," as a man "truly inspired by God." So it is not inappropriate for the *Weekly* to sustain the notion and say, "We believe Dr. Townsend's perception of such an idea is not an accident but rather an answer to the prayers of tens of millions of organized children of God lost in a wilderness of doubt." And the lieutenants of the movement in the great conventions are sure of a cheer when they state that "someday men will talk of Dr. Townsend as we now speak of George Washington or Abraham Lincoln." Robert Clements is regarded as the modern Alexander Hamilton or the General Grant of earlier days. Because of this adulation, Townsend himself needs no fanfare or rhetorical tricks to get the rapt attention of an audience. When pitted against such orators as Gerald Smith and Father Coughlin, it was possible for Dr. Townsend to read his speech in what reporters described as a "dry, flat voice" and to receive a "thunderous applause." The leader is quick to sustain this identification and to show his followers that he is what he is only because of them.

> The movement is yours, my friends . . . Without you I am powerless, but with you I can remake the world for mankind!

Symbols and songs. Townsendites are given many opportunities to identify themselves publicly with the movement. Buttons may be purchased for ten cents, special Townsend license plates, radiator emblems, and tire covers may be purchased for the automobile. Slogans are numerous. Some samples are: "The three emancipators —Washington, Lincoln, Townsend"; "First we laughed—then enlisted"; "Honor thy father and thy mother"; "Enact the Townsend Plan in this Congress"; "The abundant life begins here and now"; "Millions of jobs for young people, billions of smiles for old people." Special Townsend songs, with words adapted to well-known music are sung at meetings. To the music of *Onward Christian Soldiers* go the words:

Onward Townsend soldiers
Marching as to war
With the Townsend banner
Going on before
Our devoted leaders
Bid depression go,
Join them in the battle
Help them fight the foe.

To the tune of *Marching through Georgia*:

All the mills will turn their wheels, the factories will run,
Youth will find activity and work that must be done,
Older folks can take their ease and have a bit of fun,
And will be grateful to Townsend.

The revised words of the *Battle Hymn of the Republic* are:

Mine eyes have caught the vision of our Dr. Townsend's plan,
Which is sweeping o'er the nation, only as a good thing can,
'Twill benefit each boy and girl, each woman and each man,
When it becomes a law.

Importance of the movement. Members are constantly being reminded that the values and plans which make up their world are the only hope of achieving a better life and that it is their honor and duty to see that the mission succeeds. The last sentence in a specially prepared *Speaker's Manual* points out that this is "perhaps the greatest composite picture of national political economy ever presented under one cover in the brevity, clarity, and completeness found here." Followers are told that their movement is composed of millions of people united in important work.

Where Christianity numbered its hundreds in its beginning years, our cause numbers its millions. And without sacrilege we can say that we believe that the effects of our movement will make as deep and mighty changes in civilization as did Christianity itself (said Dr. Townsend).

At the Chicago convention he stated:

For every 100 delegates here assembled today a million prayers go up to the God of Justice that our efforts in this convention may not fail. We dare not fail. Our Plan is the sole and only hope of a confused and distracted nation . . . We have become an avalanche of political power that no derision, no ridicule, no conspiracy of silence can stem.

And Townsend disciples say that "Dr. Townsend is leading a greater army than has ever been known in history."

Authorities accept the Plan. Since the details of the operation of the Plan are often difficult to figure out and since the whole thing is likely to appear fanciful, the leaders constantly emphasize the fact that experts who really understand such complicated matters are wholeheartedly back of the idea. In the official description of the Plan,[38] the reader is told that "this plan has been submitted to able statisticians and economists, and their testimony is that it is thoroughly sound and workable." They point out that "economists estimate that each person spending $200 per month creates a steady job for one additional worker at good pay" or that "money circulates under the present system or it does not circulate in accord with whims or fears or emotions of a few men or institutions that control the major portion of the money of the land." The same document quotes the reasons given by "a nationally known lawyer, author and lecturer," by a "nationally known statistician," by a "learned jurist," a "noted educator," a "former Lieutenant Commander of the Navy," and the "editor of a daily newspaper in one of the flourishing cities of a great state, a man who is successful in business, and whose business it is to know the hearts of human beings, know the facts which control human lives, know the conditions of life, of business, of industry." After reciting the testimonials of these men, the founders conclude:

> These are the witnesses. Judges of Courts, Commanders of Battleships, Editors of Newspapers—are these the ones who seek lazy lives at the expense of others? Are these the unthinking and the followers of vagaries? Or are they the patriots who love their country, the humanitarians who love humanly, the thinkers who are able to recognize Truth?

The *Weekly* reports to its readers that a "noted university teacher" pointed out "with facts and figures, not only the workability of the Plan by sound economics but that in truth and in fact the Plan itself or something very similar to it will have to be made the law

[38] Townsend and Clements, *op. cit.*

of the land before any permanent prosperity or measure of security for the masses can be expected to obtain in this Nation."[39] It was delighted to print Kathleen Norris's comment that she thought the plan was "audacious, original, inspired." Sometimes, apparently, big names are used rather loosely. The leaders have quoted statements which they claim were made by a nationally known statistician, formerly chief statistician of the Department of Labor and the Department of Commerce. But this statistician swore before the congressional committee that he never made any such statement.

It is not difficult for the national headquarters to counteract unfavorable statements that the followers may learn from other sources. The leaders prohibit the sale of any literature at club meetings that has not been approved by national headquarters. They point out that all newspapers other than the *Weekly* are against the plan because the transactions tax would cut into their incomes. The adverse criticism of economists is not taken seriously. The Townsend system of economics "outrages the economists," according to one advocate of the movement, "probably because they never thought of it."[40] Other economists who condemn the Townsendites are not highly respected since "they don't seem to have solved much themselves." Townsend has outbid all competitors.[41]

[39] *National Townsend Weekly*, May 4, 1936, 5.

[40] M. J. Dorman, *Age before Booty*, New York: Putnam, 1936, 24.

[41] The way in which serious criticism is officially handled may be illustrated by an editorial from a small pro-Townsend paper which is reprinted in the *Weekly* (*National Townsend Weekly*, April 13, 1936, 10). The editorial under the headline, "It Is All Great Hoax, Say Professors," is an answer to the widely publicized, thoroughly documented and closely reasoned analysis of the plan prepared by the University of Chicago Round Table (*The Economic Meaning of the Townsend Plan, op. cit.*).

Up to within a few weeks ago the Townsend Old Age Pension Plan received but scant recognition from brain trust leaders and the great American press, allegedly always ready to print the news. But, presto, a simple twist of the wrist, a quick shifting of the political kaleidoscope and now Townsend Old Age Pensions get editorial and news space galore which everyday looms before the reading public. True, most of the space devoted to the subject is defamatory, explaining how it just cannot be done, but the change of attitude is most apparent. The other day 21 brain trust professors from the University of Chicago, all of them being "experts in the field of economics, taxation, public welfare and public administration," reported their findings concerning the Townsend Plan. Everyone of the brain trusters are highly paid; not a single one would be able to live on less than several hundred thousand annually; not a mother's son of them caring a tinker's how the old folks live or die, but they were unanimous

So much for the history of the movement itself, the characteristic of its organization, and the techniques it uses to sustain the interes of its followers. We have said that the movement has many follower Who are these people and just how does the Townsend Plan fit int their lives?

THE TOWNSENDITES AND THEIR SUPPORTERS

Observers of Townsend Clubs, picnics, and conventions hav drawn pictures of the "typical" Townsendite. According to on of them:[42]

He is a tired American. His face is lined with weariness and age. His shoulders are bowed. He is part gray, part bald. He is clean, well-dressed, seldom fat. He is perhaps a small-town merchant, or a farmer, or a banker, or a clerk. He is a worker, with himself, and a wife, and perhaps a few children to support. He is not a pauper, nor even very near to poverty. But he is a man who feels, now that it has been pointed out to him, that he deserves as an elementary right what all his life he has been working for—economic security. "I paid all my taxes, all the time," you hear him say. "The country owes me that $200 a month. Old people should be allowed to live in peace. If we retire, the young can work."

A similar individual is constructed by another observer:[43]

in the opinion that money for paying the $200 a month pension cannot be raised by any sort of transactions tax.

So that group of 21, most of whom probably pay no income tax, and who are averse to the privileged class being asked to pay, dismantled old-age pensions in their own minds and made public their views, what they claimed was an unbiased opinion of the facts. It would be "insanely extravagant, they alleged, to pay $200 without regard to need." In other words, an old man and wife, both of whom have toiled through the years to bring up the children, who have suffered poverty and undergone hardships untold, are not entitled to as much as the old couple who have lived in ease and idleness, but now, through chance, are without funds. The capacity of one to spend money "intelligently" makes it necessary that he receive more.

Well, those fellows ought to have the dose they propose administered to themselves. Mental and bodily suffering is something that cannot be measured in terms of dollars and cents. But in all their wisdom, those 21 failed to offer a better plan. Their whole plea for defeat of the Plan lies in the fact "that taxes would fall unjustly on everybody who got in its way and could not evade it in some way." That the rich simply refuse to pay their just share of the transactions tax is the sole reason for all opposition to those $200 pensions.

[42] S. Pass, Life begins at 60, *Christian Century*, 1935, **52**, 1411 f.

[43] Russell Porter, Looking for utopia along the Townsend trail, *New York Times Magazine*, Feb. 5, 1939.

Mr. X is over 60. He has a wife about the same age. They have grown children, probably married and with children of their own. Most likely Mr. X is a farmer, small-town storekeeper, clerk or mechanic. He has been thrifty and industrious all his life, but the depression caught him at a bad age. He lost his job, or his home, or his savings, or all of them, and he did not have the strength or the wit of a younger man to regain them. Of course, there is Mr. Y, also, typical of the shiftless and lazy in the pension movement, but he can be taken for granted. Mr. X grew up in an era when country people were devoutly religious, and he and his wife are regular churchgoers and readers of the Bible. All his life he has been accustomed to the biblical picture of an honorable and venerable old age. He has looked forward to his declining years as a period in which he would be one of the elders of the community, his words heeded with love and obedience in the family circle and with respect by all, and his sere and yellow days passed in slippered ease and contentment.

Now he has suffered cruel disillusionment. He has the aches and infirmities common to all old people—he finds himself poor, lonely, friendless and haunted by the specter of insecurity for himself and his family. He feels unwanted and unwelcome. He may be getting old-age pension and his sons may be on home relief or WPA. His pension is public charity and he feels, in the words of the psalm, that "the righteous are forsaken and their seed begging bread" . . . He complains that New Deal social security means little or nothing to him. If he is employed he would have to work twenty years more, or until he is over 80, before he could receive substantial insurance payments under the present set-up. If he is unemployed now, he says, the best he can hope for is what he calls "pauper's relief." He says he must wait until he is 65 and then get a "pittance" in most states.

It is, of course, difficult to know just how accurate such portraits of the "typical" Townsendite are. Somewhat more reliable knowledge of the members or supporters of the plan are available from two sources: a nationwide survey of persons who approve the Townsend Plan and case studies of a few Townsendites.

People who favor the plan. In January of 1939, interviewers of the American Institute of Public Opinion were asking a representative sample of the population all over the country, "Have you heard of the Townsend Plan?" and, if you have, "Are you in favor of this Plan?" Ninety-five per cent of those questioned had heard of the plan. When this 95 per cent was asked whether or not it favored the Plan, 12 per cent had no opinion, 35 per cent said "yes," 53 per cent said "no." No significant differences appeared between persons who live in different sections of the country: New Englanders and persons in the east-central states were no less enthusiastic than middle or far westerners.

However, as one would expect, significant differences do appear when the population is divided according to age and economic status: older and poorer people are more in favor of the Plan. But of these two determinants of opinion, economic status is far more important than age. From Table IV it can be seen that the difference

Table IV

People Who Favor the Townsend Plan—Divided Separately
by Age and Economic Status (Figures in Per Cent)

Age	Yes	No	No Opinion
Under 30	31	53	16
30–50	34	53	13
50–60	37	54	9
Over 60	46	46	8
Economic Status			
Above average	17	76	7
Average	28	59	13
Poor	49	42	9
On relief or old-age assistance	69	26	5

between people under 30 and those above 60 who approve the Plan is only 15 per cent, whereas the difference in the "yes" answers is 21 per cent between people who are relatively well-to-do and those who are poor, and the difference jumps to 52 per cent between those who are well-to-do and those who are on relief or who are now receiving old-age assistance.

But Table IV obscures a cardinal point: people in the lower economic brackets tend to be more in favor of the plan than those in the higher income groups *irrespective* of age. For the American people, the Plan has clearly become a remedy to relieve general economic insecurity. It is no longer a Plan whose benefits are felt to be restricted to the old folks. The approximate rank order of people most favorably disposed toward the Plan would be:

1. Reliefers, over 50 years of age
2. Poor people, over 60
3. Reliefers, under 50
4. Poor people, under 50
5. Average-income people, over 60
6. Average-income people, under 60
7. Well-to-do people, over 30
8. Well-to-do people, under 30

Table V

PEOPLE WHO FAVOR THE TOWNSEND PLAN—GROUPED BOTH ACCORDING TO
AGE AND ECONOMIC STATUS (FIGURES IN PER CENT)

Economic Status	Age	Yes	No	No Opinion
Above average	Under 30	7	81	12
	30–50	16	78	6
	50–60	18	76	6
	Over 60	21	72	7
Average	Under 30	24	59	17
	30–50	28	59	13
	50–60	30	62	8
	Over 60	36	57	7
Poor	Under 30	41	42	17
	30–50	41	39	20
	50–60	46	39	15
	Over 60	68	32	0
On relief or old-age assistance	Under 30	60	27	13
	30–50	62	24	14
	50–60	73	19	8
	Over 60	70	21	9

Case studies. If the hopes, and ambitions, the worries and responsibilities, the record of the past and the dreams of the future of several hundred Townsendites could be woven into case studies, the statistical picture of those who favored the Townsend Plan would be greatly enriched and made more psychologically relevant. For the indices of age and economic status we have found so important are, at best, substitute indices which give the psychologist clues to look for. What he is interested in primarily are the mental contexts and the motivations that result from age or economic environment. Owing to limitations of both time and money, it has been impossible to make an exhaustive series of case studies. But a dozen Townsendites in different parts of the country were interviewed and these reports give us some insight into the way the Townsend Plan fits into the lives of a few real people. Three of these case studies are reported below.[44]

Case 1. Mr. Henry Stone is now 73 years old. He was born and raised on a marginal farm. He finished the sixth grade of school. Stone's first job was as a driver in a livery stable. Then he worked as a lumberjack for several years, but found he needed a more regular income and got a job in a glove factory. This work also proved to be seasonal, so he tried farming for 15 years, worked on the roads, drove teams, and started a small junk business. Then he went back to the glove factory, where he has been for the past 20 years. He has always worked hard and has never been idle. It wasn't until the depression in the early 1930's that he got really worried about making a living, and even then he managed to stay off relief.

He lives with his wife, a daughter, grandson and a fellow worker who pays the Stones $11 a week for his room and board. Until a few months ago the daughter, who is divorced and has a nine-year-old boy, was employed in a shoe factory. Her wages averaged between $8 and $10 a week, but she lost her job when the company heard that she had made a complaint to the Wages and Hours Administration. The family pays $18 a month rent for an old, dark house much in need of repair. It has no cellar, and the heat is supplied by an old-fashioned round stove set up in the dining room. The furniture is shabby and worn, but only the daughter seems to be troubled by these poor surroundings. Mr. Stone himself has no "dress-up" clothes and never thinks of dressing differently on Sundays or holidays from the way he does on regular days.

Mr. Stone has had good health and until recently always looked younger than his years. Now he is developing a bad heart. Last year he earned $450. He has always been a great talker and his speech is liberally sprinkled with profanity. He spends his spare time sitting on the front porch reading or arguing with friends.

"So you want to know about the Townsend Plan, hey? Well, come in and sit down and I'll tell you whatever you want to know. I guess I'd rather talk about that than anything else. People tell me they can't understand me because I can talk for it and against it, but that's just the way I'm built I guess. Ain't very much fun sometimes when you're both talking on the same side of the question.

[44] The writer is greatly indebted to Mr. Paul Grainger, who made these interviews for him. The narratives are reproduced exactly as Mr. Grainger recorded them. All names or other identifying characteristics are fictitious.

"I guess there never was such a thing to talk and argue about before. They can thank Dr. Townsend for that, anyway. He got a lot of people out of their houses and made them think about doing something about politics and about their government and representatives and what good they were getting out of it all.

"The Townsend Plan would be the best god-damned thing that ever happened for this country—if they'd only give it a chance. And I'll tell you why it don't get a chance. People are too damn lazy to take any interest in a good thing like this when they've got a little money and a job, and there's more people like that than there are old ones and unemployed. The only time you can get anything done to help the people is in depressions, when they're all poor and worried. Then the Congress knows its gotta pass things like the Social Security and Employment Insurance, because they know the whole country wants it.

"I'll tell you how I got into the Townsend movement. I used to go down to old Tom Haley's feed store and sit around and talk. Tom was a pretty smart fella. He was a Republican, but nevertheless he could see on both sides of the fence, and I took quite a lot of stock in what he said. *We read some about the Plan in the papers and old Tom thought it might be a pretty good thing.*

"That night a man came along in a car and he asked Tom if he cared if he parked out back of the store and eat a bit of lunch he had with him. Old Tom said, 'Sure, go ahead.' So the man did. Later on he asked if he could park and sleep in the car there all night. Tom said all right, and he asked the fellow what his business was. It seems that this man come from a state out west where the Plan was going strong, and he was trying to organize groups around here, too. So as he talked we got enthusiastic about it, and old Tom talked with some people and they got a meeting called for the courthouse one night. Old Tom see me and asked if I wasn't going up, and I said guessed I would—*wouldn't do no harm to see what they had to say. So I went an' I got all fired up over the Club,* and I entered my name and my wife's and Fred's (the roomer), and a couple of others. Paid 25 cents apiece dues.

"Only thing I never did like about it was them talking $200 a month all the time. I couldn't see that and never will. Can you see the United States government giving every old couple a nice car to ride around in? No. It didn't seem to me that it was balanced right. Two hundred dollars is more than a lot of old folks need and they wouldn't know what to do with it. Wouldn't be doing them any favor to make them spend $50 or $100 a week. They ain't geared up to living like that. Some could use it good, but most of them only want enough to get along on. If you ask for too much you're not apt to get anything. One speaker they had here kept harping on that $200 a month and he made me mad.

"So I got in when it first started here. My wife didn't think much of it though, so I had to take her name off after the first year. Fred is real enthusiastic about it, though.

"I get mad at some people. They like the Plan all right and they hope it passes, but they won't even buy one of our 10 cent buttons to wear. It takes money to run a club and pass a law and you can't do much on 25 cents a year. When they have meetings they usually pass the plate, and if they want eats they ask you to bring something or donate. I can't afford to do that so much any more. I took the *Townsend Weekly* for two years, but I've stopped now because I can't afford that either. I don't go to all the meetings any more either, since my hearing ain't what it used to be. I could follow the speaker good in the old clubrooms, but there's something about the new rooms so that I can't hear good. I'd like to go and I read all I can about it and listen to speeches on the radio, but it seems as if I don't care so much as I used to. Probably because I don't feel as good as I did.

"The newspapers don't print much about it. I guess these big advertisers and newspaper men don't want to see this Townsend Plan passed. That's the trouble with people like that. They never want to see any change of any kind. Afraid it'll take a dollar out of their pockets.

"The Social Security is a good thing, but not for me. I went over to the post office and asked the man about how much I could get, and he said he thought about $18 to $20 a month. He asked if I wanted to make out an application, and I told him I couldn't get along on that. Even the $450 I earned last year ain't enough. *Social Security is all right for the young men just starting in, but no good for us old ones. So you see it can't take the place of the Townsend Plan for us. I'll tell you one thing Townsend has done. He's made the Social Security payments higher than they first thought they would be.*

"I don't even expect to get anything out of the Townsend Plan. I really don't know if it'll ever be passed or not. If it is I probably wouldn't be here. Well, I didn't put much into it, and I never expected to get much out of it. If they came out for $50 a month, they might get somewhere. I don't think Townsend is the right man to head the thing now. He made too many enemies in Congress and he's not the right type anyway. He's a good talker all right, but when it comes to the questions they fire at him he can't answer them."

Case 2. Mr. Barber is now 63 years old. He was born on a farm in northern Pennsylvania and lived there until he was 23. He attended a rural school, completing the eighth grade. Because of an accident which badly crippled his father, Barber had to support his mother at an early age. His first job was in his uncle's general store, which also served as the local post office. Barber worked there for 15 years and was postmaster for the last few years. The store was finally disposed of to settle the uncle's estate and Barber moved to an eastern city. He and his wife were very poor when they moved to town and he had difficulty getting a good job. Finally he became janitor and caretaker for two churches and did gardening on the side. For the past 10 years he has done fairly well at this and is now buying the old-fashioned house in which he lives. One of his three sons is a minister and the whole family is very devout.

People who know Barber say he is one of the finest, gentlest, most unselfish, and hardest working men they know. For years he has been superintendent of a Sunday school. He was the first president of the local Townsend Club and is now its secretary-treasurer. He is regarded by the members as an ideal officer who exercises a needed restraining influence during the meetings.

"Yes, I was the first person in the county to join the Townsend movement. The first time we had a meeting here I got the speaker, paid his expenses, and hired the hall. That was all out of my own pocket. I first became interested in the Plan because it *sounded very reasonable to me. I had complete faith in Dr. Townsend. It is my conviction that the plan can do what it set out to do. It should make it possible for people between 60 and 95 to go on living like Americans should. In a rich country like this our old people shouldn't be objects of charity.*

"*The Plan will bring about an enforced circulation of money and in that way help the unemployed and the manufacturers and producers.* I am sure it will bring about better social and economic conditions. It has been tried out in the West, but it wasn't on a large enough scale to provide a practical test. I think that Townsend has tried to be sensible about what he said the Plan will do. I haven't any idea about how soon the Plan can be put into effect. Much depends on getting more members of Congress to sign the petition to get the Townsend resolution out of committee. We had 101 signers last year and this year there are 130. So you see we are getting stronger all the time. It may take several years, but I really think we're going to see the Townsend Plan, or something very like it, in this country. The Social Security Law cannot take care of all old people because they don't all contribute to it. The Townsend Plan covers all classes.

"It is difficult to say how many of these Congressmen, politicians, and businessmen, who say they're for the Plan, are sincere or not. Senator Downey is a good man for us. He spoke for three hours in the Senate on the Plan, and *they say* the speech had effect. Our local papers won't give us much space. Whenever they do print something in our favor, they add a few lines on the end that kind of destroy the good impression created above.

"We have 4 clubs here now and the Townsend Youth Movement has just been started. The No. 1 Club has 300 members and No. 3 has 65. I don't know how many 2 and 4 have. We have almost enough for a business and professional peoples' Club now. We have 25 out of a necessary 30 for a charter. There's more business people than you think in favor of the movement but they want their own club. I guess they don't want to mix in with the 'riffraff.'

"The $200 a month is really required to give business the big boost it needs, but no one could get that much at first. They figure now that the first pensions would come to about $40 a month. It is the New Dealers and these people working on the Social Security Act who are fighting the Townsend Plan. It's not the capitalists and manufacturers. *They* know what the Plan would do for them, and they understand it is designed for them as well as old people. Our tax is fair because it would fall on everybody equally. It wouldn't increase prices much—only about one-fifth of a cent on a loaf of bread. If a young man makes $15 a week now he'd get about $18 then, so why should he mind paying out a little more in taxes. Take the merchants. They pay more than 2 per cent to advertise and get business. They'd get much more under the Townsend Plan.

"I think I can truthfully say that outside of my family the Townsend Plan is my chief interest. *Of course I am a little selfish about it, but on the whole I think I can say that I'm thinking more about all poor old people than about myself and what I'd get.* Nothing which has been suggested can equal the Plan. And *the Plan has done so much good already by giving some people a new interest and purpose in life.*

"I went to the Cleveland Convention as a delegate, and I received the deepest impression there of the value of the Plan. You could see in the faces of those 2,000 people that they believed in it so thoroughly as a godsend to this country that they'd stake their lives on it. In helping old people today, and posterity, by bettering national economic conditions, buying power is everything and that is what the Townsend Plan would supply. I believe so strongly in all that I've told you that I wish I didn't have to earn my living. I'd like to spend my time, all my time, just working for the movement, talking about it to people and selling them our literature. You see my desk here and all these letters, books, and pamphlets. I spend most of my evenings up here working on the club business and keeping up to date on our literature. My wife says she has become a 'Townsend widow.' We have meetings once a week and card parties once in a while. *You have to have activities to hold people's interest in the Clubs.* I have to spend quite a bit of time like that—getting donations, seeing members and new prospects, and so forth."

Case 3. Billy Carver runs a filling station with his brother in a small town. Others who have operated this station have always failed and Billy is now on the ragged edge. He is now 18 years old.

Billy was brought up on a small farm. Although his father worked hard on the farm, he could not make it support his large family, and whenever possible he supplemented his farm earnings by working in a factory, on the roads, or as a garage mechanic. Billy got interested in cars while he was helping his father. He left high school at the end of the third year to try to earn enough money so he could take some technical training. He is a quiet, well-mannered, good-looking young man.

"Yes, I joined the Townsend Club—that is, the Club for younger people—about two or three months ago. They were just starting the Townsend Youth Movement here then, and there was some fella staying here from one of their headquarters, I guess, who was helping the local people get it started. He come in here and talked to us one night trying to sell us the idea of joining up in it. He said what a good time all of us young people would have if we only got behind it and put it across. And of course he told about all the good the Plan could do for the old people by giving them something to live on after they get so they can't work or find a job anymore. I thought the Plan would be a pretty good thing.

"I had heard quite a bit about it before, because my father and some of his friends were kinda interested in it. Dad wasn't a member or anything, but he was in favor of the Plan, so I knew quite a bit about it before this Club started. I kind of liked the idea of being in the Club and helping the movement along at first, but lately I haven't been able to get to the meetings at all because we've had to be here, and I'm more interested in getting this business going than anything else.

"*I wonder sometimes what us young people can do,* because older people aren't used to listening to young ones—that is, an older person mightn't have much faith in an idea that we were arguing for. They'd figure we hadn't enough experience to know what we were talking about.

"I don't think the Plan can do all that they say it will, but it ought to help some if it only had a chance. *One thing sure is that a lot of old people would quit working, give younger ones a chance to get jobs. A young fellow can't get a job anywhere these days except when you don't need any experience, and those jobs don't amount to much. Employers always ask what experience you've got, and how is anybody going to get experience if they never get a chance.* No, they don't talk any more about $200 a month. They know they couldn't get anywhere near that to start with. All they can do is divide up equally the money they get in from the sales tax.

"I don't believe it would affect me or my people much if it did go into effect. It'd take a long time for the pensions to have much effect on business. Two hundred dollars is more than the average man earns anyway. Maybe they wouldn't know what to do with it. If I had it I'd put it into the business. Lately I have been a bit doubtful about the whole thing. Some of the guys who come in here don't think much of it, and when they know you're in it you have to take a lot of kidding. It'd be a nice thing all right if it worked, but there seems to be just as good arguments against it as for it. *Still it seems as if something has got to happen to take care of all these people out of work or business'll never get like it used to be. Wouldn't do any harm to give it a try anyway. The way things look, pretty soon they'll be having sales taxes all over—just to pay for the government, and the old folks and taxpayers will be left holding the bag—with no pensions or anything.*

"This Social Security is all right so far as it goes. *I don't know very much about it* because it doesn't affect any of us. *But from what I hear,* they aren't going to pay very much. Wouldn't be any better than the old-age pensions for most people.

"I don't know what is holding up the Plan now. No, there aren't any of my friends that belong to the Club or care anything about the Townsend Plan. Maybe if I could go to more meetings I'd be better able to answer your questions. I don't think the Young People's Club is going to go over very big here. They lose interest in anything pretty quick, especially with summer coming on. *I don't just see what we can do anyway for it*—just sign our names and pay our 25 cents a year is about all."

WHY THE TOWNSEND MOVEMENT FLOURISHED

Our description of the movement, the historical setting in which it occurred, the people who participated in it, is ended. It now remains for us to summarize the psychological reasons for the movement's appeal. As psychologists, we are not so much interested in the Townsend movement itself as we are in the psychological reasons why economic panaceas of its type arise from time to time. If this case study is to serve as a prototype for similar occurrences, then, we must go beyond journalistic description, economic or sociological analysis. We want to know *why* the Townsend Plan flourished. There are at least four important reasons.

1. *Satisfaction of needs.* It is obvious that the Plan, as outlined by the leaders and as believed by the followers, would ease the material burdens and wants which we found so prevalent in the culture when the plan was proposed. In addition to the simple, primitive needs for food, clothing, and shelter, the Plan would presumably also satisfy derived needs, such as those for automobiles, travel, radios, and inside plumbing. The Plan would theoretically provide security, employment in congenial tasks, medical care, education. All these are derived, yet widespread, and very real desires of men in modern life.

A questionnaire, sent out from the national headquarters of the Townsend movement, asked the followers: "How would you spend your $200 a month?" The "first replies received to this question" are reported by the founders and reveal the needs of the faithful:[45]

[45] Townsend and Clements, *op. cit.,* 27. No details of the questionnaire or the population sampled are given, hence it is impossible to check the reliability of the results. However, when compared to other knowledge of the followers, the returns seem reasonable. The fact that medical and dental attention rank highest is not surprising if one peruses the *National Townsend Weekly.* The advertising in the paper is largely concerned with remedies for "diseases of the blood," blood pressure, piles, eczema, bunions, constipation, deafness, sinus, colitis, poor eyesight, false teeth, etc.

The results of one trial of the Townsend Plan in Chelan, Washington, are also illustrative. The local Townsend Club gave $200 to a sixty-three-year-old couple.

Oculists, doctors, dentists, nursing care, sanitariums	392
New, warm clothing	276
Self-improvement, travel, lectures, books, theaters, etc.	315
Remodeling, repairing, painting, additions to home	272
New automobile	229
Payment on taxes, debts, and mortgages	227
New furniture	222
Buy or build a home	198
Additional help in house, driving, working on lawn, etc.	153
Electrical appliances (other than radio or refrigerator)	121
Electric refrigerator	107
Insurance of various types	83
New radio	81

If this is a sample reflection of what the followers would do with extra money, it is no wonder that they flock to a man who says, "How would you like to have $200 a month to spend? You can buy that new car you have long wanted. You can travel You can pay off the mortgage. You can get little Mary that dress she wanted. You can put in a new bathtub. You can gratify any of the desires which for years you have been unable to fulfill."[46] It is no wonder that they nod with approval when a leader tells them, "We want you to have new homes, new furniture, new shoes and clothes. We want you to travel and go places. You folks have earned the right to loaf, and you're going to do it luxuriously in the near future."[47] And with the old folks provided for and distributing money, the needs of young people would in many ways be alleviated.

But other programs have made similar promises. The EPIC Plan and technocracy, launched about the same time, were also to provide for the needs of people. Socialists and Communists in this country have been trying for decades to gain converts to their proposals for a more abundant life. The contention of those who propose all these programs is that they would provide the more abundant and secure life that so many people crave. Why have they not been believed, why have their schemes not swept over the country as Dr. Townsend's has? The fact that the Townsend Plan would provide for needs is a common denominator in all these proposals. Other characteristics must differentiate it.

First they paid their Townsend Club dues, then they gave $1 to the church, then they bought some toothpaste, the Mrs. had her hair done, and they then spent the bulk of the money in paying off some debts and in storing up canned goods. *News Week,* Jan. 30, 1937, 9 f.

[46] Roosevelt, *op. cit.,* 12.

[47] E. B. White, One man's meat, *Harper's,* 1939, 179, 553-56.

2. *The Plan is simple enough to be understood.* When people are in need of food or clothing, a filling in a bad tooth or a vacation; when they work to earn money which they find is inadequate or when they would be willing to work if they had a chance; when they find circumstances pounding them for what appears to be no fault of their own; when they find themselves at the mercy of institutions, laws, or forces entirely beyond their control, they are very likely to wonder what it is all about, why they should not have at least some of the things they see others have. They need an explanation that makes sense to them. They want to give some meaning to their conditions. If they are to do anything to lessen their dissatisfaction, they must understand the causes of their dissatisfaction before they can direct their remedial energies. When people who are thus bewildered are people who have had relatively little education, when they have had neither the opportunity, the time, nor the interest to learn something of the intricacies of modern government and finance, they have no adequate frames of reference, no reliable standards of judgment by means of which they can interpret the many schemes they are told are designed to improve their lot in life. They are highly suggestible, lacking in critical ability.[48]

Because of the interdependence and complexity of various phases of modern governmental and economic machinery, only an expert can predict what effect a certain change in one part of the system would have on other parts. And even the expert realizes that his knowledge is limited, while some experts may be aware that their interpretations are restricted by their basic assumptions. In brief, any adequate remedy for the general increase in the standard of living is bound to be enormously complicated. Any one who has seriously studied banking and exchange, labor relations, social security, cooperative buying, and international finance will know this; anyone who has tried to compare the presuppositions and mechanisms of capitalism and socialism soon learns that neither system is simple.

One very obvious reason, then, why the Townsend Plan recruited so many followers was its enormous oversimplification. Like its offsprings, the "Ham 'n Eggs Plan" or "Thirty Dollars Every Thursday," the Townsend Plan neglects all basic economic problems, pulls the whole standard of living up by its own boot straps. Its terminol-

[48] See ch. 3.

ogy is not clear. The question period in one Townsend meeting shows how lightly even Dr. Townsend skips over fundamental problems.[49] As the observer reported, when the question period opened Dr. Townsend "began quietly to come apart, like an inexpensive toy."

"How much would it cost to administer?" inquired a thrifty grandmother, rising to her feet.

The Doctor frowned. "Why, er," he said. (This was the first "er" of the afternoon.) "Why, not a great deal. There's nothing about it, that is, there's no reason why it needs to cost much." He then explained that it was just a matter of the Secretary of the Treasury's making out forty-eight checks each month, one to each state. Surely that wouldn't take much of the Secretary's time. Then these big checks would be broken up by the individual state administrators, who would pay out the money to the people over sixty years of age who qualified. "We're not going to have any administrative problems to speak of," said the Doctor, swallowing his spit. The little grandmother nodded and sat down.

"Can a person get the pension if they hold property?" inquired an old fellow who had suddenly remembered his home, and his field of potatoes.

"Yes, certainly," replied the Doctor, shifting from one foot to the other. "But we do have a stipulation; I mean, in our Plan we are going to say that the money shall not go to anybody who has a gainful pursuit." An uneasy look crossed the farmer's face: very likely he was wondering whether his field of potatoes was gainful. Maybe his potato bugs would stand him in good stead at last. Already things didn't look so simple.

"How much bookkeeping would it mean for a business man?" asked a weary capitalist.

"Bookkeeping?" repeated the Doctor vaguely. "Oh, I don't think there will be any trouble about bookkeeping. It is so simple. Every businessman just states what his gross is for the 30-day period, and 2 per cent of it goes to pay the old people. In the Hawaiian Islands they already have a plan, much like mine, in operation. It works beautifully, and I was amazed, when I was there, at how few people it took to administer it. No, there'll be no difficulty about bookkeeping."

[49] This description is taken verbatim from E. B. White, *op. cit.*, with his permission.

"How will the Townsend Plan affect foreign trade?" asked an elderly thinker on large affairs.

Doctor Townsend gave him a queer look—not exactly hateful, but the kind of look a parent sometimes gives a child on an off day.

"Foreign trade?" he replied, somewhat weakly. "Foreign trade? Why should we concern ourselves with foreign trade?" He stopped. But then he thought maybe he had given short measure on that one, so he told a story of a cereal factory, and all the corn came from some foreign country. What kind of way was that—buying corn from foreigners?

Next question: "Would a person receiving the pension be allowed to use it to pay off a mortgage?"

Answer: "Yes. Pay your debts. Let's set our government a good example!" (Applause.)

And now the gentleman down front—an apple-cheeked old customer with a twinkle: "Doctor, would buying a drink count as spending your money?"

"A drink?" echoes the Doctor. Then he put on a hearty manner. "Why, if anybody came to me and wanted to drink himself into an early grave with money from the fund, I'd say, 'Go to it, old boy!'" There was a crackle of laughter, but the Doctor knew he was on slippery footing. "Don't misunderstand me," he put in. "Let's not put too many restrictions on morality. The way to bring about temperance in this world is to bring up our young sons and daughters decently, and teach them the evils of abuse. (Applause.) And now, friends, I must go. It has been a most happy afternoon."

Questions are not asked if people do not have either a certain skepticism or a sophisticated frame of reference sufficiently grounded to see that a specific problem *might* arise. And, if questions are asked by an alert Townsendite, the chances are that the frame of reference which prompts the question is based on such meager information that he is completely unable to check the validity of the answers he receives. When the interpretation provided by the Plan has been accepted, it provides a rather rigid frame of reference that only with difficulty can be dislodged by the critics. The relevance of criticism simply cannot be comprehended, since the details of the Plan itself are not explicit. The Townsendite is sure that his leader or one of the authorities who has endorsed the Plan knows the right answers.

This Plan, then, was simple enough to be understood. And, once understood, it gave people a meaning. It showed them how their desires could easily be satisfied. And it showed them that these desires could be satisfied, not in some dim and distant future, but right here and now.

> Put one billion six hundred million dollars a month into circulation, and we wouldn't have to wait thirty days—nor ten days—after the passage of the law before factory wheels would be turning fast. Almost immediately everyone would get work. We know that from experience.[50]

3. *The Plan fits old norms.* Even though Townsendites lack frames of reference adequate to interpret economic schemes, we must not suppose that their mental context is entirely blank. The overwhelming majority of them are Americans who have absorbed many of the norms of the culture in the course of life. And no matter how much the Plan would provide for needs and no matter how simple it might appear, it would not have been so swiftly accepted by thou-sands of people if it had not been clothed with certain norms especially dear to the hearts of lower middle-class old folks. As we have just pointed out, the Plan succeeded partially because people were highly suggestible, owing to the lack of frames of reference, by means of which they could check the soundness of a particular proposal which was simple enough for them to understand. And their suggestibility was further increased because the Plan so congenially reinforced certain standards of judgment that they already cherished and jealously guarded.

For one thing, the Plan is indigenous to the American way of life. The founders state:

> It is a simple American Plan dedicated to the cause of prosperity and the abolition of poverty. It retains the rights of freedom of speech and of press and of religious belief and insures us the right to per-petuate and make glorious the liberty we so cherish and enjoy.[51]

"The Plan should make it possible for people over 60 to go on living like Americans should," said Mr. Barber in the interview reported above. "The Townsend Plan Is True Americanism," runs a slogan.

[50] Roosevelt, *op. cit.,* 34.
[51] Townsend and Clements, *op. cit.,* 7.

Meetings are generally opened with a salute to the flag and the singing of *America*.

Furthermore, the leaders believe that their Plan will save capitalism. To the question, "Is not the Plan you advocate a definite leaning toward the Socialism advocated a few years ago by Debs and Hilquist and Sinclair?" the official answer is "No, it is the very antithesis of Socialism. Socialism demands the abolition of the profit system. We believe that the profit system is the very mainspring of civilized progress."[52] An automobile tire cover can be purchased with the motto, "The Townsend Plan Will Save America from Radicalism." It is also claimed that the Plan will ease income taxes, reduce real-estate taxes, and that the 2 per cent transactions tax will make it possible in a few years to pay off the national debt. No capitalist could ask for more.

The movement is not only good Americanism, but it is good Christianity. "The Townsend Plan is religion in action." Religious ideology and ritual play an important part in the meetings. Frequently the Lord's Prayer is recited and hymns are sung. It is assumed and stated that God is on the side of the Townsendites. Many district leaders are retired ministers. Dr. Townsend often refers to his religious background. "I have come nearly four thousand miles to see you," he said in opening one meeting. "You look like good Methodists, and I like that. I was raised in a Methodist family, so I know what it means."[53]

Thus, there is nothing foreign or revolutionary about the Townsend movement. It not only fits but also promotes three of the most widely held patterns of value in the country: Americanism, capitalism, Christianity. One does not have to sacrifice any of these more fundamental ideologies to join the Townsend ranks. One does not run the risk of being called a foreigner, a Red, or an atheist. One is everything a nice person ought to be.

4. *The Plan preserves or enhances self-regard.* Our explanation of the Townsend movement would be incomplete if we failed to place the needs of the followers and their mental contexts into a personal motivational framework. To say that the Plan is accepted because it satisfies needs, because it provides meaning to puzzled citizens,

[52] *Ibid.*, 30.
[53] White, *op. cit.*

and because it does not contradict accepted values does not give us the whole story of why people are so enthusiastic about it or why, once they accept the Townsend interpretation, they defend it so consistently.

The American culture has always put a high premium on youth. The energy, stamina, and idealism of relatively young people was needed in earlier days to settle the country. At least the energy and stamina of youth are prized now in a day of precision machinery when labor is plentiful. Our culture has made remarkable, if by no means adequate, strides in providing for the education of young people; our doctors have reduced infant mortality; our YMCA's, Boy Scouts, and the like receive handsome contributions to assist young people through adolescent years; our novelists have immortalized typical American boys; our orators talk freely about the opportunities and responsibilities that lie ahead of the younger generation. Throughout the whole process we have tended to neglect the other end of life.

This is no place to speculate on the reasons for such neglect, but it is an important consideration if we are to understand the Townsend Plan. For Dr. Townsend has given old people a place in the scheme of things. They are made important cogs in the wheel. Over and over again they are told that because of *their* efforts our country has progressed, that after lives of sacrifice and devotion *they* deserve attention and comfort, that because of *their* training and experience *they* alone are peculiarly equipped to be the sensible disbursers of the money which will start and keep the ball rolling. In brief, they are promised a status which they have so far found only in their dreams. *Their* self-importance is raised.

Thus, when they identify themselves with their leader or when they realize what they *might* be if the Townsend Plan were put into operation, their egos are enhanced, the latent values which they hoped might be realized seem less distant. Hence, the frame of reference provided by Dr. Townsend is one that enormously involves their egos. Not only can they understand it, but they also can understand its significance in their own lives. Thus they cling to it tenaciously, countering criticism and political defeat, not with argument or fact, but with sorrow and despair. "I don't ever expect to get anything out of the Townsend Plan. I really don't know if it'll ever be passed or not. If it is, I probably won't be here," said seventy-three-year-old Mr. Stone in his interview.

Not only old people but young and middle-aged Townsendites, too, believe that, if older people were provided for, *then* their own desired place in society could be achieved. *They* could then have the jobs they wanted; *they* could assume responsibilities of the sort society valued; *they* could be free to plan for themselves alone, without including the oldsters in their budgets and their holiday plans. So they, too, accept the Townsend Plan avidly because their own self-regard, as well as their desire to have their wants satisfied, is so intimately involved. "One thing sure is that a lot of old people would quit working and give younger ones a chance to get jobs," said Billy Carver. "A young fellow can't get a job anywhere these days."

The Townsend Plan must be regarded only as a symptom, as a single illustration of the type of social phenomenon we must expect from time to time until the culture can accommodate people more satisfactorily. What will stop such movements? Townsendites claim that "only God can stop our Plan." Some of them even doubt God's omnipotence in this direction. Of those who favored the Townsend Plan in 1936, 71 per cent voted for Roosevelt in spite of their leader's admonition to vote against the New Deal, or for the Republicans.[54] Even those who approve the Townsend Plan apparently were not willing to accept the all-or-none principle of the founder. No doubt they felt the Social Security Act was a step in the right direction. But it and other meliorative measures can be regarded as only a step. Both bodily and derived needs are insistent. The widespread desire for a "place" in society that is somewhat commensurate with ambitions cannot be forever ignored. And it seems unlikely that the critical ability of people will be increased rapidly enough to enable them properly to evaluate the schemes presented them. Somehow, then, if we wish improvements in security and comfort, those who better understand the problems of government and finance, of capital and labor, and of youth and of age have the task of seeing to it that needs are better provided for, that meaningful and reasonable goals are substituted for panaceas, and that a large proportion of the population does not feel that the discrepancy between its hopes and its realizations is so unbridgeable.

[54] Data obtained from the American Institute of Public Opinion.

CHAPTER 8

THE NAZI PARTY

In 1919, a handful of disgruntled men were holding weekly meetings in a run-down Munich beer hall. They discussed the plight of Germany, the remedies needed, the possibility of Germany's rebirth. Like so many other groups of that period, they formed a political party. By 1933, this apparently insignificant band of beer-mug philosophers had been transformed into a mass movement that swept its leader into power. Soon one European country after another fell into its orbit. People in many corners of the world gradually became aware of the fact that they could not forever remain indifferent to the teachings and tactics of this new organization.

The story of what happened in those few crowded years has been told often and well by observers and scholars.[1] And these chroniclers have not all been content merely with the unraveling of tangled historical threads. Some historians have carefully analyzed what they believe were the main reasons for the phenomenal growth of the Nazi Party. One proposes a psychoanalytic interpretation;[2] another finds the key in the economic determinism of Marx,[3] a third believes that Nazi success is due largely to the use of hypnotic tactics and the appeal to an instinct to be dominated.[4] Others point out that the final victory of the Nazis can only be understood by the frank acceptance of the pluralistic explanation which they suggest.[5] These latter pluralistic accounts seem especially sound and convincing. Yet

[1] See T. Abel, *Why Hitler Came into Power*, New York: Prentice-Hall, 1938; R. A. Brady, *The Spirit and Structure of German Fascism*, New York: Viking, 1937; K. Heiden, *A History of National Socialism*, New York: Knopf, 1935; G. B. Hoover, *Germany Enters the Third Reich*, New York: Macmillan, 1933; S. H. Roberts, *The House that Hitler Built*, New York: Harper, 1938; E. A. Mowrer, *Germany Puts the Clock Back*, New York: Morrow, 1933; F. L. Schuman, *The Nazi Dictatorship*, New York: Knopf, 1936.

[2] Schuman, *ibid.*

[3] John Strachey, *The Menace of Fascism*, New York: Covici Friede, 1933.

[4] Ernest Kris, *New York Times*, Dec. 8, 1940.

[5] Abel, *op. cit.*; Hoover, *op. cit.*

he social psychologist wants, somehow, to add to these explanations
rovided by the political scientist, the economist, or the sociologist.
Ie cannot accept certain psychoanalytic assumptions about mind in
general which result in what, so far, seem to be oversimplified explanations of Nazism. The question of *why* the Nazis were successful
s not satisfactorily answered for the social psychologist until he has
ranslated the conditions, circumstances, and events recorded by
others *into their psychological consequences for the individuals who
supported and who were the Nazi movement.*

The task is not an easy one. For, contrary to the expectations of
many laymen, columnists, or students in other fields, the psychologist
has few rabbits up his sleeve. He cannot find evidence to support
glib claims about the innate, militaristic, barbaric, or submissive characteristics of the "German people"; he cannot convince his colleagues
that there is some hidden lust for power in people who inhabit a
certain geographical portion of the earth; he cannot content himself
with a simple analysis of Hitler's undoubted genius for organization,
propaganda, demagogy, and grand political and military strategy.
The best the psychologist can do is to apply to the data already
accumulated by others various tools of analysis, various conceptual
frameworks, in the hope that he can better understand the why of
Nazism.

Because both the idea and the name of National Socialism can be
found in German political history even before the first World War,[6]
our analysis must begin with the historical setting of the Nazi movement. What were the circumstances which made such an idea click
at one time, when it had failed at another time? What were the
conditions of the German people during the period when Nazism
developed? What were their needs, frustrations, and ambitions?
When this picture has been outlined we shall be in a position to
understand the appeals and the tactics of the Party itself. Finally,
we shall try to bring together the psychological reasons for the
growth and success of the Nazi movement in Germany.

HISTORICAL SETTING

German nationalism. The Germany that Hitler and his colleagues
discussed in 1919 can be fully understood only if we take a quick

[6] Heiden, *op. cit.*

glance at its history. People think and talk so much in terms of nations that they are likely to forget that nations, as we know them are comparatively recent developments, and that differences important to the psychologist exist in the life history of modern states And Americans, particularly, conscious of their recently won place in the Western World, are likely to think of Germany as an "old" nation. In reality, the United States, as a homogeneous political federation, is almost a century older than Germany.

During the long years of the Holy Roman Empire, what we now know as Germany was essentially a large number of small principalities or states, dominated by either secular or church authorities. To all intents and purposes, they were quite independent of the powerless emperors who came and went. England and France had achieved a national unity centuries before. They continued not only to consolidate their power but also to extend it. During the long years when the various German states were competing with each other, England and France were discovering new territory, colonizing in Asia, Africa, and America, building up empires that were well outlined by the time German nationality was achieved.

It was not until late in the nineteenth century that the hundreds of separate states in Germany had been juggled down to a workable number of twenty-two, to be more or less brought together by Bismarck. Yet even these separate states were relatively independent. Each had its own legislative body, its own ruler, its own government. Some even had their own armies, railways, and postal systems. All were dominated by Prussia, which gave the Kaiser-king wide powers. As rulers and governments came and went, civil servants carried on the mechanism of government with the routine efficiency for which the *Beamter* was famous. The central government at Berlin, however, settled matters of great national importance. Thus the unification of local governments into what we know of Germany was not accomplished until the Franco-Prussian War of 1870.[7] From then until the first World War, Germany was ruled as an autocracy. Close behind the Kaiser stood the army officials, the powerful landowners, and the wealthy industrialists.

There are two important psychological consequences of this history. In the first place, the great masses of the people had been

[7] Italy was not unified until about the same time.

aught submission and obedience to authority. Laws, traditions, customs, and social values of all kinds perpetuated and encouraged political docility. The responsibility of citizens to participate in government and to steer the ship of state was, as we shall see, something the people were neither prepared for nor unequivocally enthusiastic about. They had become conditioned to autocratic leadership—they knew little else—and to be freed from routine demands was not an unmixed blessing for the majority.

In the second place, the German people were not so accustomed to national unity that they could take it for granted and submerge it in their thinking. At the time of the first World War, the people were, like the young man who has just had his first shave, highly self-conscious. They felt that they were superior Nordics with a Fatherland. One might almost say that they were overcompensating for a feeling of national and cultural inferiority, a feeling reflected by the fact that French usually was spoken by the aristocracy and the members of good society in Germany as late as the eighteenth century. The people had been taught that their army was invincible, that the war they entered in 1914 would be a short one. For years they heard nothing but reports of victories. And as winter followed winter during the war, suffering became more acute. Terrific sacrifices were made for the Fatherland, for the splendid army in the West. The news that the lines were breaking and that defeat was imminent came to the German people as an unusually profound shock. "German nationalism was wounded at the height of its pride," a historian points out.[8]

The chaos and turmoil that were to follow the defeat of the army were due, in part, to these psychological consequences of the course of German history up to the summer of 1918. By this time German culture was composed of a people generally characterized as efficient, determined, energetic, and talented, who had a strong desire to make their nation second to none.

Postwar confusion. When the government asked the Allied powers for an unconditional armistice on October 6, 1918, intense resentment burst forth on all sides. Many people realized that they had been misled, that stringent regulations had been imposed on them by persons who they now realized could not be trusted. Hence, they con-

[8] J. T. Shotwell, *What Germany Forgot*, New York: Macmillan, 1940.

cluded that the government no longer deserved respect or obedienc
and there was an immediate breakdown of all authority

A German writer, now exiled, has tried to recapture his impression
of these hectic days.

> When I think back to that time I have strange memories of grey,
> empty, dirty streets on which fell a steady, mist-like rain and where
> the sun never shone. The despair must have been that intense, and
> it was enhanced by the crumbling stucco of the houses, the dim
> flickering gas lamps, worn-out shoes, empty gaping store windows,
> and the other aspects of ruin.
>
> Starvation, lack of coal, grippe epidemics, strikes, political coups
> and the increasing insecurity of private life are characteristic of this
> period which assumed more and more the form of a civil war. I
> remember street fights which lost their local character and trans-
> formed the town in which I lived and the surrounding countryside
> into a battle ground for the period of one week. Burned mansions,
> houses shot to pieces, the dead in the street, barricades, the thunder
> of tanks and the hollow ring of the alarm bells in lightless nights,
> brought the terror of war into a country which had not yet become
> acquainted with it.[9]

The police and state officials refused to carry out their regular
orders. There were riots for food, mass demonstrations demanding
the abdication of the Kaiser, mutinies in the navy and army. Local
governing councils were set up by sailors, soldiers on leave, and
workers. The vocal sections of the people wanted to banish the old
regime but keep the social and economic structure of society about
the same as it had been. Both the middle class and the proletariat
craved a return of order and stability under somewhat more democratic auspices. There was no systematic, widely articulated demand

[9] This quotation and some others included below were taken from life histories
written by Germans who left the country after Hitler attained power. The authors
participated in a prize competition arranged by E. Y. Hartshorne, S. B. Fay, and
G. W. Allport, all of Harvard University, whose purpose was to select the most
adequate life histories on the subject, "My Life in Germany Before and After
January 30, 1933." None of the material has yet been published, but analyses of the
life histories by Hartshorne and Allport, J. S. Bruner, and E. M. Jandorf are in
preparation. The writer is greatly indebted to these men for permission to use short
extracts from their rich source material. All names and identifying characteristics
are fictitious. The writer is grateful to the contestants who have kindly permitted
him the use of their documents. The quotations used were selected and translated by
Jandorf of Harvard University.

or radical change in the distribution of power and wealth. The people had not been prepared to take political responsibility in their own hands. But, because of the general disintegration of authority and the desire for new leadership, the stage was set for a real revolution. However, no party was sufficiently organized to assume immediate power. There was no leader. On November ninth, the workers in Berlin revolted. Troops, sent to quiet them, joined the cause of the workers. The Kaiser was forced to abdicate, and at noon on that day the leader of the Social Democrats announced that "the monarchical system had collapsed" and that a German Republic had been born.

The new government received wide moral support. It was backed by most of the people whose chief objective was to rid Germany of the Kaiser; it was hailed by the majority of workers because of the social legislation for which the Social Democrats stood; it was enthusiastically received by liberals who looked forward to greater freedom under Germany's first democratic state.

This movement did not mean, however, that everyone unequivocally supported the Republic. Bitter dissension arose on both the left and the right. The Communists regarded the new government as a major defeat of the working class and, following the pattern of the Russian Revolution, urged that power be retained by the councils of soldiers and workers. When they militantly tried to wrest control from the newly formed government, they were vigorously suppressed. In this task the government was aided by bewildered soldiers, returning untriumphantly from the battlefield—soldiers who felt they had been betrayed by their former leaders and who could not stomach the sudden reversals of power, the degradation of their own status, which they believed the rule of proletariat councils meant. As one of them wrote later:

> No one who has not himself experienced it, can imagine what went on in our young hearts when, on the night of November 9, 1918, we were roused from sleep with the words of treason and revolution. Who had betrayed us? Our fathers, our brothers? No! A thousand times no! We looked at each other aghast, and with no particular information at hand, we realized that, if these things were true, there must be something decidedly rotten somewhere; the enemy must be behind the front as well as before us. We grew more and

more wide-awake as news kept drifting in. We waited in vain for orders to strike out against the traitors . . . The so-called soldiers' council presented all manner of requests and orders, demanded that we remove the decorations from our uniforms, and so forth. In reality, it was politely put up to us that we proceed to map out our own dismal existence. When, however, we were ordered to give up our flag in exchange for a red rag, our patience gave out. Shame reddened our cheeks and anger constricted our throats. Clearly there were people at work intent on turning things upside down. Heroism had become cowardice, truth a lie, loyalty was rewarded by dastardliness. We shouldered our weapons and put this extraordinary delegation behind lock and key.[10]

In addition to the Communists whose leaders were killed and whose organized effectiveness was broken, there were many disorganized but potentially powerful elements in the population who looked askance on the new parliamentary regime. Conservatives, government officials, and great landowners, with vested interests in the old system, opposed democracy for its own sake. During the early months after the revolution, these groups remained quiescent. Later, when the time was more appropriate, when the enthusiasm and hopes of their enemies were not so high, they contributed their share in opposing the successful establishment of democratic government. Aligned with them, at least temporarily, were numerous workers and soldiers who saw little difference between the parliamentary government and the councils advocated by the Communists. The new government was indiscriminately characterized as "Red" and was regarded as responsible for the stab in the back, the betrayal inside, which brought defeat. The feeling that must have existed in many people is described by a German farmer who had been conscripted for the war.

Despite the efforts of the leaders to ingratiate themselves with the workers, the revolution of 1918 was a crime, not only against the workers, but also against the entire people. What became of peace, freedom, bread? So many catchwords, thrown to the furious masses, so that the so-called people's tribunals might have a better hold on them for their own sinister purposes. I need not emphasize that this criminal and forcibly induced development was a slap in the face of every decent German. Were these the fruits of my sixteen years of

[10] Abel, *op. cit.*, 27.

service in war and peace? Was it for this that the fresh youth of Germany was mowed down in hundreds of battles? It almost seemed as if that might be the answer—treason to Fatherland and people celebrated veritable orgies. All that still reflected the glory of the heroic deeds of our old army was derided and trampled in the gutter . . . Shallow pacifists inflated themselves and sputtered high-sounding phrases. Spineless men and the sickening offshoots of exploiters triumphed over the decent part of the population.[11]

The resentment of the soldiers on account of what they regarded as a betrayal, however, was not turned against the government because Hindenberg and others in the military caste agreed to support the Social Democrats if they, in return for this service, would militantly stamp out the radical elements of the population. The bond uniting the new government and the old army was, therefore, a tenuous one, not founded on any common ideological interests. And, during the first hectic months of the new regime's reign, the cooperation of the army was perhaps the main stabilizing force on the home front. All evidence would indicate that the great majority of people, at least passively, approved the onslaught against those of the extreme Left Wing. People, above all else, wanted a return of stability and order, not further drastic change. When the first National Assembly met at Weimar on January 19, 1919, the various coalition parties, led by the Social Democrats, received approximately three-quarters of the popular vote. A new constitution was adopted, a leader was elected, and the first parliamentary government of Germany was officially launched.

Versailles Treaty. The first blow the new government received and which was destined to undermine permanently the success of democratic government in postwar Germany was the Versailles Treaty. It aroused unequivocal and furious resentment among the people. It was a final insult to the hard-won German nationalism. From all quarters demands flowed into the government that it should reject a treaty which made Germany entirely responsible for the war, demanded impossible reparations payments, and gave German territory to states that were somewhat artificially created. A typical resolution of the period read:

[11] *Ibid.,* 26.

> We prefer to sacrifice everything and fight to the last man rather
> than accept as cowards a peace that is against our honor. Contemp-
> tible is the nation which does not offer its life gladly for the sake of
> its honor.[12]

Mass meetings and demonstrations of all kinds were staged. Patriotism and nationalism were again the watchwords.

Government leaders were helpless. There was nothing for them
to do but sign on the dotted line. The blockade was continuing.
Allied armies were still intact and ready to pounce if the treaty was
not promptly ratified. And, as soon as the representatives of the
German nation had signed the treaty, the animosity that had arisen
against the treaty was inevitably transferred to those who had signed
it, even though the signers themselves were as vigorous as any nationalist in denouncing its terms.

> Under the right leadership . . . we might have swept the worm
> gnawing at the vitals of our people out of sight. Never, never could
> we conceive how people who called themselves our fellow Germans
> could deprive us of our last remaining possession, our national honor.

Thus wrote a professional man later, when he recalled the day
immediately after Versailles.[13] A government worker said:

> It was a bitter injustice that this nation, exposed to an overwhelming
> number of foes, should thus be humiliated, in a manner that did
> little honor to the conquerors themselves. It seemed to me unbearable
> to think that there had been men who acquiesced in Germany's
> alleged responsibility for the war. Could a nation that had become
> great through decades of steady efforts for peace, suddenly precipitate
> such a conflagration? Could men who, in their own country, led lives
> of usefulness and devotion, and who, as I had ample opportunity to
> observe, reared their children in love and piety, suddenly turn
> barbarians in the land of the enemy?[14]

A student wrote:

> We had come back in 1918 from the battlefields, no longer boys but
> men, hardened in the forge of war. Now we had to shape our life.
> The German people was in misery and distress, enslaved by unjust
> enemies. We fought it out. We young Germans knew how to bear
> our fate.[15]

[12] *Ibid.*, 31.   [13] *Ibid.*, 33.   [14] *Ibid.*
[15] From the life histories obtained by Allport, Hartshorne, and Fay, *op. cit.*

With such sentiments widespread, it is no wonder that the two parties that had voted to sign the treaty lost eleven million votes in the next election (June 1920).

Political turmoil. Since the new government was based upon the principle of rule by a democratic majority, there followed twelve years of struggle for the majority vote. Yet, because of the Weimar constitution, which gave each party proportional representation, and because of growing factionalism, it became practically impossible for any single party to obtain the majority vote necessary to carry out any consistent program. There were, among others, the following political groups contending for power: the Nationalists, representing the die-hard Tories and composed of many wealthy people and landed gentry; the Conservatives, from industry and trade; the Democrats, representing liberal leaders from commerce and the professions; the People's Party, which included industrialists who could not qualify for the Nationalist party; the Centrum Group of Catholics, which cut across class lines and was conservative when liberals were in power and liberal when conservatives reigned; the Socialists, made up largely of relatively conservative people who had small profits or savings to protect; the Majority Socialists, containing many trade unionists; the Independent Socialists, who were more revolutionary but who stood for pacifism; the Communists, and the Nazis. In addition to these there were secret, counter-revolutionary military organizations, which often operated as the watch dogs of industrialists or wealthy landowners who, themselves, were openly identified with other parties. The *Freikorps*, composed chiefly of army officers, was one of these, with a militant nationalistic, anti-Semitic program. For veterans of lesser rank, the *Stahlhelm* had its appeal. Separate and rather diffused radical groups with anti-Semitic programs also arose. It is significant of later developments that, when these armed bands tried to overthrow local or state governments, they were only mildly punished; but, when they took up arms against Communists and other radicals, the latter received severe treatment from the government for resisting.

In the midst of the hammering from right and left, the middle-of-the-road parties could stay in power only as long as they compromised. Since they accepted the principle of majority rule, it was quite impossible for them to create any new political or economic machinery to meet the incessant emergencies which arose. They retained many of the old army officers whose experience they needed to crush radical revolts; they did what they could to maintain the army, which alone safeguarded them in a hostile world; they employed the same diplomatic corps; the same judiciary.

> Only a few judges were politically active in behalf of the Weimar republic. Most judges adhered to the parties whose aim was to bring about a change in the republican form of government. This opposition found an expression in the extraordinarily lenient sentences handed down in political slander suits. Grave but unfounded accusations against *Reichspräsident* Ebert, the *Reichskanzler*, or the other ministers, were punished with small fines where the law provided options of several years imprisonment.[16]

No drastic attempts were made to rearrange the balance of economic control. Hence, what has often been called a "revolution" was more a struggle of a republican government to stabilize a society that had grown up under a monarchy.[17]

Whatever parliamentary majority gained power was caught by the circumstances of events. Any strong measures to counteract political opposition or to relieve economic strains would most certainly have destroyed whatever democratic government attempted them. The governments that came and went were operating within a set of assumptions written into law by a constitution, which made it impossible for them to carry out reforms necessary to consolidate power. Aside from the traditional factionalism within the state, the Allies were pressing for fulfillment of treaty obligations, obligations which continued to be resisted by the people and which cast an unpleasant aroma on any government that transferred Allied pressure to the shoulders of the people themselves. In 1923, the Germans found insult added to injury when Poincaré marched troops into the Ruhr because of Germany's "criminal" failure to meet reparations payments. It was not until 1932, just before Hitler came into power, that the Allied powers sufficiently revised the terms of the treaty so that they might have been met.

Thus any government that was formed depended for its existence on the toleration of various coalitions. Coalition governments, whose

[16] From the life histories obtained by Allport, Hartshorne, and Fay, *op. cit.*
[17] For a more complete discussion of this point, see Hoover, *op. cit.*, ch. 3.

foreign policies pleased the conservatives, almost inevitably had domestic politics which alienated the liberals. Under these conditions,
lobbying and bargaining were rampant and many elections reduced
themselves to the overthrowing of specific coalitions or political personalities. Parties on the right, especially the Nationalist Party, could
not gain popular support because of their aloofness to the needs and
interests of common men. "Before elections we were always welcome; once the elections were over, however, the voter was something of a nuisance," wrote a clerk who had nationalist sympathies
but could not bring himself to join the party.[18] The Communists on
the left could not gain public sympathy because their appeals were
so foreign to the traditions of the people. "I could never develop
any enthusiasm for the utopian idea of a 'unity of nations,' " said
one man whose patriotism was probably typical of the average citizen.[19] Yet the right and left enlisted sufficient support to harass
the middle. And the constitutional structure of the republic plus
the iron hand of the Allies prevented the creation of any government authority strong enough to gain the respect and confidence of
the masses. A young man who wanted a picture of the President of
the Republic received the following information from the shop he
had written for the photograph: "We regret not to be able to fill your
order of the . . . since we do not carry pictures of Herr Ebert and
similar traitors."[20]

Postwar economy. Interwoven into the political scene as partially
causing the constant shifts of cabinets and ministers were the economic conditions existing from the time of the revolution to the
advent of Hitler. The exorbitant reparations' burden hung heavy,
not only over the heads of the people, but also over the organized
governments which they created. By 1923, government borrowing
from the Reichsbank to meet national debts had reached such proportions that the only way out was the issuance of notes. As the fear
of inflation and the consequent loss of purchasing power spread, the
circulation of money increased and inflation itself was accelerated.
The mark fell to a ridiculous figure. An American dollar in 1923
could buy three or four billion marks.

[18] Abel, *op. cit.,* 128.
[19] *Ibid.,* 139.
[20] From the life histories obtained by Allport, Hartshorne, and Fay, *op. cit.*

A major consequence of the collapse of the mark was the practical liquidation of the middle class. Small investors who had put their money into savings, bonds, stocks, or mortgages lost practically everything they had. Those who did manage to retain any valuable assets or those who were later able to borrow moderate sums to finance businesses were bound to feel insecure after bitter experience. Only well-established industrialists and huge property owners could borrow abroad. Thus economic power became increasingly centralized, a group of *nouveau riche* arose, and both the small propertied man and the aristocrat found themselves relatively powerless. As one German wrote later:

> We wandered Sunday mornings into the environments of the city. We tried to pick up something from the peasants. Of course only on a basis of barter, for money was valueless. That was the time when the peasant felt himself master . . . And when we men came home . . . the prettiest girls were awaiting us. It required a good bit of self-control to resist them, when, for a handful of potatoes, one could buy the most beautiful girl for a whole long night. If you ask me, what has harmed Europe's culture most, I shall answer without hesitation: not the war, not the revolution, not the civil strife between parties, but the inflation. Morals, ethics, faith, love, and loyalty—all were destroyed in the delirium of inflation.[21]

Following the inflation of 1923, a period of comparative prosperity set in for the working man. Some social legislation with respect to wages and hours, unemployment benefits, housing, and education was inaugurated. And besides, capitalist economy throughout the world was enjoying a short boom period. But the depression of 1929 did not leave Germany unaffected. The national income of over 72 billion marks in 1928 had fallen to 48 billions by 1932. Whereas wages and salaries amounted to approximately 44 billion marks in 1929, they fell to about 25 billions in 1932. As reflected in the average wage of the skilled worker in the metal trades, this meant a drop in the weekly wage from 54 marks in 1928 to 30 marks in the fall of 1932; while the weekly pay of an unskilled worker in the same trade dropped from 42 to 21 marks during this period. Little was done by the Brüning government to reduce taxes on the wage earner. And the worker became aware that a share of his tax pay-

[21] From the life histories obtained by Allport, Hartshorne, and Fay, *op. cit.*

ments was being diverted to subsidize agriculture on the estates of the large landowner.

Unemployment in Germany, as in the rest of capitalist society, increased rapidly after the depression. In 1929, the monthly average of unemployed was about two million; by 1931, it had risen to over four and a half million, and, by the beginning of 1932, it had jumped to six million, almost one-tenth the total population. Industrial production was nearly cut in half during this three-year period. And at the same time unemployment benefits were cut. The government at this time tried to complete a credit agreement with neighboring Austria in the hope that the economic conditions in both countries would be somewhat stabilized. But this attempt was frustrated when the Bank of France withdrew its credit from Austria, causing the collapse of its banks and humiliation in Germany.[22]

It has been estimated that in 1932, half the German population was living on almost a starvation level. People were so miserable that the subtle arguments of politicians and traditional economists failed to interest them. The common man was desperately aware that something was radically wrong. In Germany, as well as elsewhere, there was the growing realization that there was potential abundance, that the machinery existed to produce food, clothing, and other necessities, if only someone would take hold and run it. Certainly nothing worse could happen than had already happened.

INSECURITIES OF DIFFERENT GROUPS

Any classification of a population into separate interest groups is bound to oversimplify the true state of affairs. And any characterization of the troubles and worries of a single group inevitably distorts somewhat the particular troubles or worries of a given individual within that group. It should already be clear from our earlier discussion that there are enormous differences between the attitudes and ambitions of people who may, for descriptive purposes, be bunched together in a particular combination. The chief justification for such a procedure is that, by and large, individuals who have similar ways of life, similar means of earning a living, similar experiences will emerge with roughly similar standards of judgment upon which they will base specific action and opinion.

[22] G. E. R. Gedye, *Betrayal in Central Europe,* New York: Harper, 1939.

Postwar Germany certainly contained large numbers of people whose backgrounds had built up in them mental contexts which made them interpret events in particular ways. Some of these people hoped for things that others feared; some were vitally concerned about problems that others did not even recognize. Hence, before we begin the story of the Nazi Party itself, we should take a more detailed glance at the way in which certain persons of various strata were affected by the general conditions already outlined.[23] For Nazism was possible only because of widespread support, support that was by no means confined to a single class or interest group.

The Junkers. This landed aristocracy had always considered themselves above the common man. Through their control of Prussia and Prussia's domination of the first Reich, they had furnished the state with many of its most able government and army officials. It was, they believed, their duty and proper privilege to continue to supply Germany with persons who were, by breeding and tradition, capable of running the state. The general point of view of the Junkers at this time is reflected in the purpose of the *Herrenklub*, a political organization founded mainly by Junkers in 1924, as a sort of private council for the aged Hindenburg, himself one of the landed gentry. The aim of the club was "to preserve that Christian conservative basis such as befits a man of political mind who feels responsible to God for his nation." The nation, presumably, was the special concern of the *Herrenklub* members who were responsible only to God.

It is no wonder, then, that the Junkers considered the state owed them a living. They were, therefore, paid enormous subsidies by the postwar governments which were powerless to shake off their political influence. Even the Social Democrats could not extricate themselves from Junker power. When Brüning submitted a tax plan and, later, von Schleicher proposed that some of the landed estates be conscripted for state use, they soon found themselves in the bad grace of President von Hindenburg.

It is also not surprising that the Junkers detested and despised all democratic, republican forms of government. They detested them because such governments obviously did not explicitly recognize the superiority of certain types of people and because the tenuous, im-

[23] For further discussion of these group characteristics see Hoover, *op. cit.*, ch. 2; Schuman, *op. cit.*, 95-108.

plicit recognition of the value of Junkers to the state might at any moment be jeopardized. They despised the republican governments set up after the war since they saw how weak and subservient they were, not only to the interests of the Junkers themselves, but also to other powerful pressure groups, especially those of industry. The Junkers were becoming more and more frightened of industrialists whose tariff policies were very much at odds with their own. They were ready to welcome a strong authority that could be relied on to counteract the power of this particular enemy and which could also assure them that they would have nothing to fear from their traditional foe, the peasant.

The industrialists. The leaders of Germany's vast industrial plants were naturally more afraid of a successful revolution than of anything else, a revolution that would transform the existing economic structure and redistribute economic and political power. The hope of the industrialists was that they could keep trade unions impotent, prevent legislation from regulating wages and hours, or providing unemployment or old-age insurance. Although some social legislation had been adopted by the new democratic governments, on the whole the industrialists were not too discouraged by events. The Communists had been disarmed, the workers could not seem to agree on any common program of action. Furthermore, the industrialists found the new governments seeking their advice, taking no drastic action to curtail their profits or power. They had, apparently, the feeling that revolutions were, after all, nothing to fear, that capitalism and private industry had proved their intrinsic merits by weathering the postwar storm. According to one observer, even shortly before the Nazis came into power, the majority of German industrialists felt that the "end of the crisis would surely come and that the economic system in Germany would remain essentially unaltered."[24]

We shall see later, however, that this was not the opinion of all industrialists. At least a few of them were apparently extremely fearful of further revolution and willing to give both moral and financial support to a political leader whom they felt they could use to their own advantage.

The middle class. The inflation brought with it not only enormous

[24] Hoover, *op. cit.*, 28.

financial loss to the small investor but also a profound sense of the futility of saving and the hopelessness of economic advancement. There was also built up, as a result of this experience, a keen resentment against "big business," against a system and the leaders of a system that had made such a catastrophe possible. If the old system had brought the middle class to that impasse, what was there to fear of new systems? Certainly they could not be much worse.

> The German *Bürger* felt his most precious value attacked—his security. With the increasing insecurity of his existence and of his personal life the whole concept of *Bürgerlichkeit* seemed to approach collapse. The plaster of the houses crumbled and with it crumbled the plaster from the façade of the German *Bürgertum* and revealed the deep-seated, inner insecurity of this class which has no inner firmness to call its own. No long tradition stood behind it. The external prosperity of a happy epoch helped erect this magnificent structure whose interior was considerably hollow. When the epoch which had lent him the appearance of security ended, the *Bürger* felt as defenseless as a mussel deprived of its shell.[25]

This cynicism seems to have been further encouraged by the continued impersonalness of the business structure itself. The little man was beginning to feel even more and more helpless and far removed. The persons who sat on industrial and banking boards and really directed things were distant and unknown. Business, in Germany as everywhere else, was becoming more and more institutionalized, more and more a complex pattern that could only be understood by experts, something that was bound to absorb or destroy the single entrepreneur who tried to make his profit by new adventures not backed by large financial interests.

In the midst of all this, salaries of government employees and white-collar workers were rising more slowly than prices. And these salaried employees, in their competition for positions, sensed the fact that their numbers were rapidly increasing in the population. Women and youth were entering these ranks, filling subordinate positions and retarding advancement. New recruits for white-collar jobs were coming more and more from the "lower" classes. A survey made in 1931 showed that only 6 per cent of male salaried employees over 50 years of age had stemmed from homes of manual workers,

[25] From the life histories obtained by Allport, Hartshorne, and Fay, *op. cit.*

while 35 per cent of those under 25 had this background.[26] There was every reason for the white-collar worker, the member of the lower middle class, to feel that his status was threatened, that he would soon be indistinguishable from a member of the proletariat.

This loss of status was the main worry of this large and growing group. In Germany as well as in all other countries that had developed under a capitalist economy, these people felt themselves superior to manual workers. They did not fit into any Marxist pattern, which neatly divided people into two classes. They could not call themselves employers, and they resisted with all their might identification with workers. The values of their society placed their mode of work on a higher plane. They were accustomed to receiving more prestige, more respect, more privileges, more social deference than members of less elite groups. They regarded their work as somehow more important to the state; they regarded themselves as somehow the necessary helpers of their employers, and they liked to feel that the halo of prestige and authority accorded the employer or the national servant also belonged to them.

Now their importance was in dire jeopardy. If their salaries were further lowered, if their jobs became more insecure it would be impossible for them to differentiate themselves in socially recognized ways from the proletariat. There was a huge discrepancy between their level of expectation and their actual level of achievement. And there were few signs that the situation would be improved, either for them or for their children.[27] In addition, these people, unlike manual and industrial workers, had no such thing as a trade union to fight for their rights, had no unemployment or social insurance to fall back on, had no political ideology rationalizing their needs, their problems, or their status.

The proletariat. The dissatisfactions of the working class were due essentially to two general influences. In the first place, the economic conditions themselves, particularly after 1928, had, as we have seen, materially affected the security and standard of living of the laborer. But in addition to this usual phenomenon, dissatisfaction was spread

[26] Hans Speier, The salaried employee in modern society, *Soc. Research,* 1934, **1,** 120. This article, pp. 111-133, gives a clear picture of the predicament of the salaried employee in postwar years and the reasons why he felt his social status was in danger.

[27] For the psychological effect of the economic changes on the lower middle class, see Schuman, *op. cit.,* 95-108.

more widely and experienced more intensely because of the long history of labor education which the working class in Germany had enjoyed. For decades workers had been shown the inherent injustices of the capitalist system; for decades they had struggled to organize themselves solidly enough to achieve social legislation and to wrest at least some control of economic power from the few who used it to their own advantage. They had seen a proletariat rule established in Russia, and in their own country the formation of a republican government under the Social Democrats had brought with it hope for real change and better days. But as time passed and no essential modifications of the economic structure were made, the workers became more and more disillusioned with their newfound leaders. The Communists were not only harassed by their internal enemies but, badly guided by Moscow, were unable to formulate any indigenous program of action which would appeal to the mass of workers. Furthermore, the multiplicity of labor unions and the intricacy of their organization made it difficult for labor itself to create any convincing, unified program and follow it through.

In brief, the proletariat were dissatisfied with their conditions, disillusioned with the new postwar governments, eager for a transition to a more socialist economy, and increasingly aware that their desires could be satisfied only through their own struggles and organization, and not by some benign ruler.

The peasants. The peasant had always been the backbone of German agricultural economy. As a small landowner he was intrinsically capitalist, psychologically aligning himself with wealthy industrialists and, at times, with the landed Junkers. By 1932, the peasant's position was desperate. The impact of world events had filtered down and shouldered him with debts. The prices he was receiving for marketable goods were declining. Bankers and industrialists were manoeuvring tariffs in such a way that he found himself competing unfavorably with Holland, Denmark, and Sweden. Neither the government nor the rulers of the economic system seemed to be listening to the peasant's protests. He seemed helplessly caught between combined forces which he could not direct because of his own lack of bargaining power.

The youth. Young people, who had been children during the war, vividly remembered their privations and sufferings when their fathers were at the front, their mothers working desperately to outwit the effects of the Allied blockade. They had been told that there was a reason for all this, that they would be rewarded later. Like youth everywhere else in the world, they expected something out of life. But postwar events shattered the hopes and plans of the vast majority. Comparatively few jobs were available. In an effort to prepare themselves for specialized positions, youth flocked to the universities and technical schools. This increase in students only aggravated the situation, producing a terrific oversupply of lawyers, doctors, teachers, and technical experts. Young people banded together into groups, expanded into "movements," crusaded for their rights. But the government, itself caught helplessly by assumptions and circumstances, did little to alleviate the frustrations of youth or even to provide encouraging promises

THE STAGE SETTING FOR NAZISM

Such were some of the troubles that beset certain groups of people. The list of grievances could be amplified with considerations of the special problems of women, ex-soldiers, professional people, merchants, and the like. In addition to the ordinary cares of life, practically no German was exempted from worries, brought to him as a result of circumstances far beyond his own control.

Many of the prewar norms had completely disintegrated. The monarchists and the older authorities had shown themselves incapable of sustaining the needs of the people. The whole superstructure with which the German had identified himself, in which he had taken pride, and by means of which he derived a certain sense of security—a certain feeling of belongingness had been undermined by the Allied victory and subsequent events. The economic system had brought him to the verge of disaster in 1923. The church no longer seemed a vital force.

With the crumbling of the old superstructure, new norms had been tried. Democracy had been instituted, power had been theoretically vested in chosen representatives of the people. But still conditions failed to improve. There had been short periods of hope with Wilson's Fourteen Points, and with the Dawes and the Young Plans for refinancing German debts. Yet the situation for almost everyone, following 1928, grew steadily worse. Apparently the old superstructure needed more than these new props.

It is not difficult to imagine the human results of the political and economic events which transpired in Germany between the end of the war and the advent of National Socialism. Excerpts from case studies collected by Abel give us intimate glimpses of the way in which typical people were affected.[28] These life histories *were written by Nazis,* with the motivation of cash prizes, to explain why they had joined the Hitler movement. Into the reminiscences *one therefore finds projected considerable Nazi rationalization.* Nevertheless, the conditions described are certainly not exaggerated and the rationalizations themselves, as we shall see later, are invaluable clues to an understanding of Nazi appeals.

Many people were in desperate need of sufficient food and clothing to keep body and soul together. Standards of living, of course, waxed and waned with the times. But even during good years, the line separating sufficiency from hunger was thin and tenuous. A feeling of security was almost completely lacking. When the standard of living was temporarily raised it seemed to be balancing precariously on the edge of an all-too-familiar precipice. An unskilled industrial worker recalled that:

> The terrible burden of the breakdown threatened to bring all economic life to a standstill. Thousands of factories closed their doors. Hunger was the daily companion of the German workingman. Added to this was the artificial whip of scarcity . . . which sent workingmen scurrying from their homes to beg for food from the farmers. For no German family received more than twenty to thirty pfennigs dole per head in the terrible year of unemployment. Housewives will readily appreciate what it means to rear a family on that. The government carried its measures against the public so far that many an honest workingman had to resort to theft to obtain food. A case in point is the extensive pilfering of potatoes all through harvest time. Burglaries, too, became daily occurrences, and the police had their hands full protecting the citizens' property. All fellow citizens, with the exception of the Communists, yearned for better times.[29]

A young man wrote:

> A time of utter misery now set in for the family. I had to leave school. Once again we came to know hunger, for it was next to

[28] Abel, *op. cit.*
[29] *Ibid.,* 126 f.

impossible to provide for a family of five on our meager dole, while my father continued to live in Düsseldorf. An abysmal hatred flared up in me against the regime that could not provide employment for a family man who had done his duty in the war.[30]

In addition to physical needs that were not properly satisfied and the desired security that was not attainable, there was for many of the elements of the population a fear that their status—the place in life which they felt belonged to them—if already reached, could not be long maintained or, if not yet reached, could never be attained. It was impossible to plant roots into shifting sands. A small industrialist reports:

My most urgent task in 1919 was to make my business a going concern once more. This was the more difficult, since throughout the long years of the war no one had had the time to concern himself with it. After much effort, I finally succeeded in getting some orders. All my hopes, however, were dashed. The inflation put an end to my endeavors. I had no money to pay my help—my reserves were gone. Hunger and privation once more held sway in my home. I cursed the government that sanctioned such misery.[31]

And, as government followed government, plan followed plan, winter followed winter, it was inevitable that more and more people should become more and more confused. They could not understand the various economic, political and international forces pushing them one way and another. Battles over personalities and specific proposals obscured the broader issues involved. The demands of the Allies, the weakness of the democratic governments, the control of business by big industrialists, the continued favoritism shown the Junkers—all hung like heavy clouds over the heads of the bewildered citizen.

If someone were to ask me what it looked like at that time in Germany, I would have to answer: "Everywhere perplexed people asked, what are we to do? . . . There was absolutely no single group, not even the peasants, which was not concerned with serious problems. For instance, in 1927 I visited a Jesuit monastery. Even these secluded men had relegated the spiritual character of their institution into the background to such an extent that they emphasized again and again the problems and questions of what the people were to do in a prac-

[30] *Ibid.*, 125.
[31] *Ibid.*, 122.

tical way to escape material and spiritual distress. The people took hold of the most amazing variety of creeds and philosophies. Sects sprang up like mushrooms . . . An honourable old violin teacher of mine joined the *Bund der Aufrechten*."[32]

An ex-service man wrote:

All any front-line fighter could do was to resign himself to existing conditions and try to shield his family from hunger and privation. The German wife and mother fought side by side with her husband in this struggle against an overwhelming fate. Strikes and revolts flared up everywhere. The fate of Germany seemed to be sealed. Momentarily there was the false boom of the inflation . . . Some thirty-five parties arose to confute the people, a very witches' Sabbath. Devoid of political training, sick of body and soul, the German people reeled giddily after the different will-o'-the-wisps . . . There was a constant tension in the air. One government followed the other. The Marxists held huge mass meetings. The population was split up into tiny parties. The atmosphere was teeming with all sorts of plans. There was no unity of purpose anywhere. It was impossible to find one's way in the Hell's Kitchen of contradictory opinions. Divided by political views, interest, class and caste, the people were so many toys in the hands of the nation's enemies.[33]

Concern with immediate problems and the growing feeling of personal helplessness, dampened the newly acquired sense of political responsibility. The rise of an anti-democratic movement was possible only after this disillusionment with democracy. What could the citizen do now? Where could he turn for sympathy and help? Who could tell him how to localize the causes of his troubles? Who was strong enough to smash whatever bonds were holding him? The answer to these and other questions was being satisfactorily provided for more and more people by one of those disgruntled patriots, Adolf Hitler, who had met in the Munich beer hall in 1919. During the 1920's, Hitler was increasingly recognized as the silver lining to the clouds. As an old saying has it, when it gets dark enough the stars come out.

[32] From the life histories obtained by Allport, Hartshorne, and Fay, *op. cit.*
[33] Abel, 123 f., *op. cit.*

Chapter 9

THE NAZI PARTY (*CONTINUED*)

Nazi Appeals

As the years pass, it becomes less and less difficult to piece together the states of mind of some German people in the years following the first World War. The genius of Hitler was his ability to sense this at the time. He saw clearly the needs and frustrations of these people, he knew they were nostalgic for the realization of certain old values. He saw the political bickering of different interest groups, the lack of direction of government policies, the disillusionment of the common man, the desperate need for positive leadership, for some focus of the widespread discontent. His earliest speeches showed his understanding. They also outlined his program, a program specific in its indication of what the Nazis were against but vague in its indication of what the Nazis were for.

Any analysis of the nature of the Nazi appeals is bound to oversimplify the story. No matter how we try to generalize our explanation, as valid for all persons who joined the movement, we are faced with the simple fact that all people are different. As we have pointed out before, personal backgrounds, capacities, ambitions, and values give every individual a mental context more or less unique. The complete account of the appeal of the Nazi program could, then, only be given if we knew the complete life histories of all the followers. Nevertheless, sufficient information is available to show us the various offerings of the Nazi repertoire. And, like the people at a circus, potential Nazi followers were able to find, in the variety of appeals offered, some particular pattern which consciously or unconsciously attracted them.

A leader provided. By 1920, the institutional structure which had held sway in Germany for several generations had broken down. Neither the state nor the church could claim the allegiance of the individual. No new institutions with promises of stability, no new social values with clearly defined goals had arisen to replace what had gone. The people of Germany were living in a culture with which they could identify politically and geographically but not psychologically. The individual felt himself a more or less isolated unit in a loosely united, multidirectional society.

Because time is required for the emergence of new institutions after a collapse of the old, if social unity is to be restored at all, it must be restored by an individual or some closely knit group which achieves power by capitalizing on the free-floating allegiance of puzzled citizens. Periods of social chaos and weaknesses of central governments have often been followed by Napoleons or Cromwells.[1] People accustomed to institutionalized life cannot plunge happily into a state of anarchy. This was especially true for the German people who, as we have seen, were not used to political responsibility, who had a tradition of political submissiveness. For institutions and social values are not entities that exist in a vacuum. If they have any reality at all, it is in the mental life of the individuals who compose them.

Hence, when institutions and social values are disturbed, it means that people are disturbed. And when people are disturbed they are anxious to regain mental stability. The easiest and most usual way of accomplishing this is to look for a leader, identify oneself with him, transfer one's troubles to him, and believe that he can always cope with things, that he always has another trick up his sleeve, that he can safely protect one against external dangers. This process, so commonly followed by children, is also frequently followed by adults when they face critical situations which prove too much for their own limited resources.[2] Confirmation of this tendency is found in the sudden rise of the number of people willing to endorse Franklin D. Roosevelt for a third presidential term just after the German invasion of Holland and Belgium. In late April, 1940, 47

[1] For a discussion of this point, see Sigmund Neumann, The rule of the demagogue, *Sociol. Rev.,* 1938, 3, 487-498. E. E. Kellett's *The Story of Dictatorship from the Earliest Times till Today* (New York: Dutton, 1937) shows the inverse relationship between the adequacy and strength of institutions and the rise of demagogues.

[2] For a more elaborate, psychoanalytic account of this process, see Robert Waelder, *Psychological Aspects of War and Peace,* New York: Columbia University Press, 1939, 25 f.

per cent of the population in the U. S. said they would vote for Roosevelt for a third term. By the end of May, 1940, this percentage had risen to 57.[3] Undoubtedly a major reason for his break in the third-term tradition was the continuation of the war crisis.

There is ample evidence that the German people during these critical years craved a strong leadership. A clerk has told how:

> Around 1923 I reached the conclusion that no party, but a single man alone could save Germany. This opinion was shared by others, for when the cornerstone of a monument was laid in my home town, the following lines were inscribed on it: "Descendants who read these words, know ye that we eagerly await the coming of the man whose strong hand may restore order."[4]

A business man in East Prussia observed:

> The call for a second Bismarck resounded throughout East Prussia. The desire for a leader was evident in every political manifestation of East Prussians. They could not abide the unholy treaty of peace, the occupation of the Rhineland.[5]

A traveler wrote:

> I made the rounds, going from place to place, from group to group, confused, bewildered, diving now and again into the mad scramble for diversion that surrounded me, but unhappy always with a nostalgia for the proud Germany of my youth. I was looking for the German soul, or rather for the leader who would know how to reanimate it, and I was resolved not to desert again.[6]

Surely one of the millions of people who called themselves German would have the necessary qualifications to satisfy this need for leadership.

It is no wonder, then, that the message of Hitler, his own obvious belief in the righteousness of his program, his sincerity, and his faith in himself made an indelible impression on those who heard him. In a period of doubt and uncertainty, here was a speaker who did not argue the pros and cons of policies but who was fanatically self confident; who did not quietly suggest that he and his program

---

[3] See releases of American Institute of Public Opinion.
[4] T. Abel, *Why Hitler Came into Power,* New York: Prentice-Hall, 1938, 151.
[5] *Ibid.*
[6] K. G. W. Ludecke, *I Knew Hitler,* New York: Scribner's, 1937, 7.

were possible solutions, but who actually shouted certainty at the top of his lungs. Witness typical impressions of people in his audiences who later followed him.

> I saw his illimitable faith in his people and the desire to set them free.[7]

> What impressed me most about Hitler was the courage with which the war-time corporal attacked all evil.[8]

> I do not know how to describe the emotions that swept over me as I heard this man. His words were like a scourge. When he spoke of the disgrace of Germany, I felt ready to spring on any enemy. His appeal to German manhood was like a call to arms, the gospel he preached a sacred truth. He seemed another Luther. I forgot everything but the man; then, glancing around, I saw that his magnetism was holding these thousands as one.[9]

Having found a leader, people rapidly identified themselves with him. His goals became goals for *them*; his program gave *them* interpretations; his sincerity and conviction gave *them* new direction. "I felt that Hitler personified all my desires for a new Germany," said one convert.[10] "At once I offered myself to him and to his cause without reservation . . . I told him the story of my life, dwelling especially upon years during and after the war when I had felt myself baffled at every turn . . . Solemnly clasping hands, we sealed the pact. I had given him my soul," writes another.[11]

Hitler was quick to invite and cement this identity. "You are mine, and I am yours," "*You* are Germany," "*We* are Germany" are typical phrases.

> If I speak to you and to millions of other workers, I do so with greater right than any other. I have myself come from your ranks. I have been among you for four and a half years in war, and I speak now to you to whom I belong. I lead the struggle for the million-masses of our brave, industrious workers and our laboring people.

These are the opening words of a sample speech.[12] The effect of these

---

[7] Abel, *op. cit.,* 153.

[8] *Ibid.,* 152.

[9] Ludecke, *op. cit.,* 13 f.

[10] Abel, *op. cit.,* 183.

[11] Ludecke, *op. cit.,* 16.

[12] Quoted by Schuman, *op. cit.,* 259.

tactics on listeners "was a tremendous surge in our hearts, a something that said: 'Hitler, you are our man. You speak as a soldier of
the front and as a man; you know the grind, you have yourself
been a working man. You have lain in the mud, even as we—no big
shot, but an unknown soldier. You have given your whole being,
all your warm heart, to German manhood, for the well-being of
Germany rather than your personal advancement or self-seeking.' "[13]
"Heil Hitler" became a greeting used not only by the people, but
by Hitler himself. Like Stalin, who is reported to clap when his own
name is cheered, Hitler has sufficiently identified himself with the
people so that even his name is something external to his person, a
symbol of the whole ideology.

Thus it was possible for Hitler to identify himself, not only with
the National Socialist Party, but with the whole nation as well. His
unequivocal acceptance by so many people provided a peculiar kind
of docile, fatalistic democratic basis for his unrestricted power. It is
not a mere euphemism to say that Hitler expressed the "will of the
people." And many of those whom Hitler chose for his close associates were careful to preserve the fiction that the leader was the
sole authority, responsible to no one. If for no other reason, the self-
interest of those who had prestige and power, because they had won
Hitler's confidence, would lead them to deify their leader.

> Just as the Roman Catholic considers the Pope infallible in all
> matters concerning religion and morals, so do we National Socialists
> believe, with the same inner conviction, that for us the leader is,
> in all political and other matters concerning the national and social
> interests of the people, simply infallible. Wherein lies the secret of
> this enormous influence which he has on his followers? . . . It is
> something mystical, inexpressible, almost incomprehensible, which
> this unique man possesses, and he who cannot feel it instinctively
> will not be able to grasp it at all. For we love Adolf Hitler, because
> we believe deeply and unswervingly that God has sent him to us to
> save Germany.[14]

So writes Göring, Hitler's most valuable servant. Under these circumstances, as a national leader with unprecedented power, it was
the part of wisdom for Hitler to refuse any titles that would connect

[13] Abel, *op. cit.*, 153.
[14] Hermann Göring, *Germany Reborn*, London: Mathews and Marrot, 1934, 79 f.

him with former German leaderships. He did not assume the title
of President after von Hindenburg's death; he did not want to be
known as a "Kaiser." He assumed a title of simple grandeur, *Der
Führer*,[15] following the example of Il Duce. And a *Führer* was precisely what the people most craved.[16]

It is important to remember that Hitler reached the pinnacle of
the German state not by the storming of any bastille, the march on
any Rome, or the forceful overthrow of any provisional government.
After the failure of his Munich *Putsch* in 1923, he decided that he
could achieve power only via the election booth. In July of 1932, his
party polled almost 14 million votes, 37 per cent of the total. On
January 30, 1933, he was appointed Chancellor by President von
Hindenburg. All this means, then, that the Nazi leader had a program
which attracted the people and their votes. What was the program?
Why was it effective? A description of some of the main Nazi theses
will show how they fit into the mental contexts of the people.

Naming enemies. One of the most important reasons for Hitler's
astonishing success was his ability to verbalize and concretize causes
of dissatisfaction, to focus attention on real or plausible sources of
trouble. He either discovered or created enemies for the people. A
later follower, after attending his first meeting of the National
Socialist Party, tells how "much was touched upon that had long
been in my subconscious mind, and was now called forth into consciousness. I went home deeply moved, thinking that, if the aims and
purposes outlined by the speaker were capable of achievement, then
life would once more be worth living."[17]

[15] For this and other characterizations of charismatic leadership, see Hans Gerth,
The Nazi Party: its leadership and composition, *Amer. J. Sociol.*, 1940, **45**,
517-541.

[16] We have deliberately left out of account the fascinating story of Hitler's life
and any analysis of Hitler's personality, abnormalities, or maternally inspired pan-
Germanic dreams. A study of Hitler as an individual is a separate story from the
study of Hitler as the leader of a successful mass movement. The secret of Hitler in
the latter capacity lies in the discovery of the relationship between the man and
his followers. The characteristics of the man himself must obviously be noted to
explain the phenomenon, but the genesis of the characteristics are outside our main
interest. The same holds true for his close associates, Göring, Göbbels. Accounts of
Hitler's life will be found in his autobiography, *Mein Kampf*; in Roberts, *op. cit.*,
ch. 1; H. D. Lasswell, The psychology of Hitlerism, *Pol. Quart.*, **4**, 373-84; J.
Gunther, *Inside Europe*, New York: Harper, 1936, chs. 1 and 2.

[17] Abel, *op. cit.*, 120.

Among the earliest enemies isolated out of the confusion was *the Jew*. In order to designate the Jew clearly it was necessary to construct a Nazi doctrine of race. This was not difficult for Nazi scientists. In learned accounts they showed the superiority of the Nordic race which, they pointed out, was found in compact groups within Germany. Aside from the common physical features attributed them, the Nordics were endowed with certain traits of "mind and soul." This race "is uncommonly gifted mentally. It is outstanding for truthfulness and energy. Nordic men for the most part possess, even in regard to themselves, a great power of judgment. They incline to be taciturn and cautious. They feel instantly that too loud talking is undignified. They are persistent and stick to a purpose when once they have set themselves to it. Their energy is displayed not only in warfare but also in technology and in scientific research. They are predisposed to leadership by nature."[18] The possession of German blood united people into *Das Volk*. It is "essential for admission into the community of German people."[19]

Hence any intermixture of blood is regrettable. "Intermarrying with races of foreign blood is as dangerous for the continuance and existence of a people as inheritable internal defects."[20] Since the hybrid Jew has obnoxious characteristics, according to the Nazis, and since the Jew is said to be the only major racial grouping with which German people have direct contact, "the first opposition measures of the National Socialists must aim to remove the Jews from the cultural and economic life of our folk."[21] The official program of the party stated:

> Only those who are members of the nation can be citizens. Only those who are of German blood, without regard to religion, can be members of the German nation. No Jew, therefore, can be a member of the nation.

Such was the rationale of the National Socialist racial doctrine, so avidly accepted by the people in spite of the fact that the "average" German falls far short of the Nordic ideal and in spite of jibes that

[18] *The Nazi Primer: Official Handbook for Schooling the Hitler Youth,* translated by H. L. Childs, New York: Harper, 1938, 20.

[19] *Ibid.,* 13.

[20] *Ibid.,* 77.

[21] *Ibid.,* 78.

the true Nordic is as thin as Göring, as tall as Göbbels, as blond as Hitler.

But for many reasons the racial myth served its purpose. It restored the self-esteem, the status of the people. Anyone who was not classified as a Jew could be classified as an Aryan. Furthermore, in Germany as well as in other parts of the world, there were overt and slumbering prejudices against the Jew. He had been persecuted often before at critical periods. For centuries he had been the favorite scapegoat. In addition to this deeply rooted tradition, "the economic position of the Jewish group within the German nation was undoubtedly superior to that of the average German."[22] The Nazis were quick to point out and to exaggerate the high positions occupied by the 1 per cent of the population labeled Jewish. One report had it, for example, that, in 1930, 57 per cent of the metal-trade firms were in Jewish hands and that, in 1928, 52 per cent of Berlin physicians were Jewish.[23] Any such statistical account obscured the true picture because of the deliberate selection of figures.[24]

It was, therefore, particularly easy to attribute Jewish success, industry, business acumen, professional or cultural attainments to unpatriotic, scheming, treasonable activity.

The fate of Germany seemed a matter of indifference to these international allied parasites thriving on the people.

The war had been a business deal for these creatures.

My observations convinced me that our honest and upstanding people had been poisoned to the marrow by alien Jews.[25]

Such were typical attitudes toward the Jew.

By intensifying this common frame of reference, by making it a respectable social value in larger and larger groups, the Nazis were able to ascribe to the Jews a multitude of evils. They were blamed for pacifism, international capitalism, Marxism, Freemasonry, Esperanto, nudism, reparations, war defeat, Versailles, democracy, inflation, liberalism, sexual immorality, and a host of other ailments of the German body politic. Practically every trouble any German ever had

[22] Hoover, *Germany Enters the Third Reich, op. cit.,* 173.
[23] Brady, *op. cit.,* 55.
[24] American Jewish Committee, *The Jews in Nazi Germany.*
[25] Abel, *op. cit.,* 157, 158, 163.

could be, and was, traced to some Jewish influence by Nazi orators and propagandists, especially by the vituperative Rosenberg.[26] Excerpts from typical party posters of the early period read:

> Today, Friday, August 12, 1921, a great public mass meeting takes place at the Hofbrauhaus. Speaker: Herr Adolf Hitler about: THE PROTEST AGAINST RISING PRICES, A JEWISH SWINDLE. Beginning 8 P.M. War invalids free. To cover expenses of the hall and posters, admission one mark. Jews not admitted.

> German Fellow Citizens! The National Socialist German Workers' Party asks you all to come Thursday, August 25, 1921 to the Zirkus Krone to a giant demonstration against the continued cheating of our people by the Jewish agents of the international world stock exchange capital. Speaker will be: Dr. A. Schilling, author, leader of the National Socialist German Workers' Party at Mährisch-Ostrau, and Herr A. Hitler, Munich, about INTERNATIONAL SOLIDARITY, A JEWISH WORLD FRAUD.[27]

Here, then, was a defenseless enemy, an enemy that could be seen, that was relatively distinguishable, that could be dealt with. One could himself directly participate in the persecution or enjoy it vicariously. Action could be taken and the results of the action observed.[28]

Other enemies to be destroyed were the *Versailles Treaty* and *those who were humiliating Germany* by accepting its provisions. Hitler was uncompromising in his belief that the German people had the need, the right, and the duty not only to restore their lost place in Europe but also to expand it so that they would never again be subjected to the degradation they were experiencing. While other political leaders of the time looked for ways and means to

[26] For Hitler's own detailed analysis of the characteristics of the Jew and the evils they caused, see his *Mein Kampf*, 389-457. (The edition of *Mein Kampf* referred to throughout this and the previous chapter is that of John Chamberlain, S. B. Fay, *et al.*, New York: Reynal & Hitchcock, 1939.)

[27] *Ibid.*, 539, 541.

[28] As Abel, *op. cit.*, 164 f., has clearly pointed out, a small percentage of Nazi followers genuinely disliked the anti-Semitic program of the party.

> Even after I joined the party I did not see eye to eye with it on the Jewish question.

> Only their statements about the Jews I could not swallow. They gave me a headache even after I had joined the party.

Thus reported some of Hitler's followers.

modify Allied demands, Hitler was pounding at the very assumptions on which those demands were made. *Das Volk* was to be reunited into a greater German state. All who stood in the way of such restoration must be annihilated. The first three points of the party program were devoted to this thesis:

> We demand the inclusion of all Germans in a Great Germany on the ground of the right of self-determination. We demand the recognition of the right to equality of the German nation with all other nations; the cancelation of the Treaties of Versailles and St. Germain. We demand land and soil (colonies) for the nutrition of our people and for the settlement of our surplus population.

Visions of a great pan-Germanic state were held before the eyes of the people by Nazi publicists and spellbinders. German territory was conceived to be all territory inhabited by Germans or "receiving its cultural imprint from the German people." Non-German popula-ations who owed their "historical consciousness, their culture, and their national character" to German influence were also designated as part of the greater German culture. Obviously pre-Hitler Germany constituted only a small portion of legitimate German territory as thus defined.

Such an ideology, vigorously expressed and defended, was precisely the nourishment needed by people whose national self-consciousness had been starved. At last someone had appeared who was willing to protest loudly and courageously against injustices which the people had long felt but had been unable to express openly. Now they could identify themselves with a man and a cause. By supporting both man and cause, by attending meetings and rallies, they could finally do something to help rid themselves of their grievances. It is little wonder, then, that the meeting announced by the following poster attracted 8,000 people.

> At last we know why the German government's reply to the Paris Note had been kept secret from us for such a long time. Instead of giving to this renewed unheard-of extortion the only right answer, that is to declare herewith the so-called PEACE TREATY of Versailles as invalid for Germany; to revoke immediately and publicly the confession of war guilt by presenting the genuine documents and to demand the calling of a new peace conference based on the 14 points

of Wilson which then were promised us as the basis, the German government has worked out a COUNTER PROPOSAL. This is known to us. Around a hundred and forty-six billions of goldmarks, that is more than 1,500 billions of paper marks, the Reich's government promises the enemy to be paid by the German people. A COMPLETE LUNACY. But what we have never doubted has now arrived. But this is not enough for these international stock exchange vultures. What they want is Germany's complete enslavement. And yet this bargaining is to be continued? We protest against this! Fellow citizens! Come today, Sunday, March 6, 1921, 10 A.M. to the Giant Demonstration of Protest at the Zirkus Krone. A. Hitler will speak about: LONDON AND US? White collar and manual workers of our people, you alone have to suffer the consequences of this unheard-of treaty. Come and protest against Germany being burdened with the war guilt. Protest against the peace treaty of Versailles which has been forced upon us by the sole culprit of the war, the Jewish international stock exchange capital; protest against the latest dictate from Paris; and protest, finally, against a Reich's government which again gives the most colossal promises without asking the German people. War invalids free. No Jews admitted.[29]

How were the bonds of Versailles to be broken? How were the people to be liberated from their slavery? The "betrayers" of the nation, the "forgetful liars" who prattle "parrot-like nonsense," must be weeded out. They were preaching, said Hitler, that miseries had to be suffered because Germany lost the war. But the war, he proclaimed, was not itself the cause of the nation's troubles "but, in turn, only a consequence of other causes."[30] What were these "other causes"? In addition to Jewish impudence, international world capital, and Marxism, there were *democratic cowardice* and *parliamentary compromising*. Hitler had no patience with representative government:

> The terrible half measures and weakness of the political guidance of the Reich in domestic and foreign affairs was due primarily to the working of the Reichstag; it became one of the chief causes of the political collapse.[31]

The nation's statesmen were branded "national criminals"; "Jewish

[29] *Mein Kampf*, 527.
[30] *Ibid.*, 307.
[31] *Ibid.*, 370.

agents," "henchmen preaching fratricidal war." Democracy with it
parliamentary machinery was called the "gravedigger of the Germa
nation and the German Reich," an institution where "cowardice an
irresponsibility presented themselves in a rarely finished type."[32]

Hitler pointed out to the people a dilemma they could understanc
If Germany were again to be strong, she must have the only powe
other nations would listen to—military might. "Oppressed countrie
will not be brought back into the bosom of a common Reich b
means of fiery protests, but by a mighty sword."[33] And "to forg
the sword is the task of the domestic political leadership of a people
to guard the work of forging and to seek comrades in arms is th
task of the foreign-policy leadership."[34] But at the same time, th
people found themselves under the control of "parliamentary dum
mies or incompetents"[35] who, by their "brutal and rude unscrupt
lousness,"[36] had "stolen and struck from the hands of the nation th
weapon of self-preservation, the only protection of the freedom an
independence of our people."[37] The only resolution of the dilemm
was the nationalization of the masses under a vigorous leadershi
that would never stoop to halfway measures. The final platform o
the party program demanded "the creation of a strong central powe
in the Reich; absolute authority of the political central parliamen
over the entire Reich and all its organizations." Hitler and the Naz
Party offered the way out if the people would only follow.

In creating these enemies, in telling the people that they wer
hated and should hate in turn, Hitler was employing an age-ol
device frequently discussed by the social scientist.[38] The proces
serves several psychological functions: it unites the people into

[32] *Ibid.*, 369.

The extent to which the Communists played into Hitler's hands by increasing con
fusion in opposition ranks is well illustrated by the fact that the underground news
paper, *Rote Fahne*, published by Berlin Communists after Hitler had assumed power
directed its attacks not at the Nazis but at the Social Democrats.

[33] *Ibid.*, 891.
[34] *Ibid.*, 891.
[35] *Ibid.*, 984.
[36] *Ibid.*, 374.
[37] *Ibid.*, 374.
[38] See, for example, E. D. Martin's *Behavior of Crowds*, New York: Harper, 192c
chs. 5 and 6. Schuman, *op. cit.*, chs. 8 and 9, extends the psychoanalytic interpreta
tion of the scapegoat technique to the Nazis.

more closely knit "in-group" by providing "outside" threats; it discourages dissension within the ranks by keeping interest centered on "common troubles"; it exonerates the people themselves from any blame for their conditions; it furnishes concrete or symbolic causes of trouble which people can conceptualize, thereby giving meanings and interpretations to bewildered souls who seek some explanation; it makes possible the directed, effective aggressive action which frustrated people crave, by creating an enemy who can be localized or specified. And, as Hitler points out, "In the ruthless attack upon an adversary, the people sees at all times a proof of its own right."[39]

The leader knew the German people well enough to discern what "enemies" they would accept. He chose enemies that were relatively safe. He concentrated his earlier attacks where he thought the chances of victory were good. "Never antagonize potential enemies. Attack them only when you can destroy them," he is reported to have told a lieutenant during the first years of his struggle for power.[40]

Visions of new social orders. The exploitation of these common enemies and hatreds provided common denominators of interest and certain positive themes in the party program. Within this framework, the Nazis offered special appeals to special groups as the need for such appeals arose. The speeches and writings of the leaders throughout the whole history of the party's development show that most of them had amazing versatility. The rich were told one thing, the poor another; the peasant was comforted by promises that would irritate the urban worker, and vice versa; a *Gauleiter* in a Bavarian lower middle-class community would emphasize Nazi theses that were just as emphatically denied by a *Gauleiter* in a similar community in Prussia. The party was never indifferent to the problems of any specific group which it wanted to attract.

Hitler knew that he needed at least the covert support of the *ruling classes* if he were to attain his objectives. In all internal party disputes, he sided with proposals that would not greatly disturb the balance of economic power. When one of his high lieutenants, Otto Strasser, persisted in arguments for a truly socialist program, he was summarily dismissed. Hitler's thesis was that "economics is a

[39] *Mein Kampf*, 468 f.
[40] Ludecke, *op. cit.*, 59.

secondary matter." But it was not a secondary matter to formulate economic appeals of various kinds when needed to win over certain important groups.

The Junkers and industrialists were naturally gratified with the nationalist emphasis of the movement. Its militarist program was the dream of an army officer so long as he felt he could use the movement for his own designs. The vituperations against Communists were everything members of the ruling classes could hope for. The creation of a strong central authority to deal ruthlessly with trade unions was a welcome prospect.

As time passed, more and more industrial leaders were beginning to see that National Socialism might serve their purposes as a counter-revolutionary movement. By the fall of 1932, confidential letters, exchanged and circulated among leaders of finance, made this point quite explicit:

> The necessary condition for any social reconsolidation of bourgeois rule possible in Germany after the war is the splitting of the workers' movement. Any united workers' movement springing up from below must be revolutionary . . . The working class will begin to turn in the direction of Communism and the bourgeois rule will be faced with the necessity of setting up a military dictatorship. This stage would mark the beginning of the phase of the incurable sickness of bourgeois rule. As the old sluice mechanism can no longer be sufficiently restored, the only possible means of saving bourgeois rule from this abyss is to effect the splitting of the working class and its tying to the State apparatus by other and more direct means. Herein lie the positive possibilities and the tasks of National Socialism.[41]

Most of the Nazi oratory and propaganda was vague in its economic program. When specific, drastic proposals were needed to win over certain dissatisfied groups, members of the ruling class were hastily assured that such utterances were to be taken with a grain of salt. For example, a Dresden party leader wrote the following letter to a factory manager in Weimar:

> Do not let yourself be continually confused by the text of our posters . . . Of course, there are catchwords like "Down with Capitalism," . . . etc., but these are necessary (unquestionably) for under the flag of "German national" or "national" alone, you must know, we should

[41] *The Deutesche Führerbriefe,* Sept. 16, 20, 1932, Nos. 72 and 75.

never reach our goal, we should have no future. We must talk the language of the embittered Socialist workmen . . . or else they wouldn't feel at home with us. We don't come out with a direct pro- gram . . . for reasons of diplomacy.[42]

When a Nazi speaker was asked about social insurance he pointed out: "Ten laws can do away with the entire mess. Traitors will be hanged. Strikers will be shot, and not many will be willing to be put against the wall on this account."[43] When Hitler was asked what he would do with the great Krupp corporation if he attained power, he replied, "Why, nothing. Do you think I am so senseless as to upset business?"[44] When great landowners expressed their worries about platform 17 of the party program, which demanded "land reform adapted to our national needs, the enactment of a law for the uncompensated expropriation of land for public purposes . . ." Hitler himself consoled them.

> It is necessary (he wrote) to reply to the false interpretation on the part of our opponents of Point 17 of the Party. Since the Party admits the principle of private property, it is obvious that the expression "confiscation without compensation" merely refers to possible legal powers to confiscate, if necessary, land illegally acquired or not ad- ministered in accordance with national welfare. It is directed in the first instance against the Jewish companies which speculate in land.[45]

Two years later, a party lieutenant pointed out that "the spirit of the whole program proves clearly that National Socialism, being a convinced and consistent opponent of Marxism, utterly rejects its ruinous central doctrine of general confiscation, and considers a per- manent agricultural class to be the best and surest foundation for the national state."[46]

It is, therefore, no wonder that National Socialism seemed a good bet to many members of the ruling classes, and that many of them gave it their moral and financial support even in its infancy.[47] "Hitler held out to us the promise of complete freedom," said an

[42] Quoted by Mowrer, *Germany Puts the Clock Back*, New York: Morrow, 1933, 149.

[43] *Ibid.*, 141.

[44] Schuman, *op. cit.*, 137.

[45] *Ibid.*, 134.

[46] *Ibid.*, 135.

[47] Mowrer, *op. cit.*, 142 f.

industrialist who had underwritten the party, but was later to be sadly disillusioned.[48]

Remedies for the particular troubles of the *middle class* were repeated over and over again. "We demand the creation of a sound middle class," began one of the points in the official party platform. The evils of the capitalist system which had brought about economic insecurity and a low standard of living were to be abolished. "We demand summary confiscation of all war profits. We demand the nationalization of all trusts. We demand profit-sharing in large concerns. We demand a grandiose extension of the old-age pension system. We demand immediate communalization of department stores and their rental at low cost to small merchants, the consideration of small merchants in purchases by the federal government, the states or the municipalities," were other avowed aims of the party. What could better appeal to the *Kleinbürgher*, a small business man who viewed with alarm the dissolution of his kind by the great monopolies? A poster publicizing a meeting of 1922 read:

> When on November 9, 1918, the German people was driven into revolution, it was told that this was the beginning of the "nation's liberation" from the bonds of "world capitalism." Today the makers of the revolution of that time admit that the whole world is ruled by a gang of Jewish stock exchange bandits, that no longer the nations but the "world bankers" decide on the destinies of this earth. In this way the true purpose of the revolution is fulfilled. While the power of the international stock exchange dictatorship, thanks to the protection by the Marxist and democratic parties, grows more and more, the last remnants of millions of independent existences are destroyed. The extinction of our retail traders and of our retail commerce is the intended final goal of our present so-called "social" policy. A fraud upon the nations such as the world has never seen before. Fellow citizens! Members of the doomed classes and professions, small business men and small tradesmen, manual laborers and officials, workers of all professions and classes! Come to the great public Mass Meeting. Our party member Adolf Hitler will speak about: THE POLICY OF THE DESTRUCTION OF OUR MIDDLE CLASS.[49]

And the appeal was especially winning since all this was to be

---

[48] Fritz Thyssen, *New York Times*, June 9, 1940.
[49] *Mein Kamp*, 552.

ccomplished without a bloody class struggle and without the danger hat members of the middle class would sink to the status of the roletariat.

What is the ultimate cause of this unheard-of weakness which makes Germany today the defenseless victim of its exploiters? It is the class struggle.[50]

(And) the regime of national concentration will, with iron fist, bring the opposing interests of the different strata of society into that harmony which is so essential to the prosperity of the German people.[51]

Thus the expanding middle class which had suffered under capitalism and which feared Communism found the sort of rationalization it had been seeking. And many members of the middle class must have looked with hungry eyes on the hundreds of positions o be vacated by the Jews when the Nazis attained power.

Hitler clearly saw that any widespread, organized opposition of *the proletariat* would have to be prevented if National Socialism were to chieve power.

The German worker is not lifted into the frame of the German people's community by the roundabout way of weak fraternizing scenes, but by the deliberate uplifting of his social and cultural position, until the most serious differences may be looked upon as overcome. A movement which establishes this development for its goal will have to draw its followers primarily from this camp . . . Unions, led by national fanatics where political and folkish considerations are concerned, would make millions of workers the most valuable members of their nationality.[52]

The leader realized that the wooing of the proletariat from its old allegiances was not an easy, short time job. "Experience shows that it will take many generations."[53] But National Socialism had to begin at once to gain what support it could from the working man.

The party's avowed intention of destroying "international capitalism" was one of the attractions offered. The program included a demand for "the elimination of income which is obtained without

---

[50] From a poster on p. 523 of *Mein Kampf*.
[51] From a speech by Göring, quoted in Hoover, *op. cit.*, 175.
[52] *Mein Kampf*, 471 f.
[53] *Ibid.*, 472.

labor or effort." Hitler furthermore promised workers that thei rights would be zealously guarded by the state. "The National So cialist employer must know that the fortune and the satisfaction of his employees are the premise for the existence and the developmen of his own economic importance."[54] To the self-imposed question "Are trade unions necessary?" Hitler replies in *Mein Kampf*, "Trade unions cannot be dispensed with, in my opinion. On the contrary they belong to the most important institutions of the economic life of the nation."[55] But like the employers, the employees, too, "are chargees and guardians of the entire national community."[56]

To break the monopoly of appeal which the trade unions and Communists, because of their legislative proposals, had for the work ing class, the Nazis freely borrowed old proletariat programs. The platform demanded that "the state be obliged, in the first instance, to provide the possibility of work and life for the citizen." A Nazi solu tion of the food problem was added: "If it is not possible to feed the entire population of the state, the subjects of foreign states must be expelled from the Reich." Various other socialistic points of the official program, already noted, appealed to old-line socialists in the ranks of the working class. The party further contended that "the state must care for the improvement of the people's health through the protection of mother and child, through the forbidding of child-labor." Also, ". . . in order to make possible the attainment of higher education for every capable and industrious German and thereby the entrance into a leading position, the state has the respon sibility to bear for a fundamental extension of our entire educa tional system . . . We demand the education at state expense of especially gifted children of poor parents without regard to pro fession or position." Here were signs of real socialism.

The party organization also provided certain democratic com panionship for members of the proletariat who were bitter about class distinctions and who asked:

Why did the higher classes of society have so many privileges? Why was the workman or subordinate treated so condescendingly? Why was one ashamed to sit down at a table with laborers? Why did the

[54] *Ibid.*, 875.
[55] *Ibid.*, 871.
[56] *Ibid.*, 875.

rich man say to his children, "You must not play with the children of workmen; they are too dirty and naughty"? Why did the master converse in a comradely tone when alone with the servant and why, when another "gentleman" was present, did he make the difference of rank so grossly evident?[57]

For the party, presumably, did away with the hated external signs of class stratification, with old titles, old fashions, old hierarchies. A party recruit recalled his first attendance at a district meeting.

At first I could hardly believe that a janitor was local group leader. Here, in the west end of Berlin, where 90 per cent of the population were intellectuals. Nevertheless, neither envy nor ill will could be perceived. This was how I had always imagined the true community of the people.[58]

Such appeals were successful in attracting some trade unionists, disillusioned radicals, and floating workers. But the majority of the urban proletariat persisted in their old loyalties and looked with fear and suspicion on the Nazis. As late as November of 1932, they were strong enough to stage an effective transport strike in Berlin. Almost six million people voted for the Communists in the election held that month.

Various promises were made for the benefit of the disgruntled *peasants*. As we have already seen, they were told that large estates would be confiscated, and the implication was clear that the peasants would be the logical persons to till the fields of expropriated Junkers for the good of the state. Peasants were promised an end of the "interest slavery" which had so long kept them in debt. They were shown how the party would rid them of the competition of foreign markets, how the expansion of the territory under the third Reich would bring new and fertile soil. which rightfully belonged to Germans. The farmer was eulogized as "the bearer of the inheritance of health, the source of the nation's youth, the backbone of its armed strength."[59] The party demand for "the freedom of all religions in the state in so far as they do not endanger its welfare or offend against the morals and sense of decency of the German race" was noted by Catholic peasants.

[57] Quotation from a case study, Abel, *op. cit.,* 219 f.

[58] *Ibid.,* 239 f.

[59] Quoted by Schuman, *op. cit.,* 135.

The party by no means forgot the frustrated *youth* of the nation.
They were told that they were the hope of the future. Hitler capitalized on what he knew were divisions within families and quarrels between parents and children, regarding steps to be taken.
Young people were told that they should not permit themselves to
suffer the consequences of a war and a peace for which they were in
no way responsible. If the "inertia and indifference of their fathers"
made the older generation "satisfied with the cheap explanation that
nothing can be done," it was clear that society would collapse unless
German youth was willing, in their own interest, to shoulder the
task of building a new state.[60] The party also held out to them their
inherent right to work and to be educated. This education, it should
be noted, advocated that "youthful brains must in general not be
burdened with things 95 per cent of which it does not need and
therefore forgets again."[61] Why, argued Hitler, should "98 thousand
have to be tortured in vain" to learn French "for the sake of 2 thousand people for whom the knowledge of this language is of some
use."[62] The new education was to concern itself with the promotion
of physical fitness, the building of character, courage, and will
power. To stamp out the growing immorality of youth, Hitler held
out the realistic solution that early marriages must be made possible
for the coming generation. The young men who joined the SA
(storm troops) were promised that they would become a part of the
police force. This would mean civil-service standing with its security
and prestige.

Finally, in devising their program, the Nazis remembered that
women constituted half the population. Hitler realized that the overwhelming majority of German women in these early years of the
twentieth century were not really fundamentally interested in assuming political responsibility, in achieving professional success. Like
their mothers and grandmothers, like women in almost every corner
of the world, they were still anxious to play their roles as wives and
mothers. So it was pointed out to them that the Nazi plan for providing jobs and economic security for men would rapidly induce
them to look for wives. And Hitler also pointed out that the state

[60] *Mein Kampf, op. cit.*, 511.
[61] *Ibid.*, 626.
[62] *Ibid.*, 627.

must take care "that the fertility of the healthy woman is not limited by the financial mismanagement of a regime which makes children a curse for the parents."[63] Many repressed, frustrated, or dissatisfied women were consciously or unconsciously attracted to the leader.

Such were some of the attractions of the party for special groups. It "has had at times to be simultaneously all things to all men."[64] But in reviewing these appeals and in locating the strength of Hitler's following, it must constantly be borne in mind that Hitler never obtained a majority vote for his party. Since the story here deals with the success of a movement and since we are forced to chart this success by trying to understand why the party appealed to different interest groups, the false impression may be obtained that the movement finally attracted the overwhelming majority of the people. As has already been pointed out, Hitler received 37 per cent of the vote in July of 1932. But once his minority group attained power, its vigorous suppression of all dissenting opinion and its ruthless dissolution of all organized opposition gave it complete authority. Just how many of the German people might have been called followers of the movement at the height of its power will probably never be known.

The appeals of the early years, like the statements and propaganda issued after Hitler became Chancellor of the Reich, represent a confused mixture of fact and fiction, of sincere promise and insincere bluff. But how could these be distinguished? Only the few who were close to Hitler could guess his basic standards of judgment; only the experience of subsequent years has told us which of these many proposals were really meant. Yet, in their time and in their social context these appeals were effective.

[63] *Ibid.,* 608.
[64] Hoover, *op. cit.,* 152. This technique of varying interpretations to suit a particular group is one of the most important Nazi propaganda devices during the second World War. For example, after the Anglo-American agreement in 1940, in which Britain leased certain territory for United States naval bases in exchange for overage destroyers, German propaganda for home consumption pointed out that this move demonstrated England's weakness, since she was giving up valuable territory for a few pieces of scrap iron. Neutral European countries were told that the destroyers would never reach England because Germany commanded the sea by her submarine fleet. People in South America were told that this was an attempt on the part of the United States to encircle and conquer them, while persons in the United States who listened to German short-wave broadcasts heard that President Roosevelt had made a bad deal and was getting his country into war.

How well the varied promises were kept after Hitler became Chancellor is a question we need not pursue here. That many early followers were very soon disillusioned is certain. The following excerpts from the life histories of a few people illustrate Nazi appeals and Nazi hypocrisy.[65]

(*A Roman Catholic priest* whose sole interest was to educate young people in the Catholic tradition. Since he had been told by the Nazis that if they achieved power, they could cooperate with him in this work, he went to Rome to study fascist youth organizations.) I returned from Rome full of hope, believing that even under the new regime I would be able to work among the youth for Christ and his church. But I was sadly mistaken. I had believed that I was dealing with upright Germans, but they turned out to be pure Bolshevists.

(*Hans* was *an adolescent who joined the party* which promised improvement of working conditions for youth. The day after attending a Nazi celebration in the spring of 1933, he returned in his SA uniform to the office where he worked, feeling disgruntled.) It is a dirty trick, nobody got anything out of the day off. We didn't have any fun. We had to march for seven hours. I'd rather deliver parcels and flirt with the salesgirls.

(*The owner of a small store.*) Small business was exceedingly embittered because all the promises that had been made concerning the abolition of the injurious department-store competition had not been kept . . . They saw themselves cheated. For what other motive caused them to cast their vote for Hitler? They had been promised a tremendous improvement in their existence and now their biggest competitors were being encouraged.

(*A skilled worker.*) Time and again a worker would say to me: "We can't understand why the party in power calls itself *National Socialistische Arbeiter Partei*. What are they doing after all for the workers? After we deduct all the contributions from our wages we work for a pittance. We are no better off than we were before."

(*A member of the lower middle class* gives his reactions to an announcement made by Hitler to the effect that the money collected by the *Winterhilfe* drive to relieve the sufferings of the poor had been used instead for rearmament.) It is quite clear that the hard-earned nickels of the little man, pressed from him by an appeal to his pity

[65] Allport, Hartshorne, and Fay, *op. cit.*

for the very poor, had not been used for this worthy purpose. They had been used cold-bloodedly for strictly military purposes. None had any idea in 1933 that these morally motivated collections were connected with such warlike intentions.

(*A former trade unionist.*) The laborers saw with bitterness the extravagant doings of the new leaders who posed as the lifesavers of the German people, who drove through the streets in the most luxurious limousines . . . "What is the difference between these Nazis, even if they wear uniforms, and the infamous party bosses of the Republic?"

Nazi Tactics

In a very real sense, the gamut of Nazi appeals just outlined was the foundation of Nazi tactics. The appeals provided the goals of National Socialism—they gave what systematic rationalization there was to the movement. When compared to the theoretical structure of Marxism, this Nazi philosophy appears patchy and opportunistic. But it is false to conclude that there was no theory at all. On the contrary, Hitler was well aware that some general formulation of principles was a prerequisite to the movement's success. Discussing the failure of Germany's fight on Marxism he said:

> Every attempt at fighting a view of life by means of force will finally fail, unless the fight against it represents the form of an attack for the sake of a new spiritual direction. Only in the struggle of two views of life with each other can the weapon of brute force, used continuously and ruthlessly, bring about the decision in favor of the side it supports.[66]

Hitler's autobiography and speeches provided the necessary Bible for the movement.[67] And because the new Bible listed enemies and goals and had no pretense of being logically or scientifically valid,

[66] *Mein Kampf*, 223.
[67] Hitler himself did not consider the value of *Mein Kampf* to be great in attracting *new* members to the cause but in providing an "intimate enlightenment" for those who were *already* party members (see preface to *Mein Kampf*). The fact that goals, objectives, and enemies are more important aspects of fascist policy than consistent rationalization is shown by Mussolini's order in 1921 that "within the two months between now and the National Congress the philosophy of fascism must be created." (Letter to Bianchi, Aug. 27, 1921, reprinted in *Message et Proclami*, Milan: 1929. 29.) At that time the Italian movement of Fascism was two years old.

the techniques by means of which the goals were achieved could be pragmatic. If one method failed, another could be tried without hesitation and without fear of ideological inconsistency.

> Every idea aimed at changing the world has not only the right but also the duty to assure itself of those means which make possible the carrying out of its ideas. Its success is the only worldly judge of the right or the wrong of such an enterprise.

This was Hitler's statement of pragmatism.[68] Once the goals were outlined, the task, then, was to get them to the people in the most effective manner possible.

The pragmatism and opportunism of party tactics were facilitated by the comparative disintegration of old norms and the disrespect for old mores. The Nazis were not hampered by the rigid, accepted standards of morality that hold sway in a culture in less critical times. It was therefore possible for them to reformulate standards of judgment, to redefine "right," "justice," "liberty," and "good" in their own terms. This complete revision of values *is* the Nazi Revolution. What people in certain parts of the world would regard as "dishonesty," "treachery," "deceit," or "barbarity" the new Nazi philosophy would regard simply as good tactics—*if* such practices brought the German people, or the nation, closer to their goals.[69] Nowhere was this revolution clearer than in the complete Nazi rejection of much that an age of reason would stand for.[70] The Nazis clearly recog-

---

[68] *Mein Kampf,* 477.

[69] It should be remembered that minority groups who want radical changes in existing norms are generally condemned. Cf. pages 117-120.

[70] The fact that the shift in values was so revolutionary made it difficult at first for some people to believe the Nazis would actually carry through proposals which conflicted so much with accepted standards. The case studies of Hartshorne, *et al.,* clearly show that for many people it took a profound personal shock to make them realize that they had been looking at Nazism through rose-colored glasses. For example, a young Jewish lawyer reported that he was looking for a job in Germany in 1935. When his prospective employer asked him why he was trying to find work in Germany at this time, he replied:

I am of the opinion that the government will be contented with the anti-Semitic measures carried out so far. Things will calm down from now on.

Only after his father and brother had died from Nazi cruelties and after violence to his own person did he realize the significance of the Nazi threat.

The wife of a Jewish manufacturer wrote:

After January 1933, the organization, Strength through Joy, had ordered that

...ized that the masses of people are not motivated by rational appeals, that the common man is inspired to action when he can incorporate as one of his ego values some abstract or specific principle—some principle which may itself be illogical, prescientific, incapable of accurate definition, but which the individual thinks he understands and which he thinks will, if achieved, bring him the kind of world he wants. Said the leader:

> The driving force of the most important changes in the world has been found less in scientific knowledge animating the masses, but rather in a fanaticism dominating them and in a hysteria which drove them forward.[71]

Hence the party tactics must be designed to create this fanaticism and hysteria wherever and whenever possible.

> The nationalization of the great masses can never take place by way of half measures, by a weak emphasis upon a so-called objective viewpoint, but by a ruthless and fanatically one-sided orientation as to the goal to be aimed at.[72]

The man who later became the Nazi Minister of Propaganda echoed and amplified Hitler's words:

> A revolutionist must be able to do everything—to unchain volcanic passions, to arouse outbreaks of fury, to set masses of men on the march, to organize hate and suspicion with ice-cold calculation, so to speak with legal methods.[73]

To persons reared in the Christian, democratic tradition, here is genius on a low level.

Simplification of problems. If party propaganda was to accomplish

all the workers and clerks must have a big trip with their employers once a year. The first year we arranged a nice trip to the Black Forest. My husband refused to take part. But all the rest of the family with my father-in-law and the maids came along. I always liked to make trips into the nice surroundings and enjoyed it very much. They sang in the cars and were tactful enough not to sing Jew-baiting songs . . . At dinner I recited a little poem I had made for this day.

Only after her husband's business had been completely taken away did she see what Nazism meant for her.

[71] *Mein Kampf*, 468.

[72] *Ibid.*, 467.

[73] Göbbels, in *Der Angriff*, Feb. 18, 1929. Quoted by Schuman, *op. cit.*, 83.

these ends it must carefully adjust itself to the thought and language of the people. It must catch their attention.[74] Wrote Hitler:

> To whom has propaganda to appeal? To the scientific intelligentsia or to the less educated masses? It has to appeal forever and only to the masses! Propaganda is not for the intelligentsia or for those who unfortunately call themselves by that name today, but propaganda is in its contents as far from being science as perhaps a poster is art in its presentation as such. A poster's art lies in the designer's ability to catch the masses' attention by outline and color . . . The task of propaganda lies not in a scientific training of the individual, but rather in directing the masses toward certain facts, events, necessities, etc., the purpose being to move their importance in the masses' field of vision.[75]

And propaganda must hold this attention, must capitalize on it by making appeals simple and oversimple.

> The great masses' receptive ability is only very limited, their understanding is small but their forgetfulness is great. As a consequence of these facts, all effective propaganda has to limit itself only to a very few points and to use them like slogans until even the very last man is able to imagine what is intended by such a word. As soon as one sacrifices this basic principle and tries to become versatile, the effect will fritter away, as the masses are neither able to digest the material offered nor to retain it.[76]

And again Göbbels echoes his leader:

> The ordinary man hates nothing more than two-sidedness, to be called upon to consider this as well as that. The masses think simply and primitively. They love to generalize complicated situations and from their generalization to draw clear and uncompromising conclusions. Our agitation has often been called unintelligent and primitive. Certainly National Socialist agitation is primitive. However, the people think primitively.[77]

[74] For a discussion of Nazi propaganda, see L. Doob, *Propaganda: Its Psychology and Technique*, New York: Holt, 1935, ch. 16.

[75] *Mein Kampf*, 230 f.

[76] *Ibid.*, 234.

[77] Quoted by Albion Ross, Göbbels edits the popular mind in Germany, *New York Times Magazine*, Feb. 14, 1937, 27.

When the Nazis were later able to control the press and the radio, they further forced decision, distorted facts, oversimplified problems.

> The National Socialist press (wrote Göbbels) does not allow the reader to come to conclusions according to his own tastes. The reader, on the contrary, is to be instructed and trained according to the newspaper's purpose and tendency.[78]

And what held for the press was true of the radio.

The leaders followed these dicta not only in the content of their arguments but also in the form and context of their presentation. Hitler pointed out in the preface of his autobiography that "one is able to win people far more by the spoken than by the written word, and that every great movement on this globe owes its rise to the great speakers and not to the great writers." He clearly recognized what later research demonstrated to be a fact,[79] that "the mass of people is lazy in itself, that they lazily remain within the course of old habits, and that by themselves they do not like to take up anything written unless it corresponds to what one believes oneself, and furnishes what one hopes for."[80] "The whole flood of newspapers and all the books that intellectualism produces year by year run off from the millions of the lowest classes like water from oiled leather."[81] Hitler points out that the speaker, unlike the writer, can adjust himself to his audience, vary his arguments to suit the occasion, repeat strategic points until even the dullest understand, anticipate all questions and objections, arouse enthusiasm and conviction which will not later be dampened by calm scrutiny of printed material.[82] To be sure, as Hitler recognized, "among a thousand speakers there is perhaps only a single one who is able to speak before locksmiths and university professors alike in a form which is equally satisfactory to both sides or even impassions them towards a sweeping storm of applause."[83] But Hitler also realized very early as the years have amply proved, that he, like Lenin and Lloyd George,

[78] *Ibid.*

[79] Cf. Paul Lazarsfeld, *Radio and the Printed Page,* New York: Duell, Sloan & Pearce, 1940. Here there is clear proof that reading increases in direct proportion and radio listening in inverse proportion to the socio-economic level of the individual.

[80] *Mein Kampf,* 705.

[81] *Ibid.,* 707.

[82] *Ibid.,* 705-716.

[83] *Ibid.,* 475.

was one in a thousand. The innumerable speeches and party demon-strations, where the leader, Göbbels, or another one-among-a-thou-sand held forth, were basic to the vigorous policy followed to im-plement this recognition of the superiority of the spoken word in appealing to the masses.[84]

Mass meetings. The mass-meetings technique had other tactical, psychological advantages. For one thing, such occasions showed the single individual that he was not one of only a scattered few with new-found convictions, that the minority group of which he was a member was organized, growing, potentially powerful. Wrote Hitler:

> The mass meeting is necessary if only for the reason that in it the individual, who in becoming an adherent of a new movement feels lonely and is easily seized with the fear of being alone, receives for the first time the pictures of a greater community, something that has a strengthening and encouraging effect on most people.[85]

This strategy is particularly effective at a critical time when old norms have disintegrated, when people are seeking emotional se-curity, when they are anxious to find their place in a new world of new norms.

The mass meeting further enabled Hitler to take advantage of other psychological conditions he clearly recognized. For example, mass meetings could be planned for the time of day or the time of the week when people are likely to be least alert and thus most susceptible to suggestion.

> This applies, of course, most of all to meetings to which people with a contrary orientation of will are coming, and who now have to be won for new intentions (he notes). It seems that in the morning and even during the day men's will power revolts with highest energy against an attempt at being forced under another's will and an-other's opinion. In the evening, however, they succumb more easily to the dominating force of a stronger will. For truly every such meeting presents a wrestling match between two opposed forces. The superior oratorical talent of a domineering apostolic nature will now

[84] Wherever written words were needed, said Hitler, they should be as short as possible, should make as much use of pictures as possible, so that "a man does not have to work with his brains."

[85] *Mein Kampf,* 715.

succeed more easily in winning for the new will people who themselves have in turn experienced a weakening of their force of resistance in the most natural way than people who still have full
command of the energies of their minds and their will power.[86]

Bodily fatigue and full stomachs dull critical ability.

Hitler was sensitive to the problem of creating the proper atmosphere for meetings. The whole setting of a mass meeting, with its
decorations, slogans, banners, lighting effects, and the like should,
in so far as possible, be conducive to the same general impression
the speaker hopes to make with his words. "The same purpose," he
observed, "serves also the artificially created and yet mysterious dusk
of the Catholic churches, the burning candles, incense, censers, etc."[87]
A person who attended many of the party meetings believed that
"the military organization, always present in full force, provided the
setting and enthused the masses. This setting gave a sense of reality
to the speaker's words and helped fanaticise the millions to believe
and trust in the man who wanted to be their leader, a leader in all
spheres of national life . . ."[88] Hitler knew the importance of past
associations, "traditional memories and images," which should be
utilized wherever possible. Meetings were staged in cities or buildings that had some special significance to the people or the party.
And, finally, the whole program of such a meeting was carefully
designed as a build-up for the important speech, generally by Hitler
himself. Bands would play Nazi songs; storm troopers in later days
would show Nazi strength. Surrounded by party officers with re-
splendent uniforms was Hitler in his plain brown suit. As Schuman
has described a typical meeting:

> The chairman speaks softly, confidentially, soothingly, like a good
> neighbor. He dwells on the misfortunes of his auditors. He shouts:
> "What is the cause of our suffering?" Mighty voices from the audience
> reply: "The System!" "Who is behind the System?" "The Jews!"
> "Who is Adolf Hitler?" "A last hope—*unser Führer!*"[89]

Then Hitler rises to speak. After the party attained power and had
all the resources of the state available, these mass meetings were more

[86] *Ibid.*, 710 f.
[87] *Ibid.*, 711.
[88] Allport, Hartshorne, and Fay, *op. cit.*
[89] Schuman, *op. cit.*, 93.

elaborate, more meticulously planned, more impressive. All the science, art, and propagandistic skill the Nazis could muster were devoted to celebrations without parallel in history.

Some party symbols were carefully planned, others arose spontaneously. The name for the new movement was created with great deliberation: *National-Socialist-German-Workers-Party*. Each word had special significance for certain groups. The red on the party banner preserved a color dear to the Socialists; its combination with white and black recalled to the Nationalists the imperial colors. The swastika reminded all of the common enemy—the Jew. The party salute, the Heil Hitler greeting, gave short-cut identifications to members of the movement, and also represented breaks from the past. Slogans arose to serve as catalytic agents, as simple, memorable rationalizations of new goals to be achieved, of old evils to be destroyed: *Deutschland Erwache, Freiheit und Brot, Gemeinnutz vor Eigennutz, Blut und Boden.*

Personal effort. But the brilliance of the great meetings staged by the party, the ostentatious use of banners and slogans, should not blind us to the fact that behind the fanfare, and supplementary to the oratorical appeals of the leader, there was quietly going on all the time propaganda of a more personal, intimate variety. This, of course, was especially true of the early years before the movement was large enough to attract wholesale attention, before individuals dared align themselves openly with so radical a program. A page from the life history of a Nazi describes this underground proselytism.

> During my numerous trips, which frequently involved extended periods in the country, I found ample opportunity to spread the National Socialist doctrine. At first it was necessary to proceed with consummate caution, since the people, but lately betrayed, were wary of everything new. It was best if one could say with a good conscience that though one was acquainted with National Socialist teachings, and though one was sympathetic to the idea, one was not actually a member of the party. By this stratagem I succeeded in the course of conversations with simple farmers to inoculate them with the National Socialist "serum." Later on, when one or another was more or less won over, there would be meetings in the tiny parlor of a little peasant cottage, to which all and sundry would come, without any

suspicion of attending a political meeting. Conversations were always planned with a view to spreading National Socialist doctrines.[90]

In this way resistance was broken by "neutral" friends or acquaintances, the futility of old frames of reference was pointed out, mental contexts were made receptive to the more direct appeals of the Leader.

Terrorism. The terroristic methods so freely used by the Nazis after they attained power were part of their propaganda armament from the very beginning. Persons who were avowedly cynical or opposed to their policies were branded "Jewish-influenced liberal intellectuals," "hidden Marxists," "grumbling philistines who prefer butter to cannons and world politics."[91]

It was gradually made more and more difficult for anyone to remain indifferent to the party. The propaganda weapons of "extortion, anonymous denunciation, and anonymous rumors" resulted in "boycott, isolation," and, ultimately, "disrepute." Every effort was made to demonstrate Nazi terror when it seemed safe to do so. For example, as early as 1922, when Hitler was asked by the Duke and Duchess of Coburg to speak at a "German Day" and to bring some of his group with him, instead of bringing a few representatives of the party, with the meager party funds he hired a special train and filled it with seven hundred storm troopers. When the storm troopers marched down the street, they were jeered by the Reds. The march turned into a hand-to-hand street fight. The radicals were dispersed. Public curiosity was aroused to new heights and the evening meeting was jammed. Hitler urged everyone to action. As soon as the meeting ended a new "Red" hunt was on. "Ruthless punishment was inflicted upon the Reds wherever they appeared, and their headquarters were wrecked. Patrols found the Reds in horrible condition, as the result of being attacked singly by groups of our assailants," writes one who participated in the affair.[92] After January 1933, the party was able to use the concentration camp, the secret trial, and execution as additional terrorist devices.

[90] Abel, *op. cit.,* 82 f.
[91] Cf. Gerth, *op. cit.,* 532 f., for a discussion of the systematic terrorism of the Nazis. For its later use in France, see Edmund Taylor, *Strategy of Terror,* Boston: Houghton Mifflin, 1940.
[92] Ludecke, *op. cit.,* 82-90.

The elaborate party structure that was gradually organized divide the nation into districts, each with a party leader. Districts were sub divided, subdistricts were broken up into local groups, these int party cells, these in turn into party blocks.[93] Such tightly knit organ zations, receiving orders from the top, made for the utmost eff ciency. Decisions taken by one man could be carried out almos immediately. Furthermore, information did not travel one way only Every good Nazi might regard himself as a spy, relaying informa tion of persons dangerous to the cause, of backsliders, of local discor tent that the party should somehow relieve in its own interest.

> I have 100,000 eyes in my territory to see that everything goes all right. I have 100,000 ears close to the bosom of the people. They report in the shortest time where disturbances and economic difficul ties emerge, where food prices are unjust, where there is a shortage of food—in short where the people feel thwarted.

Thus wrote a district leader in 1937, when the mechanism ha attained a perfection impossible in the first years but neverthele already in process of formation.[94]

Party composition. By means of all these appeals and tactics, th handful of disgruntled men we first encountered in the Munich bee hall had become transformed into a vast yet compact organizatio of almost 850,000 by January 1933, when it was about to assum the reins of government. From what parts of the population wa this huge membership recruited? What people had been most su ceptible to the Nazi suggestion? A few statistics on the compositio of the party just before it attained power give us some insigh When classified by occupation (Table VI), we find the middle classe overrepresented, the manual workers and peasants underrepresentec

The membership also was overrepresented in the younger ag groups: whereas only 31 per cent of the total population was betwee the ages of eighteen and thirty in 1933, over 40 per cent of the Naz membership fell within this age group.[95] Among the political leader of the party almost half were ex-soldiers. Of almost a half-millio political leaders recorded by the party census in 1935, almost a thir were former school teachers, chiefly from the elementary school

[93] Gerth, *op. cit.*, 522.
[94] *Ibid.*, 540.
[95] *Ibid.*, 529 f.

Table VI*

PERCENTAGE OCCUPATIONAL DISTRIBUTION OF
NAZI PARTY MEMBERSHIP IN 1933

Occupational Classification	Party Membership	Total in Population Gainfully Employed
Manual workers	31.5	46.3
White-collar employees	21.1	12.5
Independents†	17.6	9.6
Peasants	12.6	21.1
Others‡	10.5	5.9

* Abbreviated from Gerth, *op. cit.*, 527.
† Skilled artisans, professional persons, merchants, etc.
‡ Domestic servants and non-agricultural family helpers.

This last figure is not surprising if one remembers that National Socialism was conceived of itself as an instrument of mass education and that German school teachers were not unaccustomed to bureaucracy.[96]

Behind the scenes, obscured by statistics, and hidden from public view were certain wealthy industrialists and landowners. In 1931, Thyssen, who had virtual control of the Ruhr, introduced Hitler to the Industrialists' Club in Düsseldorf as "the savior of Germany."[97] Rumor and some evidence have it that financial aid from industrialists was not confined to German capitalists alone. Some funds to support the movement undoubtedly came from England, France, the United States, and Holland. But just how much was contributed and by whom may forever remain a closed secret. Certain Junkers, diplomats, and army men were involved in the complicated intriguing that surrounded the aging von Hindenburg and facilitated Hitler's victory. The details of the political machinations, preceding the final triumph on January 30, 1933, lie far outside our present concern. But there can be little doubt that many members of the ruling classes saw in Hitler a leader whom they could use to stamp out the threat of Communism, to stop its westward penetration. His first acts as Chancellor must have encouraged them. The estates of the Junkers remained intact. Within a month Hitler apparently had a cordial meeting with leading industrialists; within two months the

[96] *Ibid.*, 524 f.
[97] Mowrer, *op. cit.*, 143.

Reichstag building was set on fire, according to Nazi plans to furnish an excuse for a thorough liquidation of the accused Communists; almost immediately after a great May Day parade of workers the trade unions were ruthlessly disorganized. But the years have shown that, as the party became more and more powerful itself, it turned on more and more powerful potential enemies. The now expatriated Thyssen warns his fellow capitalists of his mistake. Nothing was allowed to stand in the way of the ultimate realization of revolutionary goals.

SUMMARY INTERPRETATION

Any adequate description of the development of the Nazi movement should make it abundantly clear that its success was not due to any single factor. It was not simply the defeat of Germany in the first World War, the Versailles Treaty, Germany's lack of colonies, the political docility of the people, the iron fist of the ruling class that caused Hitler to emerge. Nor can any adequate interpretation of the movement's development be based on any simple and sovereign psychological theory. A systematic analysis must take into account a multiplicity of conditions and their psychological consequences.

Collapse of old norms. Nazism was possible only in a critical period when old norms, old cultural standards, were no longer able to provide the framework necessary for a satisfying adjustment and orientation of the individuals who composed the culture. It was not merely a few scattered norms that had become inadequate, not merely the norms particularly treasured by a single group or class of the population, but the whole pattern of standards which constituted the Germany of 1918. The attempted revision of some norms by republican governments proved insufficient for psychological adjustment.

Nazi racial doctrine with its vision of pan-Germanism reaffirmed latent but unexpressed values held by wide segments of the population. More specific goals of the party program were variously emphasized, not infrequently at the expense of consistency. Nazism, rather than Communism or some democratic compromise, arose because a greater number of people saw in it the possibility of breaking away from assumptions that were binding them or the possibility of constructing a new framework that would solve their own problems. Because its goals were so general and all-inclusive, its promises so varied and widespread, Nazism proved to be a thorough and complete revolt from the past. It promised whatever the heart desired.

Satisfaction of needs. The orientation people craved was one that would bring a satisfaction of the needs so thwarted during the postwar period. Since different personal backgrounds, traits, and capacities inevitably create different desires, probably almost every individual in the culture had a unique pattern of needs to be filled. We do know, however, that many people were underfed, that economic difficulties kept young people from marrying and satisfying sexual urges in accepted ways. In addition, and probably more important, certain derived needs were completely frustrated in a large proportion of the population. The desire for steady, useful, agreeable work was far from satisfied. There was little economic security for most people. And this economic instability meant that for many individuals the desires for recreation, education, homes and families, medical attention, and a whole host of other demands identified with modern life were thwarted. The Nazi program not only recognized these demands but pointed out to the people why they were not being accommodated, how the Nazi Party would see that vigorous and prompt action was taken to do so.

Appeal to the feeling of self-regard. We have seen how in 1918 people of various positions were afraid that their status was threatened by existing conditions or circumstances that might soon transpire. The middle class was practically dissolved economically, but not psychologically; the ruling class felt the danger of Communism and organized labor; the peasants saw themselves squeezed on all sides. To each group the Nazis promised what it desired. Nazi promises were believed because the standards they set up and against which status was measured were vague and nebulous. Levels of aspiration were focused along racial, nationalistic lines. Once these were achieved—so the people thought—status would be secure. By identifying themselves with the *Volk*, with the third Reich, with the leader who was to bring about the new order, individuals saw their own aspirations fulfilled.

In addition to the appeal of a restored or enhanced status, the movement promised a redefinition of status for those who were unwilling to include as part of their ego values the accepted criteria of status in the existing social order. Many members of the under-privileged classes, for example, saw in the Nazi program a destruction of the snobbery, aloofness, and disdain which had characterized the upper classes. Some radicals and progressives viewed Hitler as the precursor of the real social revolution which they hoped would rid Germany and the rest of the world of economic injustices, the uncontrolled scramble for profits, the age-old imperialism of competing nations. By identifying themselves with the Nazi movement, projecting their own unpopular goals into its program, their feeling of self-respect and personal integrity could find expression and they could enjoy the companionship and encouragement of an active organization.

Meaning provided. We have given ample proof of the widespread bewilderment in Germany during the postwar period. Innumerable and little understood circumstances had caused and were perpetuating social and personal chaos. The bickering and compromising of parliamentary governments and the intellectualism of communist propaganda failed to give most people any concrete understanding, any positive program. The Nazis pointed their fingers at enemies to be destroyed, broke through the maze of economic and political argument that surrounded the puzzled citizen, showed him solutions in his own language, showed him how these solutions would affect him personally if he would only lend his support. Simplification and oversimplification turned confusion into conviction, despair into direction.

The Nazi movement, as well as many other social movements, has often been called *irrational*. This irrationality can be explained in large part by the oversimplification of solutions and by the psychological conditions already described which lead people to accept such oversimplification. The new values proposed by the leaders become a part of the follower's ego. Hence, those who do not subscribe to the new values must be regarded as enemies of the movement or, from the point of view of the individual follower, as *my* enemies. This enemy, once concretized, can be both feared and hated.

A reasonable resolution of a conflict between a social movement and other elements of society with which it may come into conflict is impossible simply because the conflict is between two sets of

sumptions or standards of judgment. Any argument or reasoning
either side is bounded by these assumptions. Hence, if the basic
onditions giving rise to the conflicting assumptions cannot be
remedied before great numbers of people have ardently and te-
aciously accepted them, then, as history shows, the individuals who
old these conflicting values must try to get rid of each other. What
eople live for, they are willing to die for.

Strategy. The clean break which Nazi leaders and Hitler espe-
ally were able to make from current norms provided enormous
ossibilities for the use of new propaganda tactics. By throwing cer-
tin older values overboard and accepting certain others, Hitler be-
ame convinced of the righteousness of his cause. His lack of respect
or the values commonly associated with capitalist democracy made
possible for him to advocate propaganda and terrorist methods
hat persons steeped in other traditions abhorred. By distorting facts,
y ruthless persecution, by wholesale hypocrisy, it was easy to prom-
e all things to all men and to undermine the popular basis of
pposing parties.

Hitler, rather than some other leader, arose because he was astute
nough to guess what would be an appealing program, because he
o clearly saw the weaknesses of his enemies, and because he possessed
he capacity, the energy, the oratorical ability, the cunning, and the
pparent sincerity to convince others and to organize among his
ollowers a political instrument of enormous efficiency. He con-
entrated his attacks on enemies that were either weak or disor-
anized. Domestic enemies, such as the Jew or the Communist, were
iquidated before opponents from industry or the army were taken
n; small countries were swallowed up before the bout with England
nd France was risked. Hitler rarely allowed his enemies time to
rganize their opposition. From the very beginning he was always
n the offensive, seldom on the defensive. He took for granted that
he Nazi cause was the correct one, and while others debated and
uestioned their own assumptions and policies to formulate a counter-
ttack, he continued to harass them with new accusations. He con-
inued to filter into the enemy camp his own solutions with all their
ppeals for those who were becoming more and more dissatisfied
y the failure of their own leaders to act. This method has become
ven more clearly reflected in Hitler's later grand political strategy.

Where confusion and dissatisfaction already were widespread, the Nazi program was vigorously and directly promoted; but, where there was already some relatively adequate political or economic arrangement in a culture, the Nazi tactic was to create confusion, doubt, dissatisfaction and then either to plant positive Nazi suggestions or to take direct military action without fear of popular uprising.

EPILOGUE

The reasons for the success of the Nazi movement can be understood and its future strategy can be accurately predicted only if its original development and its subsequent spread are seen in relation to the whole social context. If the democratic opponents of Nazism oversimplify its causes, overemphasize the importance of the single man who happens to lead it, fail to appreciate the reasons why disgruntled people turned to it, their analysis will be dangerously, perhaps suicidally, superficial. Long ago most close observers of the movement forecast that it could be stopped only if there were some powerful revolt from within or if military might were great enough to crush the war to which the whole Nazi system was inevitably leading.

What was a small microcosm in a single culture became the macrocosm spreading over many older cultures. If its spread is to be arrested, some organization stronger and more efficient than the Nazi organization will have to do it. But, if any nation or combination of nations is to become sufficiently strong and efficient without falling into Nazi tactics in the process, they must take care that the needs and frustrations within their own boundaries are satisfied so that appeals characteristic of the Nazi program will fall on deaf ears. And if these potential domestic problems are to be solved and their psychological consequences avoided, the conflicting interests of various groups in what we know as democratic countries may have to be settled in ways that will make a redefinition of workable democracy necessary.

INDEX

ABEL, T., 210, 216-218, 221, 230-232, 235-238, 240 f., 251, 263
Achievement level, 48, 140, 227
ADLER, A., 49
ALLPORT, F. H., 31 f.
ALLPORT, G. W., 19, 31-33, 35 f., 49, 51, 56, 77, 214, 218, 220-222, 226, 232, 254, 261
American Institute of Public Opinion, 14, 42, 86, 112, 174-179, 191, 209, 235
American Jewish Committee, 240
ANDERSON, S., 64
ARNOLD, T. W., 143
ASCH, S. E., 19, 26, 69
Aspiration, level of, 48, 140, 227
Attitudes: dimensions, 19, 28; vs. frame of reference, 20 f.; vs. standards of judgment, 20 f.; directionality, 28; intensity, 28
AUSTIN, H. W., 155
Autoerotism, 146, 163

BANCROFT, H. H., 80
BARNES, J., 67
BARTON, BRUCE, 171
BEARD, C., 92, 120
BEARD, M., 92, 120
BEGBIE, H., 145, 147
BLACK, ASSOCIATE JUSTICE, 22
BLOCK, H., 19, 26, 69
BOURKE-WHITE, M., 92, 115
BRADY, R. A., 210, 240
BROWN, E. V., 138
BROWN, J. C., 145
BROWN, K., 157
BROWN, P. M., 147, 151
BRUNER, J. S., 214
BUCHMAN, F. N., 148-168
BUCHMANISM, see Oxford Group
BURKE, K., 66

CALDWELL, E., 79, 92, 115
CANTRIL, H., 12, 19, 25, 70, 72, 76 f.
Capitalism, and Townsend Plan, 207
Catharsis, 161
Causality: individual's understanding of, 39; mob members' confusion regarding, 118

CHADBOURN, J. H., 79, 83
CHAMBERLAIN, J., 241
CHILDS, H. L., 239
Church affiliation: and economic status in South, 85 f.; and illiteracy, 85
CLEMENTS, R. E., 170-172, 180
Closure, 61
Commission on Interracial Cooperation, 79, 82
Conditioned response: vs. standard of judgment, 25; and meaning, 55; in suggestion, 71 f.
Confession: functions of, 161 ff.; inadequacies of, 164
COUGHLIN, C. E., 184, 186
Critical ability: definition, 75; conditions of display, 76 f.; "self-objectification," 76
Critical situation: definition, 63; in the culture, 64; and overthrow of values, 64; suggestion in, 64 f.; rise of new leaders in, 66; "escapist" solutions, 68; in Germany, 213 f., 266

DARLEY, J. G., 19, 26
DAVIS, A., 87
DEMBO, T., 61
DEWEY, J., 29
DIVEN, K., 29, 73
DOLLARD, J., 49, 84, 87, 116
DOOB, L., 49, 84, 116, 258
DORMAN, M. J., 189
Drives: derived, 33, 164; and the ego, 35; and desire for meaning, 60; desire for congenial work as, 176; economic security as, 176; maintenance of status as, 176

EDWARDS, A. L., 19
Ego: development of, 35 f.; extension of, 36 f.; variations in, 36 f.; composition of, 37 f.; definition, 40 f.; level, 48; and achievement level, 48 f.; violation of, 49; concept, use and misuse, 50 f.; involvement and suggestibility, 73
Experience, degrees of organization of, 62 f.

FATHER DIVINE: description of kingdom, 123 f.; biographical accounts, 124; names in kingdom, 128; conflicts within king-

FATHER DIVINE—(Continued)
dom, 130 f.; influence on constituent's voting, 134; impact of external world on kingdom, 135 f.; reasons for existence of kingdom, 139 f.; "righteous government" platform, 141
FAY, S. B., 214, 218, 220-222, 226, 232, 241, 254, 261
FERGUSON, C. W., 144 f.
FOOT, S., 149, 152, 154, 156
Fortune poll, 175-177, 179
Frames of reference: definition, 20; vs. attitudes, 20 f.; overlapping, 21 f.; short-circuiting, 23 f.; differential organization of, 25 f.; ego involvement and, 27 f.; structuration, internal, 56 f.; and suggestion, 64 f.; and critical ability, 76; Negro-white relations, 87 f., 110 f.; "Four Absolutes" of Oxford Group, 166; and opinions, 177 f.; rigidity of concerning "American way," 179 f.; provided by Townsend Plan, 205 f.
FRANK, J. D., 48
Freedom of speech, 178 f.
FREUD, S., 32, 36, 50
Frustration and aggression, 49
Functional autonomy of motives, 33

GEDYE, G. E. R., 223
GERTH, H., 238, 263-265
GIDEONSE, H., 172
GÖBBELS, 240, 257 f.
GÖRING, H., 237
GOULD, R., 48
GRAINGER, P., 194
GUNTHER, J., 238

Habit, 15
HARRIS, H., 180
HARTMANN, G. W., 19, 26
HARTSHORNE, E. Y., 214, 218, 220-222, 226, 232, 254, 256, 261
HARTSHORNE, R., 143
HEIDEN, K., 210 f.
HERTZMAN, M., 19, 26, 69
HIGH, S., 155
HILGARD, E. R., 55
HITLER, A., 13, 26, 152, 210-270
HOLT, E. B., 31   [253
HOOVER, G. B., 210, 220, 224 f., 240, 249,
HOPPE, F., 48
HORNEY, K., 50
HOROWITZ, E. L., 5
HOSHER, J., 124, 127, 131, 134, 136, 139 f.
HOVLAND, C., 84

HUNT, W. A., 24
HUNTLEY, C. W., 46

Id, 32
Identification, 37 f.; in mobs, 119; with common goal of Oxford Group, 163; with leader, Townsend, 185 f.; with leader Hitler, 234 f.
Impression of universality, 142
Income: distribution of in U. S., 173; family amount needed, poll on, 174; expenditure of if increased, 175
Instincts, 32
Intolerance, 178 f.
Invasion from Mars, susceptibility regarding 70 f.

JACOB, P., 13
JAMES, W., 15, 35-37, 77, 144
JANDORF, E. M., 214
Jews, as scapegoat of Nazis, 239 f.
JOHNSON, J. W., 44, 115

KAHN, E., 49
KATZ, D., 77, 178
KELLETT, E. E., 234
KÖHLER, W., 55, 58, 61
KOFFKA, K., 36, 46, 58
KORNHAUSER, A. W., 11
KRIS, E., 210

LASSWELL, H. D., 238
LAZARSFELD, P. F., 11, 22, 259
Leader: desire for in Germany, 233; Father Divine as, 132; Dr. Townsend a 185 f.; Hitler's appeal as, 235 f.
LEBON, G., 118, 120
LEMKE, W., 184
LEUBA, J. H., 144
LEWIN, K., 36, 48, 58
LEWIS, S. L., 170, 180
LIEBLING, A. J., 124
LIPPITT, R., 58
LOE, K., 181
LUDECKE, K. G. W., 235 f., 245, 263
LYNCH, C., 80
Lynching: definition, 79; mob, definition 80; mob, contrasted with other mob 117 f.; statistical trends, 80 f.; crimes responsible for, 81 f.; punishments fo 82 f.; economic foundations, 83 ff.; r ligious affiliation and, 86; and populati density, 91 f.; and improved Negro statu 92 f.; "Bourbon," 94; "proletariat," 9 descriptions of, 94 ff.; attitudes of pa

Lynching—(*Continued*)
ticipants, 108 ff.; as solution of threats to status, 112 f.; and sexual perversion, 115 f.
LYND, H., 72
LYND, R. S., 72

McCORD, S., 171
McDOUGALL, WM., 31 f., 36, 42
McGREGOR, D., 28
McKELWAY, S., 124
Macrocosm, 114; and microcosm, incompatibility of, 137 f.
MARPLE, C. H., 74
MARQUIS, D. G., 55
MARTIN, E. D., 120, 244
Meaning: external structuration and, 57; desire for, 59-62; and needs, 59 f.; and derived drives, 60; and goals, 61; and personal values, 60 f.; and Oxford Group, 168; and Townsend Plan, 203 f.; provided by Nazi ideology, 267 f.
MECKLIN, J. M., 144
Mein Kampf, 241, 243-245, 248-250, 252 f., 255-261
Microcosm, 114, 119; and Father Divine's kingdom as, 123 f.; conflicts within, 130 f.; impact of external world on, 135 f.; reasons for existence of, 139 f.; creation of, by "sharing," 161; Townsend movement as, 185
Mob: definition, 79; personnel, 106; conditions of formation, 117; persecutory, 117; revolutionary, 117 f.; mind, 118; members, characteristic mental processes of, 118-120
MOORE, G. F., 144
Moral Rearmament, *see* Oxford Group
MOWRER, E. A., 210, 247, 265
MURPHY, G., 12
MURPHY, L. B., 12
MURRAY, H. A., 29, 61, 73

National Resources Committee, 173, 175; report of, 173 f.
Nationalism: reasons for in Germany, 211 f.; effect of Versailles Treaty on, 217 f.
Nazi Party: appeals used, 233-253; disillusionment with, 245 f.; tactics, 255 ff.; propaganda, 257 f.; terrorism, 263 f.; composition, 264 f.; strategy, 269 f.
Needs: and desire for meaning, 59 f.; satisfactions of in Father Divine's kingdom, 126 f.; satisfaction of in Townsend Plan, 201; satisfaction of by Nazi program, 267

Negro: lynching ratio, 81; subservient position of, 87 f.; stereotypes regarding, 90; improved status of, 92 f.; educational expenditures for, 96
NEUBERGER, R. L., 181, 185
NEUMANN, S., 234
NEWCOMB, T., 12

O'CONNOR, H., 150, 155, 157
ODUM, H. W., 83, 92
OGDEN, C. K., 143
Oxford Group: history, 145 ff.; aims, 147 f.; plans for industry, 152 ff.; members, character of, 154 f., 166 f.; relation of growth to events, 165 f.

PARKER, R. A., 124, 139
PASS, S., 190
Personal involvement and suggestibility, 66
PIAGET, J., 36
PORTER, R., 190
Prestige suggestion, 142; in Townsend movement, 188 f.
PREYER, W., 36
Propaganda: frames of reference and, 29; of Nazis, 257 f.
PRUDEN, D., 97
Psychological worlds, 39; constriction of in mobs, 118 f.
Public-opinion polls, 10, 13 f., 22, 42, 112

Race prejudice: acquisition of, 7 ff.; and mob behavior, 90 ff.; and Father Divine, 129, 135; and Nazis, 239 ff.
RAPER, A., 79, 81 f., 84, 86, 91, 94, 96 f.
Rationalization, 23 f.; and self-regard, 48
Reflexes, 32
Religion and Townsend Plan, 207
ROBERTS, S. H., 210, 238
ROOSEVELT, N., 172, 181, 202, 206
ROPER, E., 43
ROSE, H. J., 150
ROSENTHAL, S. P., 73
ROSS, E. A., 31
RUGG, D., 12
RUSSELL, A. J., 145, 153, 162

SCHUMAN, F. L., 210, 224, 227, 236, 244, 247, 251, 257, 261
SEARS, R., 84
Security: and mobs, 110; and Father Divine's kingdom, 139 f.; and Townsend movement, 192 ff.; lack of in Germany, 223 f., 230 f.

Self-regard: relation to ego, 41 f.; and self-integrity, 44 f.; maintenance of, 46
Senate Judiciary Committee, 79
Sentiments, 41 f.
SHAY, F., 79 f.
SHEARON, M., 174
SHERIF, M., 8, 24, 35 f., 67, 69, 75, 123
SHOEMAKER, S. M., 145, 148, 150, 152 f., 165 f.
SHOTWELL, J. T., 213
SILCOX, D. E., 151
SINCLAIR, U., 170
Slogans: use, in critical situation, 67; use, by Buchman, 160; of Father Divine, 124 f.; of Townsend movement, 186 f.; of Nazis, 262
SMITH, C. E., 74
SMITH, G., 184, 186
Social context: nature of, 3 ff.; transmission of, 5 ff., 19; motivation and, 34
Social norms: definition, 4; conflicts of, 10 f.; interiorization of, 5 f., 19; individual modifications of, 11 f.; and education, 12; and personality, 12; disintegration of in prewar Germany, 229, 266
Social values: definition, 6; acquisition of, 7 f.; conflicts of, 10 f.; personal significance of, 40; and needs, 50; revision of by Nazis, 256 f.
Songs, use of in Townsend movement, 186
SPEIER, H., 227
SPENCER, F. A. M., 163
SPRANGER, E., 37
Standards of judgment, 19; and attitudes, 21; and frames of reference, 21; overlapping of, 21 f.; short-circuiting, 23 f.; organization of, 25 f.; ego involvement and, 27 f.; and ego, 39 f.; and suggestion, 64 f.; and critical ability, 76
Status: definition, 42; relation to norms, 43; defense of and lynching, 110 f.; enhanced in Father Divine's kingdom, 141 f.; through "sharing," 161 f.; loss of in middle classes in Germany, 227; improvement of promised by Nazis, 267 f.
STEELMAN, R., 85

STERN, W., 36
STRACHEY, J., 210
Structuration, 56-59
Suggestibility: conditions of, 64 f.; to majority opinion, 74 f.; prestige, 75; sex and age differences in, 75; and mass meetings, 260 f.
Super-ego, 35
SWING, R. G., 171
Symbols: use in critical situations, 67; polarization around, 132 f.; in Townsend movement, 186; in Nazi Party, 262

TANNENBAUM, F., 83
TAYLOR, E., 263
THOMAS, N., 184
THYSSEN, F., 248, 265, 266
Townsend Plan: history, 169 ff.; practicability of, 172 f.; membership, character of, 190 f.; popularity of in different groups, 192 f.; members, case studies of, 194 ff.

VAIHINGER, H., 143
VEBLEN, T., 50
VETTER, G. B., 73
VOLKMANN, J., 24

WAELDER, R., 234
WATSON, W. S., 19, 26
WERNER, H., 37
WHITE, E. B., 202, 204, 207
WHITE, R. K., 58
WHITE, W., 79 f., 80, 82 f., 85, 90, 92
WHITEHEAD, A. N., 30, 56
WHITEMAN, L., 170, 180
WILLIAMS, C. S., 153
WILSON, D. J., 151
WOOFTER, T. J., JR., 84
WORK, M., 81 f.

YOUNG, E. F., 92

ZEIGARNIK, B., 61